PRINCIPLE AND PROPENSITY

PRINCIPLE AND PROPENSITY

Experience and Religion in the Nineteenth-Century British and American Bildungsroman

Kelsey L. Bennett

The University of South Carolina Press

Published by the University of South Carolina Press
Columbia, South Carolina 29208

www.sc.edu/uscpress

Manufactured in the United States of America

23 22 21 20 19 18 17 16 15 14   10 9 8 7 6 5 4 3 2 1

Library of Congress Cataloging-in-Publication Data

Bennett, Kelsey L.

Principle and propensity : experience and religion in the nineteenth-century British and American bildungsroman / Kelsey L. Bennett.

pages cm

Includes bibliographical references and index.

ISBN 978-1-61117-364-2 (hardbound : alk. paper) — ISBN 978-1-61117-365-9 (e-book) 1. English fiction—19th century—History and criticism. 2. Bildungsromans, English—History and criticism. 3. American fiction—19th century—History and criticism. 4. Bildungsromans, American—History and criticism. 5. Bildungsromans—History and criticism. 6. Self-actualization (Psychology) in literature. 7. Self-realization in literature. 8. Religion in literature. I. Title. II. Title: Experience and religion in the nineteenth-century British and American bildungsroman.

PR868.B52P75 2014

823'.809354—dc23

2013036699

To my husband, David Klingsmith, and our daughter, Elizabeth,
for every day they graciously accompanied me to the library door.
And to Julien, who came next.

CONTENTS

PREFACE

The simplicity of this book's premise is contained within the observation that the word *Bild* has metaphysical dimensions to it. That people are made in the "image" of God is of course the most important instance of this connection. Since this is so, curiosity alongside a certain intuitive gravity drew me into considering what this might mean in relation to the bildungsroman, the genre of self-formation that has long been held to be a product of secular modernity. The following pages accordingly offer a renewed approach to reading this genre through a close attentiveness to the spiritual formation of selfhood. This is a book both about the bildungsroman and about the religious and intellectual traditions that inform it. While some readers may prefer it to be devoted either to one or to the other, it has been my conviction from the beginning that such a sundering is, for my own interdisciplinary predilections and aesthetic sense, impossible. Likewise those looking forward to an exhaustive revaluation of the genre will not, I am afraid, find it here in these pages. Nor will they, however, find a collection of isolated observations about evangelical religion and its influences upon four discrete nineteenth-century novels. I aim for something between these extremes: I have sought to provide the intellectual and religious history to lend substance to my approach to reading the bildungsroman, and *Principle & Propensity* lays a careful and suggestive foundation upon which others might find new, fruitful directions for continuing studies of their own. Most essential, I envision my overall argument as deepening the complexity, opening and exploring new dimensions, of the ways in which readers appreciate this versatile and most engaging literary genre. If nothing else, this book invites the reader to reexamine the pervasive assumption that self-formation, and writing about self-formation, is an activity necessarily and exclusively controlled by the material conditions of a culture.

ACKNOWLEDGMENTS

I wish to acknowledge the support of many people who have helped me to realize this work. At the University of Denver, Clark Davis and Eleanor McNees shared encouragement, conversation, and their respective expertise in American and British nineteenth-century literature as I developed earlier versions of the manuscript. Also thanks are owed to Ann Dobyns and Victor Castellani, and to Gabi Kathöfer for her valuable suggestions for my translations from the German. I am further indebted to the three anonymous reviewers for their practical and thoughtful responses. I also extend my appreciation to the editors and publishers of *Brontë Studies* (www.maneypublishing.com/journals/bst and www.ingentaconnect.com/content/maney/bst) for permission to reprint material from chapter four that originally appeared in this journal. I am obliged to the National Museum of Western Art, Tokyo, for permission to reproduce Vilhelm Hammershøi's painting *Interior with Ida Playing the Piano,* also to the Metropolitan Museum of Art for permission to reprint Goya's *The Sleep of Reason Produces Monsters.* The collaboration of ARTstor and IAP (Images for Academic Publishing) with the Metropolitan Museum provided the excellent service that enabled my access to high-quality digital images of artwork from the collection. Finally I extend my gratitude to the capable editorial and production staff at the University of South Carolina Press and especially to Jim Denton for his belief in and patient helpfulness with this project throughout.

INTRODUCTION

> The author of a work of imagination is trying to affect us wholly, as human beings, whether he knows it or not; and we are affected by it, as human beings, whether we intend to be or not.
>
> T. S. Eliot, "Religion and Literature"

In book 7 of Goethe's *Wilhelm Meister's Apprenticeship*, Jarno recalls lines from a letter Lothario wrote as he was preparing to return to Germany from America: "I will return, and in my own house, my own orchard, in the midst of my own people, I will say: *Here, or nowhere, is America!*" (264). This vivid declaration from an aristocrat who fought alongside the French on behalf of the Americans during the Revolutionary War embodies the spirit of this study. In a rare instance of Continental importation of American cultural currency, Lothario's words employ the project of *bildung*, or the formation of the individual estate (in both inward and outward senses), to link the two continents.

Given the formidable literature surrounding the bildungsroman genre, the question of why one would undertake yet another study at the beginning of the twenty-first century is pertinent. Many view bildung as a summation of the eighteenth century's impossibly utopian Enlightenment ideals such as rational individual integrity or wholeness, man's basic goodness, and the progressive, organic growth of the personality in harmony with one's environment. Furthermore the term *bildungsroman* has become the familiar nomenclature that critics (particularly those outside German studies) have come to apply to virtually any novel that in some way describes a young person's path toward maturation. Based upon either perspective—bildung as a misguided ideal or, in literary form, a commonplace equivalent to the "coming of age" novel—bildungsroman criticism often finds itself rehashing what has come before or engaging in disputes over increasingly narrow generic issues. It is, in my view, precisely these circumstances that support and indeed call for a critical renewing, refreshing, and expanding of our understanding of the genre, particularly with respect to its attributes that have been frequently overlooked.

This book reexamines two long-held beliefs about the nineteenth-century bildungsroman: that it is based primarily upon secular individual growth and that it is a genre exclusive to Europe. If we begin with the idea that self-formation, or bildung, originated as a religious exercise in the context of discrete Protestant theological traditions associated through the international revival movements in eighteenth-century Germany, England, and America, the question becomes: How do these traditions manifest themselves in literary contexts? Naturally these spiritual traditions found ways into the bildungsroman, the literary genre most closely concerned with the relationship between individual experience and self-formation. Though *Wilhelm Meisters Lehrjahre* (Wilhelm Meister's Apprenticeship), Goethe's prototype of the genre, was a library staple for most serious writers in nineteenth-century England and in America, these latter writers also had their own religious traditions of self-formation to draw from. This added dimension provides a richness and distinction to each respective nation's version of the standard genre. The primary works I consider in this regard include Charlotte Brontë's *Jane Eyre,* Charles Dickens's *David Copperfield,* Herman Melville's *Pierre,* and Henry James's *Portrait of a Lady.*

To be sure many scholars of the novel have acknowledged the partial contribution of religious self-examination to the rise of the novel generally, and yet critical approaches to the bildungsroman tend as a rule to privilege its secular over its spiritual properties.[1] Part 1 of this study discusses the attributes of parallel national traditions of spiritual self-formation as they convened under the auspices of the international revival movements: the Evangelical Revival, the Great Awakening, and the renewal of Pietism in Germany as led respectively by John Wesley, Jonathan Edwards, and Count Nikolaus Ludwig Zinzendorf.[2] Just as Goethe's Lothario was inspired by his time in America, each of these spiritual leaders variously saw America as a field sown with potential converts awaiting cultivation. More particularly America provided a geographic locus and proved to be an environment hospitable to cross-pollination among the mid-century international revival movements. It was here that German Pietism intersected both with the Great Awakening and the English Evangelical Revival through what appears to be a series of fortunate coincidences: John and Charles Wesley had their first contact with a small group of German Pietists on a ship sailing for Georgia in 1735. Wesley's favorable impression of the group's conduct during a sea storm began a long association that eventually led him to travel to Germany and meet with their spiritual leader, Count Zinzendorf. Pietism's connection with the Great Awakening occurred under similar circumstances. By 1740 the first Moravian colony in Savannah had failed, and those remaining had decided to relocate to Pennsylvania.[3] The ship that took them there happened to be owned by Calvinist George Whitefield. A growing association subsequently developed between Whitefield and the Pietists, which moved Whitefield to offer the Pietists philanthropic work on a tract of land he had recently acquired and planned to develop. Eventually, however, theological differences and financial difficulties caused their separation.[4]

Almost Jonathan Edwards's exact contemporary—born in 1700, just three years earlier—Zinzendorf himself came to America in 1741 for fourteen months. Among his intentions was to found in Pennsylvania the Congregation of God in the Spirit—a superlative Moravian church that still retained centralized powers in Europe. During that time he attended the interdenominational Pennsylvania Synods and attempted to evangelize the Indians (Mohicans) by traveling and baptizing in Indian country.

The international revival movements and the thought of their leading figures provide a common basis for the many individuals obsessed with the questions "Who am I?" and "How shall I reconcile myself with the world as I experience it?" The ultimate goal for all was teleological: to ensure individual salvation and the eventual reuniting with God. I first consider the ways in which the three traditions variously sought to answer these questions through the experience of spiritual self-formation. Part 2, in turn, explores the ways in which these traditions manifest themselves in the nineteenth-century bildungsroman in England and America.

The following introductory sections provide background on the history of bildung as an idea and outline the various ways critics have sought to apply this idea to the novel in Germany, England, and America. The subsequent discussion of bildung and the bildungsroman in Germany will likely be familiar to comparativists and scholars of the novel; I include it because it provides the basis from which (1) to discuss my approach to the related issue of gender and (2) to compare those less familiar but parallel ideas of spiritual self-formation in England and America and the centrality of the conversion experience to both the religious and literary contexts under discussion.

From Speculation to Application: Bildung in the Eighteenth Century

The idea of *Bild* appears at the source of identity in its metaphysical dimensions. The King James version of Genesis 1:26–27 reads: "And God said, Let us make man in our image, after our likeness. . . . So God created man in his *own* image, in the image of God created he him; male and female created he them." Luther's version of the same text reads as follows: "Und Gott sprach: Lasset uns Menschen machen, ein Bild, das uns gleich sei. . . . Und Gott schuf den Menschen ihm zum Bilde, zum Bilde Gottes schuf er ihn; und er schuf sie ein Männlein und Fräulein." In these verses Luther collapses the separate Hebrew words for *image* and *likeness* into one, "*Bild*."[5] New Testament interpretations insist on Christ as the sole embodiment of God's image. While the fall did not obliterate the image within the individual, it did cause the spiritual "senses"—by which it is possible to experience the divine image's renewal—to become "obscured, unused, atrophied" (Runyon, "Role" 189). In this position the individual's internal capacity to renew God's image directly depends upon his or her proximity to Christ. The Reformation of course played a key role in this transformative process by refusing undue interference of the clergy and insisting on the priesthood of the individual. The responsibility for spiritual formation, then, shifted directly to the individual, whose primary source of external inspiration and guidance became the Bible itself.

The *Historisches Wörterbuch der Philosophie* supports this connection in its identification of the origins of bildung not in humanistic or pedagogical contexts but in mystical-theological and speculative natural-philosophical areas of knowledge. Only in the latter half of the eighteenth century, around 1770, did it take on the particular Enlightenment applications to pedagogic and humanist ends. In "The Transformation of Bildung from an Image to an Ideal," Susan L. Cocalis details the international influences informing this shift in emphasis from mystical and speculative realms toward more immediate and secular ends. She locates the first tradition as understanding the verb *bilden* to indicate seeking the image of God within man, into which Meister Eckhardt and later divines incorporated Plotinus's concept of "emanation and reintegration" (400). Each individual soul, tainted by contact with matter, experiences an "odyssey" in order to purify the self, to gain "self-recognition," and to integrate itself once again into God's image.

On the other hand, perhaps somewhat surprisingly, Lord Shaftesbury's *Characteristicks of Men, Manners, Opinions, and Times* (1711) had significant influence on Germans' concept of bildung when his works were first translated into German in 1747 (Cocalis, "Transformation" 401). Shaftesbury's secular concept of the "formation of a genteel character" (translated as bildung), emphasizes self-formation as a means toward establishing the ultimate goal of civic responsibility. In order to be an effective leader, the young man must cultivate a cosmopolitan sensibility or "have seen the World." This includes the acquisition of general cultural knowledge—from other nations' laws to amusements and the fine arts—which experiences such as the Grand Tour supported and celebrated.

While the presence of these two traditions indicate that the term *bildung* had been in use throughout the eighteenth century and much earlier in religious circles, it did not gain the kind of intellectual currency for which it has come to be known until late in the eighteenth century. Cocalis duly notes that as late as 1774 *bildung* appeared in Adelung and Campe's dictionaries most frequently to indicate physical appearance; only by 1807 did the definition expand to encompass its intellectual dimensions (400).[6]

By the 1770s many secular writers in Germany had become interested in bildung and wrote numerous influential works involving the concept. Cocalis credits Winckelmann and Christoph Martin Wieland with introducing the term and investing it with intellectual significance (402), while Todd Kontje considers Johann Gottfried Herder most suitable for that distinction (*German* 2). Other celebrated artists and thinkers of the time who contributed to the discussion include the Weimar classicists Goethe, Schiller, and Wilhelm von Humboldt.[7] For Kontje these writers shared the optimistic ideals of personal and cultural freedom and progress: in sum "transformation into the perfect unity of God turns into the development of one's unique self. In this view, no fall from grace has occurred; humans, like the rest of God's creation, are essentially good" (2). And yet these and related beliefs had significant limitations in their actual applications, including political complacency (gradual bildung instead of revolution, for instance) and availability restricted predominantly to males of the upper classes (7).[8]

Bildung and the German *Roman*

Even this brief account of bildung as it evolved in eighteenth-century Germany—from a mystical concept centered upon self-recognition in God to cultivation through experience of the world—intimates a rich array of potential transpositions of the concept into the novel genre. Though critics have traced a clear literary-historical lineage of the term *bildungsroman* as it first appeared in Germany, given the slippery concept of bildung itself, it is not surprising that few, if any, appear to agree on exactly what it means when applied to the novel.[9] For the sake of clarity, then, the following outlines some general taxonomic distinctions. The first major division involves Germanists vis-à-vis literary scholars of other national traditions; the second includes those who approach the genre as requiring a more-or-less established set of criteria and those with more inclusive approaches (which allow, for instance, its "nonfulfillment" or its significance as an indicator of extraliterary ideas such as modernity itself).[10] The present work finds itself in basic accordance with the two latter approaches—that is, that the bildungsroman is a genre that extends beyond German borders and manifests itself in different periods beyond the Age of Goethe. Further, along with Martin Swales, I grant the original creative work the primary power to indicate genre rather than approach it with a static set of criteria that dictate its generic fulfillment or nonfulfillment.[11]

As with any comparative work committed to translating culturally specific ideas and genres such as German bildung and the bildungsroman, I am mindful of the objection that the process inevitably involves a diffusion of meaning in proportion to its movement away from its period and cultural origins. To this I reply, first and most obviously, that criticism confining itself to understanding bildung in the Age of Goethe is far from consensus upon the term's original meaning either in itself or as it applies to the novel. At the same time, I take it for granted that while the novel is indeed in large part a product of its time and place, it is foremost a work of art. As such it has the capacity to overcome categorical restraints critics across the centuries would impose upon it. By means of a powerful aesthetic malleability and philosophic capacity, the novel, particularly the bildungsroman, is fully capable of resonating with meaning in a number of widely divergent quarters.

Traditionally humanists have understood the aim of *Wilhelm Meisters Lehrjahre* to be the hero's realization of the Enlightenment ideal of "true humanity" through the organic, harmonious synthesis of his inner faculties. Most critics generally attribute this reading to Wilhelm Dilthey's widely cited discussion in *Das Erlebnis und die Dichtung: Lessing, Goethe, Novalis, Hölderlin* (Poetry and Experience, 1906). While Dilthey did not in fact coin the term *bildungsroman,* he was responsible for its popularization in critical discussions of the novel.[12] Though some have attempted to overcome his account, subsequent accounts (particularly those of non-Germanist critics) tend simply to refer to Dilthey's work without further discussion or, by relying on secondary material, risk confusion in attribution.[13]

Among descriptions of humanist bildung as it applies to the novel, Dilthey's ideas are, I believe, still relevant and in some respects unsurpassed. Since his work may be less familiar to readers outside German studies, I provide a brief outline of Dilthey's thought on the genre within the greater context of his thinking about Goethe's poetics. Apart from the fact that his work on the bildungsroman was and continues to be influential, the emphasis he places on inwardness in Goethe's poetics helps to shed light on why this genre seems to be particularly accommodating to spiritual concerns.

The essay "Goethe and the Poetic Imagination," from *Poetry and Experience,* is a sensitive if quasi-hagiographic appraisal of Goethe's position in the pantheon of European literature among figures such as Aeschylus, Dante, and Shakespeare. Dilthey characterizes Goethe's role as harbinger of a new type of poetry in Europe, whose works arose from an unparalleled literary synthesis between modern science and the poetry of the imagination (142). By means of a comparison between Goethe and Shakespeare, Dilthey identifies Goethe's poetics as inwardly oriented, which finds its complement in Shakespeare's—and, more generally, the English—emphasis on the outward "experience of the world" [*Welterfahrung*] (152).[14] "Goethe's characteristic gift," he continues, "is to describe the conditions of his own soul, the world of ideas and ideals within him."[15]

This is not to say that Goethe's poetics are merely solipsistic—inward versus outward distinctions are, of course, a matter of emphasis and degree, and both poets utilize both—but through the "remarkable energy of experience" [*außerordentlichen Energie des Erlebens*], Goethe repeatedly transforms and intensifies the formlessness of experience into the poetry of image and form (127). The same might be argued with respect to Shakespeare; however, Dilthey's emphasis on Goethe's preoccupation with inner poetic bildung is directly commensurate with his often-cited definition of the bildungsroman as it appeared in his 1870 biography of Friedrich Schleiermacher: it is "of the school of *Wilhelm Meister*," which depicts "human development in different stages, forms, epochs of life" (282). Later, in *Poetry and Experience*, he takes the characterization further in his essay "Friedrich Hölderlin" in a subsection detailing the Romantic poet's novel *Hyperion*. Dilthey counts Hölderlin's work as a part of the larger bildungsroman legacy that begins with Goethe's *Wilhelm Meister*: "From *Wilhelm Meister* and *Hesperus* on, they all represent the young man of their time; how he enters into life in a pleasant dawn, searches after kindred souls, encounters friendship and love, then how he comes into conflict with the hard realities of the world and so matures through myriad life-experiences, finds himself and comes to know his calling in the world."[16] It is, in sum, a genre of the "optimism of personal development," which "has never been expressed more serenely and vitally than in Goethe's *Wilhelm Meister*: an immortal radiance of life-enjoyment lies within this novel."[17]

Dilthey identifies four qualities of the genre that set it apart from others: the first derives from the political culture of eighteenth-century Germany from which many artists felt alienated and consequently focused on individual and psychological rather than political themes (272–73). The second related point is its biographical quality, with the emphasis on the hero's humanity in the universal sense. Next it concerns itself with the commensurability of world-experience with inner aptitude. Lastly it is philosophical in the sense that it aims for an "Ideal der Humanität" by charting a coherent development that is always modulating.

Though Martin Swales differs from Dilthey on certain points, he does not contradict Dilthey in his basic contrast between the representatives of the two national literatures. Novelists both in Germany and England share a concern with the tension between individual potential and the limitations of finite experience. But for those more empirical-minded English readers, the reputation of the German bildungsroman is that of a mystical and indeed mystifying "rarefied epic of inwardness" with a greater regard for metaphysics than for narrative cause and effect ("Irony" 52). The Victorian novel, on the other hand, expresses the conflict between the individual growth and limitations as a "palpable, outward enactment . . . plotted on a graph of moral understanding" (66–67). In *The*

German Bildungsroman, Swales elaborates further on this basic distinction: whereas the English novel up through Joyce's *Portrait of the Artist as a Young Man* confronts particular external pressures—societal, institutional, psychological—which militate against the hero's quest for self-fulfillment, "the obstacles facing the hero of the German bildungsroman are less susceptible of realistic portrayal for the reason that they tend to be ontologically, rather than socially, based" (35). In this respect, as we shall see, certain nineteenth-century American authors bear more affinity with their German counterparts than is generally assumed.[18]

Transatlantic Critics of the Bildungsroman

Any study concerned with the bildungsroman genre's incarnations in nineteenth-century England and America must face at the outset the fact that the term did not appear as a literary category in English criticism until the 1910 edition of the *Encyclopedia Britannica.* And in this instance the term is mentioned in the Goethe entry and applies not to works in English but explicitly to Goethe's *Wilhelm Meisters Lehrjahre.* While the author criticizes the novel for its apparent "formlessness and loose construction" and critiques the hero's instability of purpose, the overall evaluation is positive.[19]

In addition to the comparative lateness of the term's entry into the discourse of English-speaking critics is the challenge of its notorious resistance to precise translation. This difficulty is apparent from a glance at the myriad renderings of the term into English, taken here, for instance, from both the *Oxford-Harrap Standard German-English Dictionary* and *Langenscheidt's German-English Dictionary.* In its simplest form, meanings of the noun *Bild* include likeness, representation, picture, image, illustration, portrait; scene, spectacle, sight; metaphor, simile. Figuratively it may mean idea, conception, or notion. As a verb *bilden* encompasses the following: to form or shape; figuratively to educate, train, develop, be; reflexively to form or educate (improve) oneself. Finally the noun *bildung* mirrors the verb form: forming or formation, constitution (of, e.g., a group), education, culture, good breeding. When the term is applied, then, to novels in English to demarcate a discrete literary genre, ambiguity increases.

The *Oxford English Dictionary* and the *Encyclopedia of the Novel* remark upon both the genre's spiritual and secular dimensions: the *OED,* second edition, defines it as a traditionally German "novel that has as its main theme the formative years or spiritual education of one person." It equates *bildung,* in turn, simply with "education." *Encyclopedia of the Novel* claims similarly that it "contains vestiges of both religious and secular notions of formation as an inner process." To complicate matters further, many subgenres are so closely related to the bildungsroman that they are often confounded in translation: the *Entwicklungsroman* (novel of development), the *Künstlerroman* (artist novel), and the *Erziehungsroman* (pedagogical novel). In line with Dilthey, G. B. Tennyson articulates the most important distinction between the bildungsroman and the *Entwicklungsroman*—of all, the two perhaps closest in aim: whereas the latter allows for virtually any kind of development, the former emphasizes the integration of a harmonious personality (138).

Susanne Howe's pioneering *Wilhelm Meister and His English Kinsmen: Apprentices to Life* has been influential outside German studies in furthering criticism's general tendency to focus on the secular properties of bildung. While at the outset Howe acknowledges the genre's debt to the "moral allegory" such as *Pilgrim's Progress,* she counts this as only one among many other influences that come together to define the bildungsroman as "the novel of all-round development or self-culture" that features "the more or less conscious attempt on the part of the hero to integrate his powers, to cultivate himself by his experience" (2, 5–6). Similarly to Dilthey, Howe distinguishes the German bildungsroman from its English and French counterparts through its unusual degree of "intensity of purpose" and "earnest, conscientious introspection" that Goethe manifested in his own development (25). After Howe critics on the bildungsroman in nineteenth-century England such as G. B. Tennyson, Jerome H. Buckley, Barry Qualls, Randolph Shaffner, and Gisela Argyle all reflect Dilthey's influence as well as cite religious ideas of bildung as background or concentrate primarily upon how these religious ideas become secularized. However, none of them devote extended critical discussion to the persisting influence of spiritual self-formation on the bildungsroman genre.

On the other side of the Atlantic, comparatively little has been written about the American bildungsroman in the nineteenth century. This is due in part first to the fact that a large part of the critical attention for the last fifty years has been absorbed in the politics surrounding defending or rejecting America's own "native" romance genre.[20] Second, this is due to the largely unexamined assumption that the bildungsroman is somehow a genre exclusive to Europe, incompatible with the literature of a democratically based culture. Franco Moretti's *The Way of the World: The Bildungsroman in European Culture* has done much to further this point of view. Without directly mentioning the American novel, only grudgingly does Moretti acknowledge the genre's "democratic" manifestations in England and then primarily in terms of its nonfulfillment. He argues that a democratic hero is in a sense oxymoronic, that "democracy is rather antiheroic; it thrives on universalistic and standardized values, around which it has to create the widest possible consensus: and no widespread consensus can come to light if the culture is too demanding, or too steeped in partiality, inequality, uniqueness" (192).

But what happens, however, when these standard ideas about the "democratic" hero transfer to nineteenth-century American fiction with the specter, or better, the *spirit* of Puritanism lingering in the periphery? Communities of saints were certainly demanding, entirely partial, rooted in the idea of inequality (souls are either saved or reprobate), and largely convinced that the experiment they were making by crossing the ocean was a unique one. Further nineteenth-century Germany and America bear certain resemblances that make the bildungsroman an especially compelling genre for authors of both nations. The *Encyclopedia of the Novel* notes that the genre in Germany answered a need "to fill the gaps left by contemporary German historical reality by recourse to speculation."[21] It is precisely this lack of historical reality in America—voiced to the point of obsession both by nineteenth-century authors and their critics—that would appear to support similar conclusions.

C. Hugh Holman and Thomas L. Jeffers are among the few commentators to discuss at any length the genre's uniquely American properties as it appears in the nineteenth century. In *Windows on the World,* Holman devotes a chapter to "the bildungsroman, American style," in which he argues that the hero typically gains some form of "philosophical stability" that allows him to enter effectively into adulthood (168). The distinguishing factor of the American bildungsroman is the presence of the hero as witness, that the initiation through which the hero or heroine must pass consists in witnessing action but not in taking action (177, 170).[22] Surprisingly Holman does not explore the contribution of the American Calvinist tradition to this type of character, and yet the feeling of being a witness to one's own and others' actions in the world certainly carries antinomian connotations.

Thomas L. Jeffers's *Apprenticeships: The Bildungsroman from Goethe to Santayana* is, to my knowledge, the only recent full-length work in English devoted to the genre both in nineteenth-century England and America, which makes it closest to the present study in scope.[23] Jeffers's work, however, takes for granted the predominantly secular properties of the genre. Furthermore he is in step with the long line of critics who emphasize the German bildungsroman's philosophical and inward orientation to the comparative neglect of national culture. He proposes that the English, on the other hand, sought to balance both "the richness of one's inner life" and the connection with one's "social environment" (35). Nineteenth-century Americans fell "somewhere in between" the Germans and the English, for while they could be "very civically responsible," at the same time their material and geographic conditions fostered "a Germanic sort of profundity about the individual self." In other words, for Jeffers the bildungsroman in England and America has more similarities—is more "Anglo-American"—than substantive differences: both seek to balance inner cultivation with social responsibility.

Gender and the "Ideal der Humanität"

While, on the one hand, feminist critics of the nineteenth-century bildungsroman in both England and America often view with suspicion Wilhelm Dilthey's definition of wholeness as the goal of bildung, many also reject Susanne Howe's subsequent approach to *Wilhelm Meister's Apprenticeship* as the model bildungsroman. Instead commentators have offered alternate, female-centered models more commensurate with the different circumstances facing women on their paths to self-formation. These revisions are due in large part to the radical differences between the kinds of education available to men and women in the nineteenth century.

The editors Elizabeth Abel, Marianne Hirsch, and Elisabeth Langland confront Dilthey's approach to the genre in *The Voyage In: Fictions of Female Development*, still one of the best anthologies of feminist bildungsroman criticism spanning the nineteenth and twentieth centuries. Based on the work of twentieth-century psychoanalysts such as Nancy Chodorow and Jean Baker Miller, they argue that "the fully realized and individuated self" traditionally upheld to be the goal of the *bildungsheld* may not necessarily apply to his female counterpart. These psychoanalytic viewpoints variously contend that, based on pre-Oedipal experience, feminine identity is foundationally different from male identity. Whereas boys create identity by differentiating themselves from their original caretakers, girls form their identity in relation to their mothers. Girls, therefore, as they mature, "do not develop the precise and rigid ego boundaries common to males" (9–10). These findings have cleared the way toward provocative readings of the texts from psychological points of view, many exemplary instances of which appear in this anthology.

Elsewhere Susan Fraiman has argued further that *Wilhelm Meister* should not be considered as a prototype for the English female bildungsroman but instead credits the "disreputable gothic novel" as a more plausible alternative (*Unbecoming* 10). Fraiman cites the imbalance of education to be a significant problem in comparing male with female development. Apart from not receiving a formal education or garnering one simply from "the world," a woman is often restricted to a single educator, her husband, which "never leads the heroine to mastery but only to a lifetime as perennial novice" (6).[24] Lorna Ellis's more moderate *Appearing to Diminish: Female Development and the British Bildungsroman, 1750–1850* emphasizes in turn the points that male and female versions of the genre share. Even the distinction she upholds for the female version, the "compromise between self-fulfillment and social accommodation," still sounds very much like Dilthey's emphasis on eventual commensurability of the environment with inner aptitude (139). But Ellis, too, looks elsewhere for a model closer to the English female bildungsroman than *Wilhelm Meister*—back to authors of early eighteenth-century amatory fiction such as Aphra Behn.

Similarly feminist critics of the nineteenth-century American bildungsroman often identify the problem of women's education (this obviously in addition to choice in marriage partner) as a central obstacle to the heroine's self-formation and social development. For models most look to the American authors' British contemporaries, from Charlotte Brontë to George Eliot. In American literary contexts, the issue of education takes on a different cast, especially since the uneducated or miseducated male protagonist holds such a conspicuous and indeed celebrated place in the American fiction of the period (in the present study, Melville's Pierre is such a one). Recently Tessa Hadley has compared Isabel Archer with Jane Eyre in this capacity—both view their haphazard efforts toward self-education "with prideful sorrows" (230). In a comparison between the same heroines, Catherine J. Golden instead distinguishes between Brontë's and James's attitudes toward female education. Whereas in *Jane Eyre* Brontë provides a meditation on the empowerment and repercussions such an education brings a woman, in *The Portrait of a Lady* James "pokes fun at the gentility argument" in Isabel's random attempts at self-culture and thereby provides ammunition for moral arguments against women's reading (59). Elizabeth Jean Sabiston further takes James to task for denying Isabel "the power of expression" (*Prison* 137). In her view this lack is directly related to Isabel's underdeveloped education—indeed education and creativity are related proportionally, the better the one, the greater the other.

More generally Dorothy Berkson likens the "classic" bildungsroman to the novel of moral initiation and counts *The Portrait of a Lady* squarely within this tradition. She includes the Puritan tradition in her description of its uniquely American attributes: its characters demonstrate a combination of Emersonian individualism and Puritan-like "intense and isolated examinations of their consciences" (53). Berkson nevertheless insists upon the distinction between male and female bildung; female initiation must perforce occur on a moral and spiritual plane because the external and social freedom of experience is denied her strictly due to her gender (54).

While these works and other feminist criticism inform my readings of the individual novels throughout this study, the overall approach I take to the bildungsroman genre is speculative in comparison. Too often these approaches, each with its many variations, have seemed irreparably at odds—with the one side charged with valuing transcendental abstractions at the expense of social and political responsibility, the other with valuing the sociological and anthropological over the aesthetic and spiritual experience that literature has the unique capacity to provide. My approach is due, first, to my own inclinations and habits of reading. I have often encountered a certain inadequacy in culturally based explanations of the novel because they typically fail to provide the kinds of tools necessary to address questions concerning the ontology of self-formation. Such approaches often result in a narrowing of the expansive dimensions of human experience that have been with us, however problematically, all along.

By looking at self-formation first as a religious practice, and how this practice changes as it filters through time and the aesthetic medium of the novel, I hope to show that for both women and men, forming selfhood has as much to do with one's metaphysics as it does with one's relation to others in the world.

Bildung as Spiritual Self-Formation

Since it is my intention to elucidate the differences between the ways in which eighteenth-century English Arminianism (as associated with John Wesley) and American antinomianism (as associated with Jonathan Edwards) respectively inform the nineteenth-century bildungsromans of each nation, an initial discussion of terminology may be useful. Arminianism originally refers to the doctrines of the Dutch theologian Jacob Arminius (1560–1609). From its beginnings Arminius's theology sets itself against Calvinism in its belief in the compatibility of human will with God's sovereignty as well as in the more inclusive belief that all, not simply the elect, may experience salvation. During Wesley's and Edwards's time, the term *Arminian* took on an increasingly vague meaning to include approaches to faith that value works over saving grace. Antinomianism (the term itself traces back to the Gnostics), lends itself even less to precise definition. In short it refers to the belief that a state of grace exempts the individual from following moral law. In its most extreme form, it distinguishes sharply between the spiritual and bodily state such that the unimportance of the latter allows for complete insubordination. It would initially, then, appear problematic to associate Edwards with such a dangerous idea, particularly since many of his contemporaries associated the opprobrious term with the impulsive excesses of the Great Awakening (Marsden, *Jonathan* 279). I take it to embody, rather, a particular abstention, not only from lawless acts but also from "works" in general because, in the Calvinist universe, all action is irrelevant to the individual's spiritual estate. In this context, then, antinomianism comes to embody an essential ontological problem: it is the paradoxical disjunction between the soul's predetermined inviolate state as it confronts the transitory world. I seek to elucidate the ways in which this metaphysical problem affects the concept of self-formation in the American bildungsroman.

In England the legacy of Wesley's Arminian vision of self-formation translated into the central importance many Victorian novelists placed on action, or what the protagonist "does." As George Levine puts it, "the question of vocation—what to do for a living—blends with the question of vocation—what to do morally" in the most exemplary Victorian bildungsromans of the period ("Jane" 90). On the other hand, in America Edwards's antinomian predicament between the fixed state of the soul in conflict with sin and the mutable world would extend quietly into the nineteenth-century American literary visions of self-formation through characters' confrontations with large-scale, life-shaping forces that become less cosmic in origin but remain nearly as irresistible. As such this legacy would appear to be comparatively indirect in its influence in comparison with its German or English counterparts, no doubt due in part to the fact that, post revolution, the very concept of "elect" had slowly metamorphosed from a static ontological condition of the individual (to "be one of the elect") into a dynamic secular activity pertaining to an entire culture—"to elect" as something one *does*.

Edwards's vision conflicts with what Tracy Fessenden questioningly calls "good" religion in American literary studies, or that which "emerges hand in hand with the new nation as a uniquely American achievement, the Puritans' sense of chosenness democratized and domesticated by Enlightenment tolerance, with the blessings of free exercise extended most liberally to matters of privately held belief and not to those allegedly irrational, regressive, or inscrutable forms of religious life . . . deemed foreign to democracy" (*Culture* 2). Indeed while Edwards's Calvinist legacy appears to pose a conspicuously inconvenient contradiction to secular rational democracy, it nevertheless persists as an indispensable and formative part of this tradition, particularly as it relates to the ways in which nineteenth-century novelists dealt with the unavoidable questions of what constitutes self-formation in the world and how to make sense of experience.

To avoid anachronism, throughout the discussion in part 1, I frequently use the phrase "spiritual self-formation" in place of bildung. Likewise as I discuss the English and American novels throughout part 2, I typically use "self-formation" in place of bildung and "novel of self-formation" in place of bildungsroman. Though the tradition of spiritual bildung did indeed exist in Germany and was practiced mostly by Wesley's and Edwards's Pietist contemporaries, I do not wish to imply that either Wesley or Edwards—or the nineteenth-century novelists influenced by them—thought of spiritual formation in precisely the same sense. I do, however, argue for the existence of parallel traditions of self-formation in all three national contexts as they are connected by the international revival movements.

The Contexts of Conversion: Evangelicalism in the Nineteenth Century

One defining feature of evangelicalism—subject perhaps as much to fervent desire in believers as to derision in skeptics—is the conversion experience or, in John Wesley's words, the "renewal of the heart in the whole image of God, the full likeness of him that created it" (*Works* 11:444). From England's Evangelical Revival under Wesley's guidance to Jonathan Edwards's American Great Awakening to Count Zinzendorf's resurgence of Pietism in Germany, all variously contribute to the greater cultural discourse of change that novelists variously interpreted well into the nineteenth century. The ways in which each nation interprets this experience alongside additional attributes unique to Methodism, American Calvinism, and Pietism respectively reveal nuanced versions of the individual's capacity for change that would have far-reaching literary effects into the nineteenth century.

The Legacies of Wesley and Edwards

Owen Chadwick's classic ecclesiastical history, *The Victorian Church,* has long since established the breadth and depth with which evangelicalism permeated Victorian culture. Apart from its presence within the Established Church itself, its influence registered from the newly emancipated Catholics of the period to the furthest reaches of Dissent. Chadwick identifies the central reason for the widespread influence of evangelical doctrine to be the perception that it represented "the authentic voice and the scriptural piety of Protestant Reformation" (5). After Chadwick, Ian Bradley's *Call to Seriousness* contributes a focused study of the deep impression Anglican Evangelicalism made on Victorian culture.[25] Queen Victoria herself was raised in a devout Evangelical household, and Bradley attributes to Evangelicalism the responsibility for "giving the Victorians their notorious seriousness and high-mindedness," which includes "the piety, the prudery, the imperialistic sentiments, the philanthropic endeavour, and the obsession with proper conduct" typically associated with the era (13, 18). Further, early to mid nineteenth-century Evangelicalism possessed a strong anti-intellectual quality that only grew more pronounced as England moved toward the Second Evangelical Revival, circa 1858 (20, 17). In place of ideas, the individual was concerned with, not surprisingly, the practical Arminian question of "What shall I do to be saved?" Bradley identifies two diverging and in some senses inherently contradictory answers to this persistent question, both of which share affinities with eighteenth-century Evangelicalism: self-examination and "ceaseless activity."

Much as it was during Wesley's time, the imperative of self-examination—"the most introspective feature of a highly introspective religion"—served Evangelicals' "sense of accountability" at the Day of Judgment, the practice of which led many to wallow in self-criticism (23–25). Ceaseless activity, on the other side, served as "the only refuge from the horrors of self-examination." This second imperative lends the movement its characteristic practical (if not somewhat neurotic) energy; individual adherents were hounded by the urge to be unceasingly *useful.* Particularly this second Evangelical characteristic had a great impact on the culture at large "if only," Bradley concludes, "because their behaviour contrasted so strongly with the indolence and apathy of the majority" (32). Peter W. Williams makes a similar argument with respect to American evangelical influence on nineteenth-century antebellum culture: the culture of Second Awakening revivalism and reform "not only shaped the lives of evangelicals themselves but became so pervasive in national life that all Americans had to come to terms with it in one way or another" (*America's* 199).

Perhaps the most obvious difference between evangelicalism in early nineteenth-century England and America is that in America, no single denomination enjoyed the privileges and powers associated with state sponsorship.[26] Though tensions nevertheless persisted among the many evangelical denominations in America, their basic cooperation on key points that would make up the Second Great Awakening gave their association a democratic tenor. Williams makes the case that Congregationalists (once Puritans), Presbyterians, Methodists, and Baptists more or less agreed upon the recognition of the Bible as the sole source of revelation, the necessity of personal conversion, and, finally, the "missionary imperative" (182).[27]

These points also belonged to the first Awakening, but the (nominally) Presbyterian Charles Grandison Finney (1792–1875) makes it clear in his lectures that between Edwards's time and his own significant changes in the theological landscape had occurred. Between the poles of Edwards's Calvinism and Wesley's Arminian doctrine of perfection, Finney and other Second Great Awakening ministers were interested in negotiating a middle ground, though one bordering closely on Arminian territory. In marked contrast to Edwards's mysticism, Finney's "What a Revival of Religion Is" (1835) is representative of this move. It begins with the words "Religion is the work of man" and continues on to insist that religious revivals are not miracles, "above the powers of nature," but rather based upon agency of the preacher as well as of the sinner (Finney 135). Particularly for the latter, conversion "consists in his acting right."

In line with this new emphasis on activism, participants in the American Second Great Awakening deeply concerned themselves with reform, which they clothed in the rhetoric of "Benevolent Empire" (Williams, *America's* 192). Coincident with westward expansion, underlying the Second Awakening were the needs for community as well as for authority—these were especially pressing the closer the revival activity came to the frontiers. One of the most noticeable signs of reform appeared in the many charitable societies founded around the time, such as Bible distribution societies, tract societies promoting temperance, and abolitionist societies such as the ethically dubious American Colonization Society (193).[28] Unlike the perception in Britain that increased as the nineteenth century continued—due largely to the class-entrenched distinctions between the Established Church and Dissent—that the second wave of revivalism was largely for the uneducated, American evangelicals emphasized the importance of education both for spiritual instruction as well as for the democratic imperative of having a well-informed electorate (202). Finally the greatest distinction between the religious climates of England and America at the time is the fact that the old Puritan conviction of exceptionalism had never quite deserted the American national consciousness. This frequently took the revised form of "postmillennialism," or the belief that the kingdom of the Book of Revelation would gradually unfold—perhaps on American soil—and climax in the Second Coming at the end of the millennium (206).

The Spectrum: Individual Conversion to Cosmic Change

If the original idea of bildung meant something like the reformation of the self into the image of God, one of the central qualities inherent in this idea is progressive change in some form. Evangelical conversion, the idea of foundational reformation in individual spiritual life, reflects microcosmically widespread cultural concerns about the nature of change as they surfaced not only in theological but also in the volatile scientific and political discourses from the mid-eighteenth into the nineteenth centuries. William James's division of individual conversion into two basic forms, either gradual (*lysis*) or instantaneous (*crisis*), draws upon this rich tradition (*Varieties* 145).[29] In its most cosmic sense, religious change manifests itself in the form of millenarianism. Premillennialists maintain that the thousand years of blessedness will follow the cataclysmic Second Coming of Christ. Postmillennialists hold that the gradual "spread of righteousness over the earth" shall precede and prepare the way for the Second Coming.[30] As Dwight A. Culler explains, the "apocalyptic temper" of the eighteenth-century Evangelical Revival affected the ways in which secular culture came to understand change: in geology, for instance, scientists were divided between "catastrophists" and "uniformitarians" or "gradualists." The first group held that the earth came to exist in its present state as a result of violent catastrophes, as first advanced by the German geologist Abraham Gottlob Werner (*Poetry* 14). "Uniformitarians" followed the Scot James Hutton, who in 1785 held that the earth formed over a series of slow and gradual processes. In the political realm, the American and French revolutions appeared to mirror and confirm the "catastrophic" view of change. As a simultaneous social and political reaction in England, Culler observes it to be no coincidence that Charles Lyell's uniformitarian *Principles of Geology* (1830–33) appeared concurrently with the first Reform Bill.

Culler conceives these contrasting points of view to have resounding effects upon the English literary imagination: the movement from catastrophism to literary uniformitarianism mirrors the movement from the Romantic to the Victorian period (15). Catastrophists, such as Thomas Carlyle, rely on "visionary imagination" and "divine revelation," whereas novelists such as George Eliot, through observation and analysis, attend to change in its slow and subtle manifestations. Jerome Meckier builds directly upon Culler's argument and raises the difference between the proponents of opposing "aesthetic ideals" into two "formidable encampments": "on one side Lyell, gradualism, Darwin, the Reform Bills of 1832 and

1867, George Eliot, G. H. Lewes, and novels like *Felix Holt;* on the other Carlyle, catastrophism, Chartists as a reminder of the French Revolution, Dickens, Collins, and novels like *Bleak House* and *Tale of Two Cities*" (*Hidden* 249). As Meckier further notes, the aesthetic gradualism of Eliot dovetails with the principle of change in Darwin's 1859 *Origin of Species* (248).[31]

Among these multifarious versions concerning what most accurately constitutes the nature of changing reality, most tend to overlook the fact that the international revival movements—with their leaders and adherents obsessed alike with the idea of conversion as an individually based, spiritually reformative activity—play a significant role in this conversation. In their introduction to *Modern Christian Revivals,* Edith L. Blumhofer and Randall Balmer argue that "most Christian revivals have as their object some sort of conversion or experience of grace in the individual," which typically takes the "instantaneous and datable" form; others seek the gradual understanding of "their spiritual lives as pilgrimages" (xi).

Most often conversion in nineteenth-century literary contexts has lost its original sense as a spiritual activity and has instead been transferred into a psychologically based phenomenon, one of many attributes contributing to the protagonist's overall development. William James's approach in *Varieties of Religious Experience* (1902), to be sure, largely informs this shift from metaphysical to psychological understandings of the conversion experience. Critics have subsequently gone on to apply James's ideas to the novel; Barbara Hardy, for instance, representatively maintains in *The Moral Art of Dickens* that typical conversion in the Victorian novel involves not a religious experience but rather "a turning from self-regard to love and social responsibility" (27). And yet not only does the experience remain pivotal in the protagonist's life, but it also affects the structure of the novel itself: the "enactment of conversion," Hardy writes, provides "the very hinge of the true novel of moral development" (56).

For those who prefer along these lines to approach the novel as a predominantly empirical genre, indeed an alternate study might focus solely on how parallel traditions of secular bildung, or self-formation, in eighteenth-century England and America apply to the nineteenth-century novels of both nations. Such a study might consider the ways in which Shaftesbury's "self-form'd," civically minded aristocrat eventually broadened to include the development of middle-class protagonists of the Victorian novel. It might, in turn, describe how in America this secular vision of self-formation underwent democratization via figures such as Franklin and Jefferson and apply this predominantly empirical, rational, and ethical model to American fiction of the nineteenth century.

Here the bildungsroman is more than simply a late eighteenth-century German import, secularized to suit the culture in which it appears; its animating principle encompasses an essential component of the way we understand the nature of change in, and the spiritually formative dimensions of, human consciousness.

Since my approach seeks to broaden the range by which the genre is typically understood by including the enduring contributions that religion has made to it, I devote the majority of part 1 to the foundational ideas of self-formation in the English, American, and German evangelical contexts. Chapter one explores how Wesley's doctrine of Christian Perfection invests the concept of self-formation with an Arminian, process-oriented ethos and optimistically maintains that salvation is available to all. Chapter two considers how Edwards's Calvinist ontology—exaggerated by the geographical precariousness of existence relative to English Calvinists—maintains a tense relationship between everyday living and the eternally fixed state of the soul. Chapter three outlines Zinzendorf's visceral-affective view of "heart religion" in order to make the elemental connection between spiritual self-formation and the international revival movements as they coalesce in the prototypical bildungsroman, *Wilhelm Meisters Lehrjahre.* In this novel Goethe incorporates the historical figure of Zinzendorf into the text itself in order to acknowledge the spiritual dimensions of bildung while at the same time expanding the concept into his own synthetic vision containing the additional forms of Romantic and Enlightened bildung. Part two develops the parallel transatlantic applications of eighteenth-century English and American ideas of spiritual self-formation to their own respective nineteenth-century novelist legatees. Accordingly each chapter in part two commences with a critical review of an author's ties to his or her respective theological tradition.

Each bildungsroman under discussion contains a pivotal conversion moment; also the protagonist of each is faced with a triangle of influences, secondary characters with whom he or she must come to terms (or fail to do so) in order to realize spiritual self-formation to its fullest extent. Chapter four commences with *Jane Eyre* because it holds in common with *Wilhelm Meister* the central concern of locating a balance between romantic and religious extremes within the character of the protagonist. In the language of Brontë's novel, the critical component of Jane's self-formation most conducive to her happiness involves a reconciliation between romantic propensity and religious principle. She accomplishes this in part by both engaging in and distancing herself from the eighteenth-century English Evangelical tradition as the cleric St. John Rivers represents it. For these reasons *Jane Eyre,* of all Brontë's oeuvre, lends itself most readily to this method of examination. In chapter five, on the other hand, partly due to Dickens's troubled relationship both with the Established Church as well as with Dissent, spiritual self-formation in *David Copperfield* is characterized more by what David rejects—for instance the various forms of counterfeit religious and romantic ways of living—than by what he directly embraces. Like *Jane Eyre, David Copperfield*'s status as one of the best-known examples of the English bildungsroman is often taken for granted. This reexamination of Dickens's most representative bildungsroman provides a new frame through which we might admire it. Both English novels, through various degrees of reorientation toward secular goals, exude an Arminian optimism about the value of work, the wholeness of the world, and the possibilities of human growth and fulfillment in it.[32]

In America, Melville struggles in chapter six with the Edwardsian dilemma in *Pierre* by subjecting his protagonist to impossible, life-determining forces that work irresistibly, and ultimately devastatingly, beyond his control. Poorly received in its own time and often overlooked in ours, *Pierre* represents an apparent anomaly even within Melville's own body of work. Nowhere, to my knowledge (and probably for good reasons), has the novel been considered to be an American bildungsroman. I do so here partly in order to highlight the radical contrast the figure Pierre casts next to his more acceptable and accepting English counterpart. Pierre is a nonstandardized figure whose development (or rather nondevelopment) proceeds outside consensus, indeed poses a direct challenge to it. Finally chapter seven shows that, due in part to the legacy of his father's lifelong engagement with Calvinism and its attendant ideas, in *The Portrait of a Lady* Henry James domesticates and refines these cosmic forces but preserves their antinomian potency in the interior life of Isabel Archer. This final work appeared roughly thirty years after the publications of *Jane Eyre, David Copperfield,* and *Pierre* (all of which were published within five years of each other, 1847–52). *The Portrait of a Lady* looks forward to the ways in which the American traditions of spiritual self-formation expand into the twentieth century: James's portrait of Lambert Strether might, for instance, appear next in line at the beginning of a new century.

In sum while the protagonist of each bildungsroman is centrally occupied with searching out that elusive principle capable of reconciling the world with the individual soul, the British and American authors offer different solutions that reflect their respective religious traditions under discussion. If Jane Eyre and David Copperfield largely confirm the reconciling properties of active Arminian experience, Pierre Glendinning and Isabel Archer retain a basic antinomian ambivalence toward experiential reconciliation with the world.

My goal is not, therefore, to present yet another study of Goethe's transatlantic influence on the Victorian and American novel. Rather I seek to contextualize the nineteenth-century Victorian and American bildungsroman alongside their Continental counterpart as each is informed by the eighteenth century's common concern for, and unique understanding of, formation of the self in spirit.

Part I

I remember by the way that you once asked me in those old Seminary days we have been talking about, to recount to you the little Iliad of my private bosom.

Henry James Sr., "Seminary Days."

1

JOHN WESLEY'S FORMATIVE "SPIRITUAL EMPIRICISM"

Things are wrong with them; and "What shall I do to be clear, right, sound, whole, well?" is the form of their question.

William James, *Varieties of Religious Experience*

Christianity, considered as an inward principle . . . is holiness and happiness, the image of God impressed on a created spirit.

John Wesley, "A Plain Account of Genuine Christianity"

Possibilities for This Life: The Evangelical Revival in England

Beyond Germany's borders, a deep tradition of spiritual formation had long been in practice throughout Protestant England and subsequently in colonial America. Indeed fundamental differences existed between eighteenth-century English and American understandings of spiritual formation that would have consequences reaching far into the nineteenth century. That is, the ways religious writers understood the role experience plays in spiritual self-formation would affect the ways in which later secular authors on both sides of the Atlantic understood the same in their fiction. The writings of Methodist John Wesley on the one hand advance a reasonable, practical, optimistic, and progressive view of personal development and the role of world experience as the individual strives for happiness, perfection, and eventually, for union with God. In contrast the often perilous contact of Jonathan Edwards's Calvinist orthodoxy with the mutable world frequently infuses experience with a paradoxical quality and fosters a mystical, transcendental longing for self-annihilation in God.

I concentrate on contemporaries Wesley and Edwards and, in connection with Goethe's *Wilhelm Meister*, Count Zinzendorf, because together they represent a nexus within the mid-century international revival movement: the Evangelical Revival, the Great Awakening, and the renewal of Pietism respectively in England, America, and Germany. While united in their basic concern with the individual's developing identity in relation to God, each leading figure advanced clashing interpretations of the fragile balance between free grace and ethical responsibility. Most simply stated, Wesley's doctrine of Christian perfection tended toward an externally oriented Arminianism on the one extreme; Edwards's (and, as Wesley would eventually charge, Zinzendorf's) insistence on irresistible grace and inward witness inclined in the opposite direction of the inwardly oriented antinomianism.

Several central currents of thought, both theological and philosophical, in Protestant England leading up to the Evangelical Revival laid the foundations for Wesley's original and fundamentally optimistic view that "Christian perfection," or reforming the self in the image of God, is possible in this life for everyone.[1] The process of perfection as Wesley conceived it necessarily involves the active concurrence between reason and the affections, faith and works, spiritual and empirical experience.

In English Protestant theology, beginning around the middle of the seventeenth century with the "Latitude-men," reason and practical ethics were elemental to understanding individual spiritual formation. In opposition to the Calvinist emphasis on free grace and innate depravity (as well as Hobbesian selfishness), latitudinarian sermons advanced the concept of individual "Primitive Integrity," that religion is wholly compatible with everyday living; in seeking happiness people will naturally recognize that it is in their best interest to pursue the religious life. By taking a commonsense approach to religion and downplaying doctrine, by the close of the century the latitudinarians had become the dominant force within the Church of England.[2]

In response Nonconformists such as John Bunyan and Richard Baxter sought to preserve the importance of grace and the distinction between the religious and the secular life that the latitudinarians had sought to minimize. Their separate dissenting traditions (Baptist and Presbyterian, respectively), however, led them to value experience ("works") differently. Bunyan showed his separatist and anti-Arminian tendencies by insisting on grace and faith as operating independently of outward circumstances. Baxter, on the other hand, identified more with the Puritan tradition (in the sense of those seeking to reform the church from within) by disapproving of antinomians and placing high value on practical works.

The larger conflict dramatized in the seventeenth century between the rational latitudinarians of the Established Church and Evangelical Nonconformists would continue into the eighteenth century within the dissenting tradition itself. The role the affections should play in relation to reason and grace as a part of spiritual formation became increasingly important to Dissenters. Up through the middle of the eighteenth century, divines in both England and America (including Edwards) would count reason and the affections not as mutually exclusive but rather as necessarily working together in the process of spiritual formation. Reason identifies and judges the soundness of revelation, but the passions are necessary for the individual to *act* in accordance with the newfound inner condition. But by using rhetoric of the affections, divines opened themselves to the charge of enthusiasm, which would become a significant problem accompanying the revivals in both England and America.[3]

It is from within this theological context that Methodism appeared as a part of the Church of England itself.[4] As for Wesley's role in shaping eighteenth-century English understanding of individual spiritual formation, Methodism offered itself as an integrated alternative to Calvinism, which, in Wesley's words, is "the direct antidote to Methodism, the doctrine of heart-holiness" (qtd. in Rivers, *Reason* 1:212). Experience and "works" in themselves are not enough to gain salvation, yet they are an integral part of the process toward it. Indeed Methodism's emphasis on process makes it particularly suitable to the concept of spiritual self-formation: as Rivers succinctly puts it, the regenerate individual, "whose life is a process of recovering in himself the image of God, will be perfect; yet this perfection is possible to all human beings."[5]

In addition to the theological precedents, some critical attention has been directed toward the philosophical contribution of the British Enlightenment to Wesley's thought, particularly with respect to his attitude toward experience. Generally, however, critics have downplayed the connection in favor of emphasizing Wesley's extrasensory or primitively emotional understanding of religious epistemology.[6] But in *Locke, Wesley, and the Method of English Romanticism*, Richard E. Brantley makes the case for Wesley's embrace of experience, worldly and otherworldly, as integral to salvation and living happiness. Experience understood in this way would, in turn, have a literary influence on nineteenth-century Britain, both for the Romantics and the Victorians (2, 211–12). Brantley contends that on the one hand Wesley understands (via Locke) that religion is significantly determined by empirical experience, and reciprocally that experience need not be empirical. This thesis is nowhere more apparent than in the language Wesley uses to describe faith in terms parallel to sense experience; he implies that "sense-perception is analogically and therefore really related to faith" while at the same time he is careful to acknowledge that spiritual and empirical experiences require distinct "senses" (48).[7]

Similarly Dreyer makes the case that experience composes the cornerstone of Wesley's thought. Where Methodism as a theological system is, finally, incoherent, epistemologically it is consistent on the principle that "nothing is known that cannot be felt" (29). "Sensible experience" was the basis of Wesley's conversion, and Dreyer offers several interpretations of what this may mean (in addition to what it does not): knowledge of God by manifest sensation or emotion; in contrast to the mystics who seek self-immolation in God, examination of the knowable self; directly perceptible witness; spiritual senses for spiritual truths (16–18). In sum knowledge and experience of faith are indissolubly linked.

Wesley's psychological emphasis on rigorous self-examination over the mystical quest to lose the self in contemplation of God marks an important contrast to Jonathan Edwards. Whereas self-examination in Edwards's "Personal Narrative" is, for instance, accompanied by ecstatic longing for the absolute experience of being "emptied and annihilated" and "swallowed up" in God, Wesley focuses on sanctification as one moment in a long, living progression toward perfection that may be applied to all of the Christian's worldly actions.[8] It is a noteworthy coincidence that to make this point Wesley uses the very same language as Edwards does: in a letter Wesley urges Ann Bolton to avoid mystics who are guilty of "refining" religion and instead to experience "humble, gentle, patient love," for "believe me, you can find nothing higher than this till mortality is swallowed up in life. . . . All the high-sounding or mysterious expressions used by [the mystics] either mean no more than this or they mean wrong. O beware of them!" (Wesley, *Letters* 5:342). The empirical emphasis on "swallowed up" here stands in direct opposition to Edwards's mystical meaning: it is the moment in which the individual confronts mortality. The highest experience in life is not the transcendental vision of dissolving into God but rather love as qualified by humility, patience, and gentleness, all of which are virtues applicable to particular situations the individual encounters daily. Similarly in an earlier letter to Bolton, he again uses the very same language of Edwards (in this case vaguely attributed to Roman Catholic writers) to show his disapproval: "They are perpetually talking of 'self-emptiness, self-inanition, self-annihilation,' and the like: all very near akin to 'self-contradiction' as a good man used to say" (5:313).[9]

Finally Theodore Runyon perhaps puts it best when he describes Wesley's attitude toward experience as "spiritual empiricism" (189). The most important transformation on which every individual should concentrate is the one that occurs in this world: for Wesley "genuine knowledge of God [should] be of such a nature that the knower is transformed in the knowing process" (193). Runyon characterizes transformation as occurring through the experience of conversion, or regeneration, in which the image of God reconstitutes itself in the individual. Experience in this sense originates neither in the affections nor as a set of innate ideas in the mind. Insofar as Wesley instead identifies experience as something originating outside the self, his understanding is Lockean. From this basis Runyon offers a new reading of Wesley's Aldersgate conversion experience that differs from the usual account of it as a prime example of religious subjectivity.[10] Rather "it is the *other* that is the primary content of experience and the self only as the recipient of the activity of the other. The sensation in the subject testifies to the revealed reality of the object and the epistemological relationship between them" (191). Applied to Wesley's conversion, then, the sensation he felt in his heart was secondary to, and a sacramental symbol of, the primary activity of God's image renewing itself within him.

Runyon's article provides a platform from which we may risk a definition of spiritual self-formation as Wesley understood it. For Wesley "knowledge is regeneration—the awakening of sensitivities within the knower which allow the knower to participate in the reality of the real world as constituted by the Creator and at the same time to actualize the full capacities of the self" (190–91). Gaining knowledge, then, through experience leads the individual to recover the image of God within and yet, utterly unlike the mystics, to preserve and improve individual identity. This hopeful, practical view of self-formation emphasizes process and a hierarchical devotion both to God and to the human community. In a sense the individual becomes a superlative version of the preconversion self, at once closely united with Christ but also fully capable of doing God's work in the world.

Perfection in Time

Perhaps the most concrete way to see Wesley's "spiritual empiricism" at work in the process of self-formation is through his autobiographical writings in combination with his explanation of the doctrine of Christian Perfection. Wesley never composed an official narrative of his conversion or a spiritual autobiography, but he does informally describe the process of his spiritual formation, including the conversion experience, in his journal for the year 1738. In addition to this, the largely retrospective "Plain Account of Christian Perfection" has been described as a "partial spiritual autobiography" with its emphasis on process and the (Arminian) importance of works (Whaling, *John* 72).

As Wesley's biographer Henry D. Rack observes, Methodist diaries served as "an aid to spiritual self-development," a quality they shared with their Puritan predecessors and Pietist contemporaries (421).[11] A representative example of this approach appears in Wesley's journal entry for Wednesday, May 24, 1738, in which he enumerates his spiritual progress from boyhood through his conversion at Aldersgate Street. The latter occurred, significantly, among his Moravian associates

(*Journal* 1:475). Though the entry dramatizes Wesley's ongoing conflict between outward and inner experience of the religious life, he emphasizes that "the image of God, was what I aimed at in all," and he proceeds to indicate that the way to reach it was through concrete actions, or "by doing his will, not my own" (1:468). He mentions earlier in the same year that his growing acquaintance with mystical writings made union with God appear to be the highest achievement in life, but he immediately recognized that this type of union came at the expense of doing good in the world (1:418). Wesley's distaste for the mystical approach to spiritual formation appears as early as 1726 when, as a young college man in his early twenties, he "began to see more and more the value of time" (1:467). Rather than cultivating a timeless inner closeness with God, Wesley recognized the importance of cultivating God's image *in time*. Understood in this way, religious self-formation is subject to the particular slowness, doubt, and hesitations that come with daily living.[12] Further that the conversion experience itself—of which Wesley famously described, "I felt my heart strangely warmed"—did not radically change these realities in Wesley's own life indicates that conversion is only one moment in a long living continuum of growing in grace. Indeed immediately after returning home on that May evening, he writes he was "much buffeted with temptations; but they fled away. They returned again and again."

Wesley's complex understanding of individual spiritual formation as encompassing advancing, wavering, retreat, falling, and rising would become central to his controversial doctrine of Christian Perfection. In "A Plain Account," not only does he allow for converted individuals to "grow in grace," but he warns that without diligence, it is possible to fall from it. And yet for those fallen individuals who had once "experienced all that [he means] by perfection," it is possible to "recover" their former state once more (11:426–27). Again Wesley appeals to experience: he is aware of many who have repeatedly regressed before becoming "established" in perfection. But most important to the process of self-regeneration is the recognition of its spontaneous beginnings, which Wesley describes with a special kind of urgency: "we are to expect it, not at death, but every moment; that now is the accepted time, now is the day of this salvation" (11:393). What gives this position its empiricism—and a large part of its controversy as well as its appeal—is the emphasis on spirituality for the living: once the individual begins the hard work of self-reformation in time, the process itself shall carry on into eternity (11:426).

This fundamentally forgiving, inclusive, optimistic approach to spiritual self-formation takes implicitly into account all obstacles that daily living, or sense experience itself, presents to the believer. Experience is not to be shunned in pursuit of inner stillness but rather through it, sometimes in spite of it; however slow the process, it is possible to reach the highest goal of re-creating the self in the image of God: "Earth then a scale to heaven shall be; / Sense shall point out the road"

(11:370). These words, from a hymn he and his brother composed, encapsulate beautifully Wesley's particular sense of "spiritual empiricism." Furthermore the practical nature of Wesley's doctrine of Christian Perfection is apparent in his affirmation that perfection and infirmity (of body or mind) may coexist as "a natural consequence of the soul's dwelling in flesh and blood" (11:394). Wesley invites the believer to accept the unavoidable flaws inherent in the human condition as well as the possibility of reaching living perfection.

The central role of experience in Wesley's religious epistemology culminates in his final account of perfection as comprising three integrated qualities: "purity of intention"; "renewal of the heart in the whole image of God, the full likeness of him that created it"; and "loving God with all our heart, and our neighbor as ourselves" (11:444). All relate directly to the individual's experience: the first signifies the lifelong dedication to God's work, the second involves uncovering Christ-consciousness within the mind, the third appeals to being a benevolent, disinterested member of the community with equal affection for all. While Wesley explicitly states that he sees no "material difference" among these three qualities, for the present purpose, the implications of the second quality with respect to individual identity bear further consideration.

As Wesley states in his *Journal* and throughout the "Plain Account," renewing the heart and mind in the "whole" image of God is possible while living. The telos of religious experience, then, becomes a particular kind of individual integrity that does not merely approximate the godlike but rather assimilates it completely. To many, particularly Calvinists, this doctrine represented a dangerous affront to the power of God's sovereignty by placing too much value on individual "works."

One of the ways in which Wesley addresses these objections reveals his understanding of the limits of individuality as it relates to "works." Good works lack perfection until they "lose themselves in God. This is a kind of death to them, resembling that of our bodies, which will not attain their . . . immortality, till they lose themselves in the glory of our souls, or rather of God, wherewith they shall be filled" (11:441). The reason why Wesley insists upon the sacrificial "death" of good works is in order to keep each good action sacred and pure by erasing the stamp of any evils attendant on individual identity such as pride and vanity. Once these evils disappear, the image of God surfaces and the individual becomes a "perfect" conduit. In creating a metaphorical parallel between good works and the body, the "death" and transfiguration of each, Wesley yet again demonstrates the deep correlation between empirical and spiritual experience.

Within the span of two short paragraphs, the very language with which Wesley describes the individual's relationship to God is encompassingly elemental: he describes love of God as "fire"; the good works return to their source "as rivers seem willing to empty themselves, when they pour themselves with all their waters into the sea" (11:441). Further he compares the soul to the air, or "a void capable of being filled with thee and by thee; as the air, which is void and dark, is capable of being filled with the light of the sun"; and finally that the "root" of good works is in God, not in "me."

Even though he adds to the above the curiously mystical image of the "abyss" into which the soul falls as it experiences "deep gratitude" to God, by using predominantly empirical language to express his highest spiritual beliefs, Wesley yet again differentiates himself from the mystics (11:441). In contrast with Edwards's desire to experience individuality being overcome by and absorbed in God (and thereby to return to God's image), Wesley understands restoration in the image of God to imply "being filled with and by" God. The idea of being filled presupposes the continuing existence of some form—in this case the individual soul—even in the case of an element as apparently amorphous as dark air, it nevertheless represents *something* capable of "receiving and restoring" God's grace and works.

Seen in this light, the otherwise puzzling epigram "True humility is a kind of self-annihilation; and this is the center of all virtues" gains a new kind of clarity (11:437). Annihilation is not the complete, absolute dissolution into God—rather the part of the self that must experience annihilation (potentially many times over) is that which harbors vanity and pride. Purged of these spiritually destructive qualities, the soul is free to act in God's image in the world and thereby embody "true humility."

2

THE PARADOX OF EXPERIENCE IN JONATHAN EDWARDS

6. Resolved, to live with all my might, while I do live.

Jonathan Edwards, "Resolutions"

Jonathan Edwards and John Wesley

Considering that Calvinism is, in Wesley's own words, "the direct antidote to Methodism," it is not surprising that most studies of eighteenth-century evangelicalism have avoided overlapping discussions of the individuals who served as their respective mid-century American and English representatives. The exceptions are notable, if sporadic, beginning in the early 1960s with Albert C. Outler. In an edition of Wesley's writings, Outler goes so far as to claim that the Great Awakening as led by Jonathan Edwards was a significant source for Wesley's own revival in England (*John* 16). Edwards himself, Outler further argues, "always minus his 'Calvinism,'" contributed significantly to the evangelical aspects of Wesley's Methodism (16n54). After Outler critics such as Charles Rogers, Gregory Clapper, Frederick Dreyer, and Richard E. Brantley have variously taken up the subject; the first three focus predominantly on theologically or philosophically based differences, whereas Brantley instead looks at their epistemological similarities.

In "John Wesley and Jonathan Edwards," Rogers points out the fact that while Edwards and Wesley neither met nor corresponded, nor do we have any direct evidence that Edwards knew Wesley's work at all, Wesley published more of Edwards's works than he did of any single other writer (22). While Rogers correctly states that the two spiritual leaders agree on the importance of the affections in religious life, one of the most important differences involves the theology of perfection. As opposed to Wesley's allowance for the truly regenerate individual to "make shipwreck of the faith," Edwards's view of a fall from grace is comparatively rigid and unforgiving. Further Rogers infers that Edwards, in a position clearly more antinomian than Arminian, would disapprove of Wesley's doctrine of perfection because it puts too great emphasis on the believer's personal powers over God's sovereignty (36).[1]

Clapper also remarks on the interest in the religious affections Wesley and Edwards share but maintains the additional important difference between the ways in which each interprets religious experience. Wesley's answer to the dangers of enthusiasm, potentially "an obsession with one's own inner experience," is to emphasize the external "fruits" of the affections or "making Christian love and joy manifest in the world through one's actions" (421). Implicitly this creates a tension between Wesley's practical, outward-oriented theology and Edwards's antinomian tendency (evident especially in the "Personal Narrative") to concern itself precisely with the formative powers of mystical-intuitive "inner experience" to the neglect of the world-oriented aspects of spiritual life.

Although Dreyer's "Evangelical Thought: John Wesley and Jonathan Edwards" presents Edwards's "rationalist" qualities in an extreme light, Dreyer makes perhaps the most suggestive case for the differences between the two divines (including the argument that Edwards is not, in fact, an empiricist).[2] Starting from the most basic point that Wesley and Edwards have in common—their evangelicalism—Dreyer insists that the similarities stop there once we consider their respective systems of thought. In large part Dreyer confronts one of the most basic problems inherent in any discussion of religious thought, which by definition is the attempt to objectify and open for analysis what is essentially the ineffable and profoundly subjective world of belief.[3] If we look at Edwards and Wesley as thinkers, the demonstrable differences between the two are many and radical.

In Dreyer's view it is not enough to make the theological distinction (Arminian/antinomian) between the two men: their differences are "not so much theological as metaphysical. Wesley is an empiricist in his basic assumptions and Edwards a rationalist. The former is preoccupied with the world of perception, the latter with the world of necessary relationships" ("Evangelical" 191–92). The evidence Dreyer advances applies to their various approaches to knowledge, existence, faith, free will and sin, and God—in other words all of the fundamental elements that together make up each thinker's theological cosmos. With respect to knowledge, Dreyer identifies two separate approaches to truth accessible either by the understanding or through perception. The first applies to Edwards, the second to Wesley. Edwards's approach to knowledge was "ontological in its basis and proceeded from the assumption of necessary being" (180). Wesley's, on the other hand, was "psychological, and proceeded from self-consciousness." Always a deductive thinker,

Edwards begins with the necessary existence of God, which he regards more "as an irresistible presupposition than a demonstrated conclusion" (182).

Other concepts that reveal Edwards's ontological position include his ideas of existence, faith, and the nature of sin. Unlike Wesley for Edwards "*being* precedes *consciousness*"—in other words the ways saints experience faith and the religious affections all depend on, and are a consequence of, the apprehension of their estate as an externally based objective truth (184). In this way faith is not so much an experience as it is a transcendental apprehension. Edwards himself only acknowledges the mind as a function of God—the only being with real, substantial existence: "In metaphysical strictness and propriety, he is, as there is none else. . . . God is as it were the only substance" (qtd. 187). By denying substance to everything other than God, Edwards in effect denies individuality (and thereby individual experience) altogether. And like faith, sin is a function not of choice or any particular actions an individual may commit but necessary to human nature itself. In sum for Edwards "things are true not because they happen but because they are necessary" (189). For Dreyer all of these elements amount to Edwards's fundamental denial of the "possibility of purpose" (187). The antinomian implications of this statement are clear: if God is the only substantial being, the individual and thereby all individual actions are insubstantial and thereby comparatively inconsequent. Spiritual identity, faith, and sin are all predetermined quantities.

As an alternative to this wholly metaphysical version of Edwards, it is certainly appealing instead to consider him in epistemological terms that seem more commensurate with present taste, as Brantley does in *Coordinates of Anglo-American Romanticism: Wesley, Edwards, Carlyle and Emerson.* Why indeed discuss any theologian's influence (in this case into the nineteenth century) in terms of largely obsolete dogma, including discomfiting ideas such as innate depravity and irresistible grace?[4] Brantley seeks not difference but synthesis of Wesley's and Edwards's shared Lockean epistemologies and their combined influence on nineteenth-century Anglo-American thought. He argues convincingly that experience is one of the most powerful connections between the seemingly irreconcilable empirical ("natural") and evangelical ("spiritual") epistemologies: in both traditions "one must see for oneself and be in the presence of the thing one knows." On this basis Wesley, Edwards, Carlyle, and Emerson seek finally to "theologize empiricism" by balancing faith with reason, myth with scientific fact, and through an inclusive "both/and" philosophical approach to theology, "they share the simultaneously rational and sensationalist reliance on experience as the avenue to both natural and spiritual knowledge" (1).

By taking this line, Brantley explicitly chooses to emphasize the "aesthetic-epistemological" over the "ontological" Edwards (9–10). Curiously while he argues for Wesley's and Edwards's "both/and" philosophy of empirical evangelicalism, he limits his own treatment of Edwards to epistemological concerns. One consequence of this choice is that the argument does not fully do justice to the fact of Edwards's Calvinism and its central role in shaping his attitude toward experience and its formation of individual identity. More attention to Edwards's theology would, of course, lead away from a synthetic vision and enter into serious and possibly irreconcilable differences between the two figures, or everything that the differences between Arminianism on the one hand and antinomianism on the other would entail.

Perfecting Perfection

It is not so much the fine points of doctrine themselves that are at issue here but rather the conflict arising from their necessary contact with the external world. The conflict may best be described as a collision between the fixed state of the soul and the mutable world of temporal experience. As for the first point, Edwards's ontological inwardness, or lifelong antinomian preoccupation with the condition of the soul, is fed by the inexhaustible mystery of the covenant of grace. Under this covenant day-to-day experience suddenly loses its formative significance because the soul's primary condition is determined by God out of time. As such it is fundamentally immune to any alteration by the affective powers the world of experience (the "flesh") has to offer.

At the same time, it is necessary to take into account the fact that temporal experience is an unavoidable, if transient, reality as are the attendant experiences of beauty, good and evil. Through contact with these variables arise enjoyment and consciousness of sin accompanied by its inevitable companion: death.[5] With both incommensurate realities before the individual—the ever-inviolable Puritan spirit in constant, forced contact with the world—through the habit of self-examination, the solution, at least in Edwards's case, appears in the form of mystical annihilation into the image of God. The complex negotiation for a balance between these clashing elements contributes significantly to Edwards's precarious sense of spiritual formation.

For a text crucial to understanding Edwards's approach to the individual spiritual estate, I turn to the 1734 sermon *A Divine and Supernatural Light.* The sermon, which Randall Stewart has called "the finest statement . . . of the experiential nature of religion," provides a suitable instance by which it is possible to gauge the value Edwards places on intuitive transcendental experience and how it defines individual formation.[6] By examining the intersection of "knowledge" with mystical intuition in the sermon, I emphasize that for Edwards the most primary formative experience for the saved individual comes not from "flesh and blood" but instantaneously from God himself. In other words the personal experience of spiritual knowledge is important and derives not from an entirely rational, nor empirical, nor yet an affective source but from a mystical-intuitive one. Immediacy is a significant element to take into account not only because it is commonly regarded as the central feature of intuition, but also because some consider it to be the defining feature of experience itself.[7] I choose to focus on *A Divine and Supernatural Light* for the additional reason that it was published just three years prior to the *Faithful Narrative of the Surprising Work of God,* which locates the sermon very near the epicenter of New England's Great Awakening.[8] That it appeared four years before Wesley's conversion is coincidental, yet this fact nevertheless allows for a convenient source for comparison to Wesley's thought around the same time.

Edwards's "Personal Narrative" (circa 1739), or spiritual autobiography, offers a particularization of *A Divine and Supernatural Light*'s general characterization of transcendental self-definition. It dramatizes, among other things, spiritual self-formation as a complex interaction between the soul's fixed eternal state and its temporal experiential growth. The most developmental moments in the narrative occur when the transcendental and temporal collide in immediate intuitive experience. While the identity of the saint is determined out of time, the narrative—because it necessarily documents lived experience—is a fitting form through which the saint may document progress or "growth" in grace. In *Cosmic Optimism* Frederick William Conner identifies the same concept as persisting in America across time and genres: "the standing paradox of transcendentalism in its evolutionary form [is] that the world is perfect but is getting better" (376n12).[9] If, then, Edwards be a "true saint," the narrative is a document revealing the truth of a soul that is perfect but is getting better. Add to this paradox the fact that Edwards was harassed by a profound consciousness of sin throughout his life, particularly after his conversion, and the result is a complex, deeply ambivalent attitude toward the relationship between temporal experience and the eternal state of the soul and the way these two apparent irreconcilables together form individual identity.[10]

Sermonizing Experience: A Divine and Supernatural Light

It probably goes without saying that Edwards would not have considered himself foremost a mystic. From an orthodox point of view, a mystic may very well fall into the same category as an enthusiast—both of whom, to various degrees of intensity, give undue authority to flights of feeling unsupported either by the Bible or by reason. And Edwards would never countenance any spiritual state to which he could not give his rational assent. Hence the sermon's consequential full title, *A Divine and Supernatural* LIGHT, *Immediately imparted to the Soul by the* SPIRIT *of* GOD, *Shown to be Both a* Scriptural, *and* Rational DOCTRINE: Edwards would have the two central authorities capable of demonstration (the Bible and reason) concur upon a single intuitive experience. Accordingly his biographer George M.

Marsden locates in the sermon Edwards's "most profound theological reflections on his understanding of true Christian experience" (157).

The opening scriptural passage for the sermon comes from Matthew 16:17 ("And Jesus answered and said unto him, Blessed art thou, Simon Barjona: for flesh and blood hath not revealed it unto thee, but my Father which is in heaven"). The two central points that he derives from it involve Simon's blessedness and the nature of knowledge. The two are directly linked in that together they answer the ever-pressing question for Calvinists: how shall I know the condition of my soul? The most important knowledge of all (Christ's identity as the son of God) Simon knew independently of all "flesh" and is thereby blessed for it. So being in a state of grace and being capable of exercising transcendental ways of knowing are related and perhaps depend one upon one another. In keeping with Edwards's antinomianism, and backed by the previous century's antinomian controversies, the sermon concerns itself more with knowing over doing.[11] Edwards makes it clear that God is the "author of all knowledge and understanding whatsoever," which includes moral and secular types of knowledge. While both forms of knowledge (human and spiritual) are gained through experience, the operative difference involves the manner by which they are transferred: the first passes on the knowledge gained by temporal experience, but spiritual knowledge, by virtue of its immediacy and truth, comprises experience in its purest form. For Edwards the meaning of this experience involves a foundational epistemological reorientation as the saint becomes aware of possessing "new principles" (as opposed to "natural" ones) (*Works* 17:410).

The discovery and following activity of "new principles" are not, in contrast to Wesley, analogous to anything in nature, nor are they available to everyone. In the elect they are "caused to exist in the soul habitually . . . according to such a stated constitution or law, that lays such a foundation for exercises in a continued course," and "those principles are restored that were utterly destroyed by the fall" (*Works* 17:411). Those fortunate enough to discover those principles that by "law" already exist within are able, through the exercise of regenerate reason, to reconstitute in themselves the image of God. For Edwards salvation is not so much a process as it is a discovery of preexisting conditions. The word *principles* of course is commensurate with rationalist thought, but it is at the same time independent of reason alone; indeed the term is something Edwards was never fully satisfied with.[12]

From this new "foundation," the spirit of God acts freely in the saint as an "indwelling vital principle" (as opposed to an "extrinsic occasional agent" in the "natural" man) (*Works* 17:411). It is upon this point the individual in a sense sacrifices distinct identity to enable the free movement of the spirit of God within, which "operates in the minds of the godly, by uniting himself to them, and living in them, and exerting his own nature in the exercise of their faculties." To this Edwards adds the mystical component of the holy spirit's ability to act on an individual and yet "not in acting communicate himself." The saint, then, is not wholly subsumed by the Holy Spirit but preserves individual faculties, such as the understanding, but exercises them actively in a new, holy way.

In what appears to be a conservative position fortified against enthusiast or mystical interpretation, Edwards defines the spiritual and divine light as "a true sense of the divine excellency of the things revealed in the Word of God, and a conviction of the truth and reality of them, thence arising" (*Works* 17:413). In other words this new way of knowing appears to be based entirely on the Bible. But a remark he makes later in the sermon deepens the complexity of his definition: while it is impossible that an individual experience the spiritual light independently of the Bible, "that don't argue, that the Word properly *causes* that light. The mind can't see the excellency of any doctrine, unless that doctrine be first in the mind" (*Works* 17:416; emphasis added). Once again it appears that only the elect, by possessing a priori knowledge of the doctrine, are able to recognize it in the Bible. The Bible contains the "subject matter" of the light, but "that due sense of the heart, wherein this light formally consists, is immediately the Spirit of God" and accessible solely to the chosen.

As it follows from the above definition of spiritual light, two distinct means of knowing the good exist in the mind: the "sense of the heart" and the rational faculty. The first represents the primary means by which to identify the light and its "excellency." It may be useful here to recall Edwards's earlier "universal definition" of excellency in "The Mind" (circa 1723) as a kind of basic affirmation: it is "the consent of being to being, or being's consent to entity" (*Works* 6:336). In that essay "being" is an aesthetic-intuitive concept that indicates proportion and complex beauty; "entity" encompasses all that is good. In order to avoid its opposite—contradiction as "the greatest and only evil"—the saint's intuitive inclination toward God is an acceptance, a "yes," to being in its most profound sense.

Applied to the sermon, then, while it is possible to make a rational judgment about God's excellency, the heart-assent to the light is what signifies most. Indeed the illustrative examples Edwards provides—the sense of honey's sweetness or a person's beauty—serve not to show that he is finally an empiricist but that in a Platonic sense the "flesh" can never reveal spiritual knowledge but can sometimes shadow it forth.

Once the saint has affirmed God's excellencies, the next step toward full apprehension is to gain a "conviction of the truth and reality" of them. In this case as well, intuition operates together with reason—the difference is that intuition determines the truth of spiritual knowledge instantaneously and is therefore the most direct way of knowing. Reason, on the other hand, provides indirect confirmation in time though participating in argument and speculation on related themes (*Works* 17:414–15). That intuitive knowledge should be instantaneous and not conveyed by anything other than God is rational, Edwards argues, for "why should not he that made all things, still have something immediately to do with the things that he has made?" (421). Experiencing this intuitive knowledge is, then, the telos of all being because it instantly connects individuals to their creator.

The only call to action with which the sermon concludes is an exhortation that all listeners engage in self-examination to determine whether they have had the experience Edwards describes. They are to seek knowledge "that which is above all others sweet and joyful" and provides the greatest consolation of all: the possibility of spiritual transfiguration (*Works* 17:423–24). The passage from Paul that Edwards instances is particularly striking in this regard: "But we all with open face, beholding as in a glass the glory of the Lord, are changed into the same image, from glory to glory, even as by the Spirit of the Lord" (2 Cor. 3:18). This passage and many others throughout the sermon make explicit that the saint effects the movement from a perceived state of separation into unity with God through an act of intuition: the experience is instantaneous and links directly with seeing, or "beholding," God's image within and without. This description presses toward the outer limits of language's capabilities: an experience based on pure sight shrouds itself, finally, in the ineffability of mystical experience.

Narrating Experience: "The Personal Narrative"

Of course by urging parishioners to examine the state of their own souls, Edwards is in line with the long Puritan tradition emphasizing self-examination as a central contribution to spiritual formation. Apart from the sermons and other public writings, some of the most urgent literary explorations offering insight into Puritans' continual, obsessive practice of self-examination appear in various forms of spiritual autobiography.[13] It may at first seem odd to use the concept of spiritual self-formation in any connection with Edwards or indeed with any Puritan. As we have seen, the very concept of spiritual formation or development in any sense in a Calvinist universe is full of paradoxes, since Calvinists concerned themselves with uncovering the individual's unchanging qualities in God over those that admit development. The soul's ontological condition excludes active perfectibility (when the soul was, is, and shall be always the same), and yet the practice of spiritual autobiography, in its many forms (journal, conversion narrative, etc.), itself demonstrates a step-by-step process toward which an individual discovers internal signs of grace. In his "Personal Narrative," Jonathan Edwards epitomizes this paradox when he expresses a longing for more time to "grow in grace" and to "increase" holiness (*Works* 16:794–95). This exercise in itself may very well be a kind of spiritual self-formation.[14]

In this connection an observation Owen Watkins makes in *The Puritan Experience: Studies in Spiritual Autobiography* is particularly fitting: "A man was what he was through the process of being remade" (238). What does this mean? The phrase indicates stasis (a man was what he was) in the midst of change (the process of being remade). This paradox stands, and in a sense must stand, at the core of Puritan spiritual identity. A saint is always a saint, and yet at the same time possesses the opportunity while living to "grow in grace." The "new" self must, then, serve as the text's narrative authority because only from this perspective is it possible to reveal coherently both identity and growth.

Critics have further pointed out a host of related paradoxes in the "Personal Narrative," including the fact that while the elect individual may notice internal signs of God's grace, the individual is at the same time worthless and the body vile: "self-transcendence required self-abasement, and self-fulfillment meant self-annihilation," which made for "an unstable emotional life." Another similar paradox the narrative invokes is the simultaneous pressure the autobiographer feels to present the self while at the same time effacing its autonomous existence.[15] Watkins offers one possible solution: the discovery of each person's "true self-image" is a movement through the alienation caused by these paradoxes toward reconciliation. Unlike secular Continental definitions, uncovering Puritans' "true self-image" does not encompass an "unlimited range of possibilities" but only a narrow pair: either Adam, which signals the "inheritance of depravity and death," or Christ—"to be made conformable to the image of Christ was not a restrictive experience, it was the only way to be set free from the chains of self-love" (227). The tensions, then, between grace and vileness on the one hand and between individual autonomy and self-annihilation on the other are all swallowed up in the all-conciliating image of Christ. Tensions that would plague the individual pre-conversion no longer apply to the regenerate individual or, in Theodore Runyon's words, "the knower is transformed in the knowing process."

As Daniel B. Shea points out in his pioneering work, *Spiritual Autobiography in Early America*, Edwards's "Personal Narrative" does not follow the usual conventions of the genre, which typically features the individual seeking signs of grace in the context of family, church, and political identity (111).[16] Edwards's presentation, on the other hand, repeatedly dramatizes his isolation from such contexts in his search for internal grace. His wife Sarah's narrative, the first-person account of which we have only the indirect presentation in Sereno Edwards Dwight's *Life of President Edwards*, conforms much more obviously to the importance of family, community, and church life in relation to individual salvation.[17]

The fact that Edwards's most significant and formative spiritual experiences occur while he is alone, outdoors, apart from the church community or any other immediate form of cultural sway suggests yet another context in which Edwards is more interested in the antinomian position of spiritual formation as "being" over "doing." Had the most important moments of the narrative occurred in political or church contexts, the emphasis would be on "doing" (as it was with Wesley), or the social activities generative of spiritual identity. Along these lines Thomas G. Couser reads the "Narrative" as avoiding the step-by-step model of exemplary action and instead cultivating an "exemplary attitude" that is inimitable yet archetypal (*American* 24). He is what he is through the process of being remade.

Edwards's "exemplary attitude," I would suggest, develops in kind with the type of spiritual experiences he describes, which increase in intensity and culminate in mystical-intuitive insight. In its barest outlines, the trajectory of Edwards's spiritual formation may be described alternately as pantheism, scriptural enlightenment, renewed sensibility, and finally seeking complete absorption into the image of God. Though excerpted often enough, Edwards's crowning conversion experience is worth quoting at length to demonstrate a concrete instance in which the temporal and eternal collide in a moment of intuition:

> Once, as I rid out into the woods for my health, *anno* 1737; and having lit from my horse in a retired place, as my manner commonly has been, to walk for divine contemplation and prayer; *I had a view,* that for me was extraordinary, of the glory of the Son of God; as mediator between God and man; and his wonderful, great, full, pure and sweet grace and love, and meek and gentle condescension. . . . The person of Christ appeared ineffably excellent, with an excellency great enough *to swallow up all thought and conception.* Which continued . . . about an hour; which kept me, the bigger part of the time, in a flood of tears, and weeping aloud. I felt withal, an ardency of soul to be, what I know not otherwise how to express, than to be *emptied and annihilated;* to lie in the dust, to be full of Christ alone . . . *to be totally wrapt up in the fullness of Christ.* . . . I have several other times, had views very much of the same nature, and that have had the same effects. (*Works* 16:801; emphasis added)

I emphasize the language of intuition through which Edwards describes the conversion experience: he had a "view"—not an idea, not a sense, not a feeling, but a "view" of God that led him for an extended period into the transcendental contemplation. This marks an important contrast to Wesley's comparable "heartwarming" conversion experience, for while the affections and emotions are without a doubt integral to Edwards's experience, in themselves they have no causative powers—these belong to God and the receptive faculty of intuition itself. In the first part of the paragraph, the "view" reflects primarily the truths he perceives. It is his consent to being. It is only as a result of perceiving and consenting to these truths that "for the bigger part of the time" he found himself full of ardent longings and awash in tears.

Of course an experience that "swallowed up all thought and conception" opens itself only with great difficulty to analysis—it is futile, perhaps, to inquire precisely into Edwards's psychology for that hour—but it seems fairly certain that while he speaks with ardent longing to be "emptied and annihilated" and "to be totally wrapt up in the fullness of Christ," the narrative stops short of claiming actual fulfillment of this desire. This suggests that while the saint may infinitely approach God's image, complete assimilation is impossible: what prevents complete immersion or "annihilation" is the encumbrance of the flesh, but also perhaps more important it is the presence of the small seed of doubt even the holiest saints may have about their salvation.[18] In addition to these obstacles, in Edwards's case the most significant hindrance is intellectual pride.

Implicit or explicit awareness of these hindrances in turn drives the narrative into a protracted discussion involving the first point in Calvinist dogma: total depravity. That Edwards devotes a considerable section to this subject after describing his conversion experience is another way to distinguish his view of spiritual self-formation from Wesley's.[19] Whereas Wesley took it almost for granted that the regenerate individual would fall into error, backslide, "make shipwreck of the faith," his focus is consistently on the practical, positively oriented concept of perfection in spite of personal flaws. Edwards, on the other hand, lest he become too self-righteous, must continually remind himself of—even dwell upon—his own depravity.[20]

One of the most remarkable features of this section of the narrative is that Edwards uses the same language to describe his sinfulness as he does to describe the circumstances surrounding his conversion. To take one example: "I have often . . . had very affecting views of my own sinfulness and vileness; very frequently so as to hold me in a kind of loud weeping, sometimes for a considerable time together: so that I have often been forced to shut myself up" (*Works* 16:802). Elsewhere, as in his view of Christ, his "wickedness" appeared to him "perfectly ineffable, and infinitely swallowing up all thought and imagination; like an infinite deluge, or infinite mountains over my head. I know not how to express better, what my sins appear to me to be, than by heaping infinite upon infinite, and multiplying infinite by infinite." In both cases, conversion and subsequent conviction of sin, the "view" is present as well as the affective response and ineffability of the experience. This suggests that for Edwards the two types of experiences are indissolubly, if painfully, bound and together significantly contribute to his spiritual makeup. Recognizing this connection in itself is a kind of knowledge that was unavailable to him in his youth.

The consciousness of his own sin, especially the personal failure of relying too much on his own intellectual strength, casts a considerable shadow over his regard for the value of personal experience and its formative potential: "The thought of any comfort or joy, arising in me, on any consideration, or reflection on my own amiableness, or any of my performances or experiences, or any goodness of heart or life, is nauseous and detestable to me" (*Works* 16:803). Furthermore the dangers of self-examination are apparent—while it allows the saint to grow in grace, it may also lead undue self-glorification in "works."

However much the narrative itself lingers over Edwards's perceived sin and "badness," a thread of determinism seems to run throughout it, from the first clause of the first sentence—"I had a variety of concerns and exercises about my soul from my childhood"—to its conclusion of God's absolute sovereignty: "I rejoiced in it, that God reigned, and that his will was done." That this is a narrative account of a saint's perseverance seems fairly certain: nowhere does it appear that Edwards will do anything—such as abandon the established spiritual course and become, say, a poet or an actor—but reach the highest point of living mystical conversion and continue beyond it to grow in grace according to God's will.

Edwards's perfectionism, his reliance on mystical, transcendental experience to define spiritual identity, provides points of intersection with Continental German Pietism, the third pillar of the international evangelical movement. Its leader, Count Nikolaus Ludwig Zinzendorf (1700–1760), provides the crucial link between eighteenth-century ideas of religious self-formation, or bildung, with the prototypal bildungsroman, Goethe's *Wilhelm Meister's Apprenticeship.* Zinzendorf's presence in the novel's inset spiritual autobiography in addition to the novel's significant engagement with Pietism signifies an elemental correspondence between the activity of self-formation specifically of a spiritual character and the bildungsroman as a literary genre.

3

PIETISM AND THE "FREE MOVEMENT" OF SELF-CULTIVATION

Synthesis and Transformation in Wilhelm Meister's Apprenticeship

I thank you very much for the copy of your novel you sent. I have a feeling, which actually increases, pervades and possesses me the further I read in it, that I cannot better express than by a sweet and inward contentment, by a feeling of a spiritual and physical health. I am willing to bet that it will be the same for all other readers.

Schiller to Goethe, 7 January 1795

What a strange man you are! You can no more shake my trust in you than you can deprive me of the hope of seeing you happy. I do not want to pry into the mysteries of your superstitiousness, but if you believe that your life is entangled in strange associations and premonitions, then I would say to you, for your consolation and enlivenment: Associate yourself with my own good fortune, and let us see whose genius is the stronger, your dark spirit or my bright one.

Wilhelm to the Harper, book 4, chapter 2

Pietism and Affective Experience

An extended comparative discussion of Count Zinzendorf's Renewed Moravian Church with the revivals in England and America warrants a separate study in its own right. In keeping with the scope and intentions of the present work, a brief overview of Zinzendorf's theology as it informs spiritual bildung must suffice to contextualize Pietism alongside its English and American evangelical counterparts.

F. Ernest Stoeffler has located the intersecting point for the international revival movements within "the Zwingli-Butzer-Calvin axis of the Reformation, which began to show its first characteristic evidences within English Puritanism and the Reformed churches of the seventeenth century. . . . Through the Wesleys it helped to shape the evangelicalism of Great Britain. In America it combined with and revitalized the older Puritan tradition to form the basic religious ethos of a host of Protestant denominations" (*Continental* 9). In another work dedicated wholly to Continental Pietism, *German Pietism during the Eighteenth Century,* Stoeffler goes into greater detail describing the overlap between Pietism and American Puritan traditions, most obviously by pointing to the existence of Pietistic Puritans.[1] For both groups the central experiences of self-examination and repentance were necessary daily activities (*German* 21). And yet Stoeffler's description of Zinzendorf's form of early Moravian piety bears significant differences from Puritanism as Edwards understood it: it is "essentially a joyful, emotional, perhaps basically romantic, attachment of the individual Christian to the 'Savior'" (159). And the nature of this attachment reveals Zinzendorf's heterodoxy in the sense that it at once affirms "the Lutheran understanding of the meaning of Christ's victory over sin and death" and emphasizes individual psychological identification with Christ's suffering (151).

D. Bruce Hindmarsh's *The Evangelical Conversion Narrative* makes a more explicit case for the nature of this psychological identification as it is informed by Zinzendorf's Christology (177).[2] Based on Zinzendorf's wounds theology, religious experience assumes visceral dimensions. Accordingly Hindmarsh characterizes Moravian conversion narratives by "the vivid devotion of the writers to the bodily suffering and wounds of Christ." Zinzendorf's own conversion was radically different from the typical Pietist understanding of the experience, which took for its traditional model the autobiography of August Hermann Francke (164). According to this model, conversion required a "painful struggle" or *Busskampf,* followed by a "breakthrough to consolation," or *Durchbrach.* Zinzendorf emphasized instead "the concrete and sensual apprehension of Christ suffering on the cross," including its aesthetic dimensions. This was based in part on his transforming encounter with Domenico Feti's *Ecce Homo,* which he encountered as a young man in a Düsseldorf gallery during his European *bildungsreise.* The work features Christ, his brow wet with blood from the crown of thorns and a coarse rope about his neck; below lies the inscription: "This I have suffered for you but what have you done for me?"[3]

Stoeffler adds that the visceral-aesthetic qualities of religious experience are further important for Zinzendorf because they contribute to individual poetic imagination and to the affections, both of which are more important than rational argument in generating sacred meaning (*Continental* 144). Thinking alone is not enough to experience God, but instead "religious apprehension involves the whole man, and preeminently his affective nature"—the importance of which clearly aligns him on this point with both Wesley and Edwards. This position, in turn, puts him at odds with the "Enlighteners" who restricted religion to categories acceptable to reason, and at the same time anticipates the burgeoning romanticism of the Sturm und Drang movement by the fact that his theology is rooted in the concepts of *Empfindung* (feeling) or *Gemüt* (something like "heart") (143–44).

Zinzendorf's theology additionally demonstrates mystical-antinomian qualities in his relative unconcern for what Christians ought or ought not to do, which would implicitly place him in accord with Edwards in this respect (153). At the same time, his antinomianism would trigger the eventual personal and theological parting of ways with Wesley as well as with other more traditional Pietists. Indeed Wesley records the rupture in his journal for September 3, 1731, the day on which the two men met and conversed at Gray's Inn Walks in London. Wesley's three major objections to Zinzendorf's doctrine were antinomianism, mystical insubordination, and "subtlety" in place of real wisdom. For his part Zinzendorf strongly objected to the Arminianism of Wesley's doctrine of Christian Perfection (2:487–500). Wesley's charge against Moravian "stillness" was, as Hindmarsh explains, from the Moravian perspective "an appropriate pastoral response to the problem of English 'enthusiasm' run amok" (*Evangelical* 163).

As Stoeffler summarily concludes, for the devout Pietist "the heart of Christian piety must not be considered a set of regulations but a joyful, affective, unutterably satisfying, personal relationship with 'the Savior.'" Elsewhere Zinzendorf would refer to the individual's achieving this Christ-centered relationship as attaining the "heart-religion." Consistent with the high value Zinzendorf places on affective response, he holds poetry to be a vehicle superior to argument to communicate the secret of "heart-religion." Once the individual experiences this deep connection with Christ—and on this point he definitely differs from Wesley and perhaps also from Edwards—all aspects of life, even the most mundane, lose their ambiguity, uncertainty, and sordidness, for the individual is continually aware of and wholly aligned with God's will. For those who possess the heart-religion, a kind of sanctity permeates existence itself: "A kind of celestial light is . . . cast upon all facets of human experience. In the deepest sense the life of the believer, both in its individual and its corporate aspects, takes on a certain provisional nature, insofar as every conscious segment of it points beyond itself to the happy state of divinely intended fulfillment" (154–55). Present experience is important because its close alignment with God's will invests it with eternal significance.

From within the dynamic and contentious cultural environment containing the currents of Pietism (promoting mysticism and the religious affections), and Enlightenment thought (advancing the optimistic freedom for individual rational inquiry), Goethe developed his own synthetic understanding of bildung that culminated in *Wilhelm Meisters Lehrjahre* (1795–96).[4]

Wilhelm Meister's Apprenticeship and the Trivium of Self-Formation

In his definitive English-language biography of Goethe, Nicholas Boyle describes the effects of Pietism on the then-inchoate German nation as less than transcendental. Boyle emphasizes that Pietism's main features (its inwardness, private gatherings, disregard for rank, and political quietism) made it a perfect complement to the "state absolutism" toward which Prussia was especially gravitating in the early eighteenth century (1:12). Count Zinzendorf was a "radical" of whom the Goethe household was wary. Rather than associating directly with the Herrnhut Brethren, the Goethes were among those nominally Lutheran families of Frankfurt who frequented less extreme, more "respectable" Pietist circles (1:75).[5] Perhaps Goethe's most significant connection with Pietism coincided with a break in his university studies (due to illness and an ensuing psychic and artistic crisis) during which family friend and devout Pietist Susanna von Klettenberg helped him to recover. During this period of convalescence, and before returning to his studies in 1770, Goethe declared a "Christian commitment," which lasted less than two years altogether (1:72). And yet the period had lasting spiritual significance on the young poet. It put before Goethe the decisive questions: "did [he] wish to live, and if so, what for?," and he knew that "any answer had to be at least as serious, at least as intimate with the inner life, as the piety at Herrnhut" (1:77). The direct artistic fruit of his acquaintance with von Klettenberg would not ripen for yet another twenty-five years—it was her spiritual autobiography on which Goethe would eventually base book 6, "Bekenntnisse einer Schönen Seele" (Confessions of a Beautiful Soul), of *Wilhelm Meister's Apprenticeship.*[6]

In *Dichtung und Wahrheit* (Poetry and Truth), Goethe's own autobiography, he describes his acquaintance with von Klettenberg.[7] One of the first characteristics he mentions is her ill health, which she regarded as an "inevitable, essential part of her transitory earthly existence" (einen notwendigen Bestandteil ihres vorübergehenden irdischen Seins) (14:370). Goethe thereby implies that von Klettenberg's best focus, energy, and intensity inclined inward: "Her favorite, perhaps sole, topic of conversation was the moral experiences which one can gain through self-observation" (Ihre liebste, ja viellicht einzige Unterhaltung waren die sittlichen Erfahrungen, die der Mensch, der sich beobachtet, an sich selbst machen kann).

She was neither "too learned" nor indulgent in sentimental religious feeling, but somewhere in between. As such she complacently saw herself "reflected in the image [*Bilde*] of Count Zinzendorf" himself. In the convalescing young Goethe, von Klettenberg found a delightful companion and potential fellow devotee. He reflects that his condition at the time—"My agitation, my impatience, my striving, my seeking, searching pondering and hesitating" (Meine Unruhe, meine Ungeduld, mein Streben, mein Suchen, Forschen Sinnen und Schwanken [371])—suggested to her his separation from God. Every one of these qualities would carry over into the character of Wilhelm Meister, and the effect of von Klettenberg's presence and conversation impressed Goethe just as the Canoness's manuscript impressed Wilhelm as he read it. Since von Klettenberg's manuscript has not survived and Goethe is not fully forthcoming on this point—in *Poetry and Truth* he does not mention a manuscript but only that the "Confessions" had "developed" from her "conversations and letters" (14:369–70)—it seems safest to assume that the spiritual autobiography is to some degree altered to Goethe's own aesthetic purposes and is therefore distinct from traditional Pietist autobiographies.

In *Wilhelm Meister und seine Brüder: Untersuchungen zum deutschen Bildungsroman*, Jürgen Jacobs argues that among many other influences, Pietistic autobiography (beginning in the late seventeenth century and extending into the eighteenth) served as a literary predecessor to the bildungsroman because it advanced an unprecedented interest in the individual experience: "with its call for constant introspection and its emphasis on feeling," it "intensified the attention to the individual in-and-of himself."[8] As Pietism advanced into the eighteenth century, Jacobs observes that what began as rigorous spiritual practice—if always with a trace of a "narzißtische Tendenz" (narcissistic tendency)—once it gained popular status, it devolved into "hypocondrische Selbstbeobachtung" (hypochondriac self-observation), morbid sensitivity, and sentimentality (31). As the *bildungsidee* became further secularized as the eighteenth century progressed, Jacobs states that the Pietist goal of aligning the self with God's will came to be replaced with the more secular problem of how to resolve the tension between the claim to individual self-realization and the validity of universal laws or "obligatory norms."[9] These "norms," for most people, meant to find and flourish in their appropriate station in society (38).

My own reading of *Wilhelm Meister's Apprenticeship* gives extended attention to book 6, "Confessions of a Beautiful Soul," because, most obviously, the fact that Goethe devotes an entire book to Pietistic autobiography within the prototypal bildungsroman suggests that spiritual self-formation is an undeniable component of bildung even if, finally, it must be subordinated to a more inclusive vision. As this spiritual autobiography undergoes fictionalization in the bildungsroman, the reader witnesses, in a sense, the historical transformation of bildung as a spiritual practice as it blends into, and is amplified by, romantic and Enlightenment concepts of self-formation.

With respect to the work as a whole, some read book 6 as a bridge between the earlier books of the novel and books 7 and 8.[10] Structurally the first five books reflect Goethe's initial conception of *Meister* as a novel on the theater, "Wilhelm Meisters theatralische Sendung" (1777–85). Goethe suspended work on it, during which time he traveled to Italy, and did not return to the manuscript again until 1794–96. Thomas P. Saine has argued that Goethe's intention that the novel be a bildungsroman did not occur until the latter period, which would in part account for the deepening philosophical concerns of the novel's latter portion (125, 131–32). In contrast the first five books read like a novel in the picaresque tradition; they document Wilhelm's adventures through the German countryside with a wayward acting troupe—among whom appear the beautifully drawn, visceral characters such as Philine, Sergio, and Aurelie—and dramatize his first extended contact with the aristocracy, the same people for whom he would come to work in the latter portion of the work.

Faced with the unusual circumstances of *Wilhelm Meister*'s composition and structural oddities, generally most German critics continued Friedrich Schiller's initial position on this subject. In a letter to Goethe dated December 9, 1794, Schiller admitted he was at first afraid that the lapse of time would have an adverse effect on the novel but dismissed these worries once he began reading it again (*Briefe* 1:767).[11] Schiller's sensitive insights into *Wilhelm Meister's Apprenticeship* and Goethe's replies together provide remarkable insight into the novel as a whole as Goethe resumed the manuscript and, to the present purpose, into the cryptic significance of the Canoness's life and book 6's function in the narrative. Few artists are so fortunate as to have a critic of both comparable powers and capacity for sympathy—mutually Goethe and Schiller realize this almost impossible ideal in their correspondence. In a letter dated August 17, 1795, Schiller critiques book 6 on the grounds that in it Goethe may have presented his ideas too subtly: "this topic is such that one is tempted to articulate what is left unspoken" (Dieser Gegenstand ist aber von einer solchen Art, daß man auch über das, was nicht gesagt ist, zu sprechen versucht wird [12:40]). Goethe's reply affirms Schiller's reading. In book 6 he meant "to conceal [his] intentions completely" (meine Absichten völlig verbergen wollte) and emphasizes that Christianity appears only in its "purest sense" in book 7 with the next generation (31:107). As we shall see, many have read these lines to serve as indirect confirmation that the Canoness's piety is in some profound way misguided.

Once public reaction to book 6 began to surface, Schiller reports a collective concern that while everyone finds the narrative "very interesting, true and beautiful," at the same time it seems to hold up the reader's progress in the novel as a whole (12:90).[12] On the following day, November 21, 1795, Goethe counters that in Weimar, the sixth book has been well received and somewhat coyly remarks that "to be sure, the poor reader never knows where he stands in such productions, because he doesn't consider that he never would take these books in hand if one did not understand how to get the best of his mental capacity, his sensation, and his thirst for knowledge."[13]

Of the many subsequent critics who have read the "Confessions of a Beautiful Soul" as an ironic critique of Pietism and its practitioners, Frederick J. Beharriell's article "The Hidden Meaning of Goethe's 'Bekenntnisse einer Schönen Seele'" shows that this has not always been the case.[14] From the novel's publication, readers of book 6 have tended to fall into two camps: one that reads it as a tribute to Susanna von Klettenberg and a sympathetic portrait of Pietism, and the other that sees "Goethe in the role of psychologist" whose concealed purpose was "to expose, through ironic insights, what he had come to believe were the hidden roots of religiosity in sickness, neurosis, and fear" (37). Beharriell bases the latter reading on the fact that by 1795 Goethe's antagonism toward Christianity was extreme, yet conflicted, because his personal "encounter with Pietism was no minor episode, but the culmination and crisis of the Christian tradition of his childhood and adolescence. His eventual rejection of Pietism meant a final break with beliefs and values of his childhood environment" (59).

Feminist critic Marianne Hirsch, on the other hand, counters Beharriell's reading in her contention that the Canoness's "imaginative creation of a context capable of affirming her deepest needs is a creative response to impoverishing and diminishing social circumstances" (31). This subversive affirmation has no real positive value as a model for bildung because it comes at the highest cost of death and loss of community: the Canoness is "buried alive, confined in the structures of her inner self and in the structures of Goethe's novel" (32).[15] Drawbacks common both to Hirsch's and Beharriell's approaches involve the marginal value each assigns to the experience of the spiritual inner life. I suggest instead that the "Confessions" provides a platform from which Goethe launches a more general and certainly not categorical critique of Christian piety and excessive self-absorption (clearly gender-neutral qualities in the novel).

Indeed the ambiguity that Schiller identifies within book 6—what, exactly, is Goethe's position on intense religious and ascetic bildung—and that Goethe cryptically affirms has proven to be a lasting riddle. By taking a close look at the contours of this fictionalized spiritual autobiography and some of the ways it connects with the novel as a whole, I will show that this broad trivium of self-formation—religious, rational, and romantic—contained in the narrative of book 6 informs Goethe's vision of bildung in the novel as a whole. The goal for Wilhelm Meister is a healthy, socially acceptable bildung. Goethe appears to suggest that in order to reach this, the isolating tendencies of extreme religious as well as romantic bildung must be brought under the auspices of a more balanced, rational approach to self-formation. These factors, among others, establish book 6's importance as a bridge between the earlier books of the novel and books 7 and 8.

Religious Bildung: Not for This World

In keeping with the goals of spiritual autobiography, the overall theme of book 6 resists conformity to secular cultural "norms"; it expresses, through a medium of serious-mindedness, the cultivation of the affections from worldly to spiritual. With a few exceptions, its basic trajectory follows more or less the conventions of the genre—the individual embarks into the world with few moral scruples, indulges in frivolities, gradually recognizes these for what they are, experiences several false convictions of faith, is overcome by a sense of sin and is thereby led to uncover true knowledge of faith, continues in a holy life with continual vigilance against sin and labor toward self-improvement. From the narrative's outset, we make the acquaintance of a delicate, sensitive, and intelligent child on her sickbed: religiousness is immediately associated with bodily illness.[16] The narrative begins, "Up to my eighth year I was a healthy child; but I have as little memory of those years as I have of my birth. Then, when I had just turned eight, I had a hemorrhage, and from that moment on I was all feeling and memory" (217). As she recovers, the influences by her family are threefold, each representative of different dimensions of bildung: her mother entertains her with stories from the Bible; her father brings her specimens from his scientific collections, "dried plants and insects . . . human skin, bones and mummified objects . . . birds and animals that he had shot"; her aunt, in service of the "Prince of this World," tells her love stories and fairy tales. About these disparate influences, she reflects: "I absorbed everything. It all took root." Significantly the fact that all of the objects representing the natural world are in the state of morbidity suggests her early indifference to the dynamic vitality of nature and highlights her inwardness. Of the remaining two influences, romance and spirituality, both of which feed her inner life, she devotes a considerable portion of the narrative to the former.

The simple story of the Canoness's youthful romantic attachments makes it easy to see that the religious serious-mindedness that early illness brought her would eventually assert itself as a way of life. The specter of death, symbolic or real, hangs over nearly every temporal relationship in the narrative beginning with her earliest attachments to two brothers who passed away before reaching adulthood. The story of her long and eventually unrealized engagement to "Narcissus," a worldly young man of the court, would be otherwise unremarkable but for the turning point it triggers within her own personal development. Just before he loses the bid for a certain position at court (a condition he needed to fulfill before their marriage could occur), she finds herself closer to a state of wholeness and health than ever before. She feels the love for her fiancé and a love of God to be in a state of equilibrium: "My love for Narcissus was quite in accord with the plan of the whole of creation, and never conflicted with my basic duties. There was no opposition here despite the immense differences. Narcissus was the only person whose image [*Bild*] hovered before my mind and claimed all my love; the other feeling was not connected with any image and was inexpressibly pleasant. I don't have it anymore and cannot give it to myself again" (227). This last melancholy line is ambiguous—surely she does not refer to her feelings toward God but to Narcissus's image. The delicate irony here, Goethe seems to imply, is that the Canoness's bildung is incomplete for the very reason that she is unable to sustain a balance between earthly love and spiritual devotion and thereby positions herself *out* of accord with the plan of the whole of creation, just as sickness is separate from the state of health.

The accompanying reason for her separation from Narcissus, and further indication of her inward nature, is her inability to enter sympathetically into the feelings of another person unless that individual have a frame of mind similar to her own. Once she discovers Narcissus is not one of those individuals, the tension increases with the striking images by which she describes the turning of her feelings *from* him: "I felt like someone wishing to warm himself in the sun when the shadow obstructs him" (229); "Much as one may enjoy drinking wine, the pleasure dissipates when one finds oneself in a fully stocked wine cellar where the bad air is almost suffocating" (230); their bond was "a glass cover enclosing me in an airless space, and if only I could summon up enough strength to shatter it, then I would be free." These images of poetic imagination—also Zinzendorf's preferred means of religious expression—are so dramatic because they constitute a reversal and rejection of what secular readers, then and now, would consider to be life-giving. Instead of viewing a life dedicated to celibacy and God as a shadow obstructing her happiness, it is precisely this way of living that, in her view, constitutes absolute fulfillment.

After their separation the Canoness continues in a state of complacency about her piety and does not gain the requisite sense of sin until much later in life, in connection with another friend, Philo. Once the Canoness discovers that he, too, has marked flaws (intimated only in the most circumspect way), it is through intense identification with his suffering that she is finally brought to a real sense of her own sin: "I didn't just think this, I felt it, felt that I was no better than he. . . . I sensed the tendency in my heart . . . now the possibility of sin had become terrifyingly clear and conceivable to me." In addition to prefiguring her conversion through identification with the suffering of Christ himself, these lines provide an instance of the operative function that Pietism allots to the affections over reason in the process of spiritual bildung. Further in line with Zinzendorf's brand of Pietism, her antinomianism is reflected in her frank dismissal of "virtuous actions"—this includes acts of charity—as a remedy for this newfound feeling of sin. Even reading moral treatises was useless; the solution could only arise from within.

This knowledge of sin and the sense that any outward remedy is useless against it clears the way toward a discovery of faith. And for the Canoness, this manifests itself in a mystical experience that realizes her longing to "reach a state of complete blissful absorption in [the] self without reference to external forms and systems" (236). The conditions by which real knowledge of faith can take root are two: the experience must be purely inward, that is, free of all images and external influences; and she must cultivate a particular concentrated frame of mind in order to experience its "effects and results" (240).

The Canoness's description of her conversion moment serves to illustrate what, in Stoeffler's words, constitutes an essential part of Zinzendorf's understanding of faith, or "man's psychological identification with the suffering Christ." In the Canoness's words, it was a "strong impulse" that lifted her in spirit "to the cross on which Jesus died" (240). She likens the experience to an impulse that propels one to a much-loved friend but culminates in a "more intense, more real" connection than any earthly associations may possibly provide. "My soul drew nigh to the incarnate, the crucified One, and at that moment I knew what Faith was."[17]

From the above it is clear that the Canoness's idea of spiritual bildung coincides closely with Count Zinzendorf's—both value affective experience in the religious life and privilege the epistemological value of poetic imagination and the affections over rational argument; with the intense emphasis on inward experience, they also share mystical-antinomian qualities. Moreover Zinzendorf and his community at Herrnhut figure significantly into the narrative itself. At first the Canoness considers Zinzendorf "a thorough heretic," but as she finds out more about the Brethren, in accordance with her ability instantly to bond in a sympathetic-affective way with like minds, she devotes herself from afar to the principles upon which Zinzendorf's community was founded. Referring to the Count, she writes, "I became extremely attached to him; and if I had been my own master I would certainly have left my home and friends, and gone to join him" (242). Politically this places her in a subversive position: outwardly she would, like others with similar sympathies, attend orthodox services at court while at the same time participate in clandestine meetings. Once the meetings were discovered, the Canoness chose to remain—in keeping, to be sure, with gender roles of the time—aloof from the controversy, which further indicates her antinomianism.

The causes that eventually estranged the Canoness from the community include insincerity and limited spiritual experience she detected in some of the members and rank (252). The first objection she tolerates until the second eclipses it once her father dies and she becomes free to associate extensively with the Herrnhut Brethren. Her fastidiousness about social rank in the spiritual community is apparent in her dismissal of one of the bishops close to Zinzendorf as "a knife grinder from Moravia."[18] He apparently wished to unite himself with her which, predictably, she resisted implicitly because of her piety and ongoing commitment to celibacy. Explicitly she explains with distaste that "his whole way of thinking was that of an artisan," and she was repulsed when she saw others in high social positions treating him as their superior. This could be due in part to her perception that the reality of Zinzendorf's ideal community was less than ideal and that people were less enlightened than they professed to be. But at the same time it shows a surprisingly worldly skepticism that defers to the status quo in the sense that, lacking authentic inward witness, it privileges and affirms secular social rank over religious hierarchy. Perhaps it is here that Goethe's own voice is coming closer than usual to the surface of the narrative.

As the Canoness's own health begins to deteriorate, she is spared additional involvement with the Herrnhutters and gradually withdraws almost completely into herself. A late intervention of a physician, clearly in line with her uncle's philosophy, temporarily counters this gravitational tendency of her nature. To regain health, he encourages her not to focus so narrowly on herself but to engage with "external things." His advice is salutary: the Canoness reflects, "I was allowed to sense from afar the presence of the creator walking of an evening in the cool of the garden. With gladness I now perceived God in Nature as clearly as I felt Him in my heart" (253). This reconciliation with living nature echoes the narrative's beginning—but now the objects have come to life, if still from afar, not of their own accord but because her religious bildung has reached a point where she perceives everything in its eternal significance. This state of continuous concentration is, in a sense, the fruit of her lifelong practice of spiritual bildung against natural tendencies toward, as she explains, "dispersing my thoughts." This scattering of concentration usually refers to external, worldly distractions, and the antidote is always recourse to the spirit, either inwardly or as it symbolically manifests itself in the world.[19]

Enlightened Bildung: "Remember to Live"

The Canoness's uncle presents an Enlightenment-based counterpoint to her views, which reminds us that the narrative is not an end in itself but serves the greater purposes of the novel and, accordingly, contributes to Goethe's expansive vision of bildung. The uncle's meticulously arranged environment affects the Canoness as previously only spiritual exercises could. Goethe emphasizes the importance of the uncle's alternative vision through the repetitions in the narrative: "Splendor and magnificence had usually led me away from myself, but here I felt led back into myself," and again, "Now for the first time, external things brought me back to myself" (244, 246). That the Canoness was able to perceive this similarity adds another dimension to her character, yet because her visit occurred after her conversion experience, his views (along with the physician's) would ultimately have a limited effect on her own. Goethe seems here to indicate that even if the Canoness cannot assimilate what she apprehends—that the ideas and feelings the uncle's environment evokes are just as ennobling as her own asceticism—the alternative is serious and open to every reader.

The uncle's this-worldly perspective becomes marked in their long discussions about religion. Human beings, he argues, hold an innate closeness to God for God to have chosen to appear in the world in human form and no other: "In the concept of humanity there cannot be a contradiction with the idea of godhead, and if we often feel remoteness and difference from the godhead, then it is our urgent responsibility not to dwell on our weaknesses and faults like the devil's advocate but to seek out our finest qualities by which we can legitimately confirm our godlikeness [*Gottähnlichkeit*]" (246). It is not enough for God's *Bild* to be innate—it is each individual's responsibility to legitimize the correspondence with God through the activity of self-cultivation. Unlike his niece, who focuses on the eternal to the neglect of the usual network of worldly associations, the uncle's self-cultivation focuses on seeking, through his great love of art, architecture, and all things beautiful, "to know the full extent of our sensual being" (246). This knowledge does not lead away from God but rather *to* everything godlike in the world.

Further, in an implicit critique of the Canoness's extreme inwardness, he indicates that individual bildung is not something that can be understood in any "pure" or abstract way, that is, apart from concrete action: "When I get to know somebody, I always ask at once what is he occupying himself with, and how and in what order. And my interest in him will always depend on the answers he gives." For the uncle knowledge of another's bildung is a direct function of action and experience, the concrete following-through toward a particular goal. Indeed he emphasizes the primacy of action over all other considerations: as long as the person has "a true sense of direction and purpose," *what* that purpose is becomes "only a subsequent consideration." In other words a universally prescriptive bildung is neither desirable nor possible—each person has a unique form to realize and, in turn, a particular position in the culture from which to act accordingly. The source of most dissatisfaction and "evil" in the world derives from those who, in the uncle's words, "have the sense that a tower should be built, but whose materials and efforts only suffice for a cottage" (247). While he may not agree with the extreme otherworldliness of his niece's "tower," that is, the internal realization of her own moral nature, he honors her serious-mindedness and persistence as materials equal to the goal as she has defined it for herself.

In contrast, then (as some would say, in *prosaic* contrast), to the Canoness's mysticism, the virtues the uncle extols are those of economy, purposefulness, sureness, steadfastness, and persistence.[20] These productive qualities all manifest themselves in the Canoness's nieces and nephews because they have all been raised by their uncle strictly according to his Enlightenment *bildungsidee.*

In a letter to Goethe dated July 3, 1796, Schiller fills out this idea beyond its merely productive and civic dimensions to encompass the full ideal of an Enlightened personality: the integrated personality is an aesthetic, harmonious balance of poetry and philosophy, spirit and flesh, and for him the character of Natalie fulfills these requirements beautifully. Schiller sees the Canoness, Natalie, and Theresa as composing a threefold vision of womanhood, with Natalie's position securely at the apex: "The first two are saints, the second two are true and human; but as Natalie is both saintly and human, she appears as an angel, whereas the Canoness is only a saint, and Therese is only a perfect woman" (12:183).[21] Due to the Canoness's asceticism, she "actually does not know love" (kennt eigentlich die Liebe nicht).

Because, on the other hand, Natalie loves what is good and true for its own sake, she does not need to withdraw into mysticism nor act out of fear. Indeed for someone whose nature accepts love as a constant reality, not an addition to it, the very concept of sin becomes irrelevant. The Canoness, on the other hand, has the serious disadvantage of leading a largely guiltless life all the while feeling oppressed by a sense of sin. And because her sense of poetry is ultimately in homage to the imageless Logos, she evidences in Schiller's words a "certain aesthetic deficiency."[22] In its place her speculative cast of mind, lacking the rigor of philosophy, devolves into Pietistic mysticism. This severe atrophying of the wide range of human possibility, Schiller seems to suggest, is no better than an exercise in religious solipsism that, in turn, brings us back to the original association between extreme religious natures and a state of unhealth.

Natalie is clearly the ideal fulfillment of that which the Canoness is only a shadow. The two look strikingly similar, and it is fitting that Goethe chooses the niece—the true "Beautiful Soul" of the novel and Wilhelm's future wife—to offer gently the final criticism of her aunt to Wilhelm in book 7. The Canoness's intense self-preoccupation, frail health, and extreme morality "prevented her from becoming for the world what . . . she might have been" (317). Natalie continues, "Every cultured [*gebildete*] person knows how hard one has to struggle with a certain degree of coarseness in oneself and others, how costly self-cultivation [Bildung] is. . . . and yet if such a fine person becomes too gentle, too considerate, too cultivated . . . the world shows no tolerance . . . for what such a person is. Persons like her are outside us what ideals are inside us, models not to be imitated, but to be striven after." In light of the uncle's overarching philosophy of bildung through action and experience (under the rule of which Natalie herself was raised) this ultrafine distinction appears to be as good as a dismissal of the Canoness's example altogether.

The Canoness's description of her niece in the "Confessions" is also not without subtle criticism, not so much directed against Natalie as against the Enlightenment program under which she was raised. The Canoness expressly voices her irritation that she was kept away from the children as an unhealthy influence. She could only observe from a distance Natalie's "ability to remain active without feeling the need for some particular occupation"—a quality of perfect feminine malleability—and her work toward improving the lives of the village's poor. The Canoness rues the fact that Natalie's actions appear to be doing good merely for its own sake because she "showed no sign of love for, or need for attachment to, any visible or invisible being such as I had felt so strongly in my youth" (255). This is not to suggest, however, that Natalie's enlightened bildung is without difficulties. While bildung would appear to be the free experiential development of individual personality, the Abbé—whom Lukács calls "die Verkörperung des Erziehungsprinzips" (the embodiment of the educative principle) of the novel, and whose views coincide closely with Goethe's own—has controlled hers from the time she and her siblings came under their uncle's care (53). The "benefits" of this control the Canoness foreshadows in her narrative: if a young woman is favored with intelligent male guidance, "she will learn more than all the universities or all her travels abroad could teach her" (226). This idea directly contrasts with the Abbé's principle that it is better to permit young men such as Wilhelm to pursue a mistaken path in order to find, eventually by inclination, the one that best suits their nature.

Accordingly Wilhelm wonders aloud that it seems Natalie has never deviated from her path. She replies, "For that I am indebted to my uncle and to the Abbé . . . for they had such a clear sense of my personal inclinations. . . . My greatest delight was, and still is, to be presented with some deficiency, some need in others, and be able to think of some way of repairing or alleviating it" (322).[23] This perfect pliancy and a universal, untiring usefulness give her character a distinctly stylized quality and deepen the irony that her name has always been the "Amazon" to Wilhelm as he tracked her throughout the novel. Her occupation is to educate, or cultivate, young women in the same pattern as the Abbé has cultivated her. By her own description of her work, it appears on the surface that she simply does not agree with the Abbé's *bildungsidee* of letting the young find their way by losing it—rather she lends stability to her female charges by providing direction when each requires it, but mostly she inculcates principles through example: "by letting them grow up in close proximity" to her, she provides them with "a sense of what is good and right" (315). Ideally for Natalie, in the truly *gebildete* person, no real conflict exists between experience and principles because no significant difference exists between the two. This recalls both the uncle's philosophy as he explains it to the Canoness as well as Natalie's response to Wilhelm when he asks her whether she has ever been in love. "Never—" she replies, "or always!" (330).

Apart from her illuminating contrast with the Canoness's extreme religious bildung, Natalie is important to Goethe's presentation of the Enlightened alternative because of the transformative effect her presence has on Wilhelm: as he compares the image [*Bild*] of the "Amazon" that he had been constructing over time with that of the actual woman, "the two would not coalesce: the former had been fashioned, as it were, by him, the latter seemed almost to be refashioning him" (316).[24]

Poetic Romantic Bildung: Not for This World

And yet finally, very peculiarly, Goethe adds the problem of Mignon and the Harper to this rational, peaceful, harmonious, and by all indications successful mode of self-formation. The Italian characters' peculiar and finally tragic defiance of either religious or scientific (rational) bildung provocatively fills out its romantic dimensions. If Natalie is the embodiment of enlightened femininity and her best teaching is by example, the serious question arises: Why does her example fail to rehabilitate Mignon? Wilhelm learns through Lothario that under Natalie's care Mignon is "wasting away" (311). Mignon's episodes of "cramps about the heart" coincide with strong emotional experiences and have become increasingly frightening. To deepen the impression of strangeness, Goethe interweaves these revelations about Mignon with Natalie's rational and peaceful discussion of her own *bildungsidee*. The physician, cohort of the uncle and the Abbé and the same man who knew the Canoness, soon appears and admits to Wilhelm that their combined efforts of "moderation and purpose" were unable to help Mignon (321). Once Wilhelm is reunited with her, she surprises everyone by greeting Wilhelm tranquilly. Her demeanor fittingly resembles a "departed spirit" as she holds on her lap Wilhelm's son Felix, who, in contrast, looks "like life itself."

It is clear that her character is not reducible to any single idea such as Schiller assigns the Canoness. Indeed Schiller goes so far as to claim that Mignon "represents nothing but mankind itself"; Eric A. Blackall calls her "the spirit of poetry" and "the guiding force of the book" (Goethe, *Wilhelm* 386). Mignon shares with the Canoness a perpetual chastity, and her wild episodes of skipping heart and convulsions are evidence that for her, too, bodily infirmity is bound up with existence and keeps her at a distance from a harmonious state of healthy bildung. How, then, is the reader to understand the immense failure of the *bildungsidee* as it applies to Mignon's personality, which, according to the physician, "consists almost entirely of a deep sort of yearning" (320)? The question may only be addressed incompletely until Augustin (Mignon's father, known throughout most of the novel simply as the Harper) is taken into consideration.

With the addition of the Harper it becomes clear that the partial failure of the Abbé's *bildungsidee* is not gender specific (if, indeed, we may consider the ethereal Mignon to be female), for Augustin's horrific catastrophe in book 8 occurs while under the Enlighteners' care. We recall that Wilhelm sent Augustin away in book 5 and placed him with a pastor who, in close association with the physician, attempted to "cure" his madness. Similarly to Natalie's, their project further reflects Enlightenment principles based on the optimistic idea that reason, order, and evenness will overcome all irrational and destructive impulses within the human consciousness. Their teaching, the pastor explains to Wilhelm, consists of minimizing individual eccentricity and supporting cooperation and community: they attempt to provide their wards with "the sense of having a common form of life and destiny with many others, and show them that unusual talent, extreme good fortune and excessive misfortune are merely minor deviations from what is normal. Then no madness will ensue, or if it is already there, it will gradually disappear" (210). He continues, "nothing maintains common sense more than living in a normal way with many people. Unfortunately there is much in our educational system and everyday life that preconditions us and our children to madness." Whereas the pastor and the physician work with those already afflicted with imbalance, Natalie's work with her charges clearly is designed to reinforce the same principles in a preventative manner.

Similarly to Mignon, once Augustin is reintroduced to the company in book 8, to all appearances the physician's rehabilitative program has succeeded. He had divested himself of his long beard and cowl, and his behavior "was completely rational"; he looked much younger and addressed everyone in calm, grateful words (364). And yet after a series of intricate plot maneuvers, in spite of the Abbé's promise to keep a close watch on him and further aid in his recovery, Augustin shocks most of the company by committing suicide.

If we presume that virtually any human being may be subject to bildung, Augustin's death in combination with Mignon's represents two spectacular failures of the Enlightenment project. On the other hand, if we do not insist too strenuously on realism in the novel, it is conceivable that Goethe himself was following the physician's advice by sacrificing Wilhelm's eccentricities and objectless yearnings because these qualities have no place in a full, active, and civically productive bildung.[25] It is in any case clear that a central dimension of Wilhelm's self-formation involves the gradual displacement of this "strange family" composed of himself, the Harper, and Mignon with his "natural" son by Mariane, Felix. The first "family" is from the beginning associated with his mistaken calling as an actor; the recognition of his paternity in turn coincides with the fulfillment of his "true" bildung as member of a large and intricately connected community, including membership to the Tower Society and work as companion and interpreter for the Marchese, Augustin's brother and Mignon's uncle. Once these civic bonds are secured, Wilhelm's "apprenticeship was therefore completed in one sense, for along with the feeling of a father he had acquired all the virtues of a solid citizen. His joy knew no bounds" (307).

Still it would be difficult to underestimate Mignon's cumulative romantic appeal to Wilhelm, especially upon the occasion of her death. The experience of sublimity that Mignon's funeral elicits in Wilhelm invests her character with a religious significance, and the feelings it evokes perhaps even the Canoness could appreciate. While everyone else gathered around the casket to marvel at the doctor's skill in embalming, only Wilhelm remained in his seat. Of this moment Goethe writes, "He could not think about what he was feeling, for every thought seemed to shatter what he felt" (353). In place of Mignon's image, Wilhelm confronts the imageless that thought cannot approach without destroying. The very experience the Canoness sought for many years comes to Wilhelm in the spontaneity of grief. Strangely this profound experience does not move Wilhelm to become a lyric poet or tragedian in earnest but rather to a comparatively flat "solid citizenry," useful mostly to the complex social agenda of the ubiquitous Tower Society.

Initially, however, Wilhelm resents the Abbé's proposed plan for his future occupation and attempts to defy it in a rare moment of self-assertion: "I don't see why I should allow conditions to be dictated to me by anybody" (348). "Because a young man," the Abbé replies sonorously, "always has cause to seek the company of other people." By the novel's conclusion, Wilhelm has submitted completely to the direction of his "friends," for "it is useless trying to act according to one's own will in this world. What I most wanted to keep, I have to let go, and an undeserved benefit imposes itself upon me" (364).

At this point the role of the Tower Society [*Turmgesellschaft*] as arbiter of Wilhelm's bildung and the Abbé's shadowy role as its figurehead require some attention.[26] It may strike some as odd that, in the prototypical bildungsroman, what would appear to be the free activity of self-formation is in fact something minutely orchestrated by a clandestine group whose motives and agenda are never fully revealed. The rather improbable series of coincidences and complicated plot machinery surrounding their activities in the novel pose an aesthetic problem over and above the ethical problem of a group assuming the right to control individuals unaware of their intentions and at times even of their presence. In its most extreme manifestations, this control becomes insidious, for instance, in the circumstances surrounding the Harper's death.

As Jarno explains to Wilhelm on the eve of his initiation into the society, "We can now justly consider you as one of us. . . . When a man makes his first entry into the world, it is good that he have a high opinion of himself, believes he can acquire many excellent qualities, and therefore endeavors to do everything; but when his development has reached a certain stage, it is advantageous for him to lose himself in a larger whole, learn to live for others, and forget himself in dutiful activity for others. Only then will he come to know himself, for activity makes us compare ourselves with others" (301). The ideas in this speech are consistent with the physician's program to "cure" madness—both advocate cooperation and conformity (in the usual religious vocabulary but with a secular ideal) as indispensible qualities that allow the individual to succeed in the world. After a strange and theatrical initiation, during which Wilhelm recognizes strangers whom he had met at different points of his life, he receives his "Certificate of Apprenticeship" filled with cryptic maxims. Later he is permitted to read the "scroll of his apprenticeship" in its entirety, which confirms that the Tower's agents have been involved in his life from a very early period and have recorded its many details. After the initial embarrassment wears away, the effect is uncanny: Wilhelm "saw a picture [*Bild*] of himself, not like a second self in a mirror, but a different self, one outside of him, as in a painting. One never approves of everything in a portrait, but one is always glad that a thoughtful mind has seen us thus and a superior talent enjoyed portraying us in such a way that a picture [*Bild*] survives of what we were, and will survive longer than we will" (309). This immediate experience allows complete assimilation of what Wilhelm only intellectually understood before: he is at once able to see himself objectively. As such his bildung is a work of art both in its representation and in its unfolding living reality (not to mention the third dimension of the novel itself). This new perspective is designed to predispose him for work that, under the Tower's "superior" guidance, will outlive Wilhelm himself. To this effect Jarno identifies "a perceptible mysticism in our organization, which thereby . . . transformed itself from craft to art" (336).

Later Jarno roguishly repudiates the entire initiation ceremony, including the certificate, as "relics of a youthful enterprise that most initiates first took very seriously but will probably now just smile at" (335). Continuing to piece these dark hints and clues together almost becomes a game in itself, something that Schiller identified as a distraction to the novel's "inner spirit" (12:193). The direct causal connection between Wilhelm and the society—why, for instance, did they select Wilhelm and not another for the elaborate apprenticeship?—remains obscure. Arguably the society's complex role in determining Wilhelm's bildung—and, more generally, its far-reaching human experiment of which Wilhelm is only a part—becomes not extraneous to but an integral part of that "inner spirit." That is the complicated familial and civic relationships that bear operative significance upon Wilhelm's development together promote the idea of bildung as an overwhelmingly *social* activity.

If we recall Kant's philosophical definition of Enlightenment as "man's emergence from his self-generated immaturity" and that immaturity "is the inability to use one's understanding without the leadership of another," it is possible in part to see *Wilhelm Meister's Apprenticeship* as Goethe's aesthetic reply. Clearly it is essential to the novel's concept of bildung that Wilhelm put aside his immaturity. Yet Goethe further indicates that Wilhelm would not have reached this point had it not been for the careful guidance from those wiser and with superior social connections.

On the other hand, isolation and obsessive self absorption, whether its source be religious or secular, is a form of madness in the novel. The "Great Physician" whom the Canoness seeks is nowhere to be found in the world beyond the one she constructs for herself; the physician's Enlightened program for the Harper and Natalie's for Mignon are unable to rehabilitate either one because each has been distorted into a grotesque through some of the deepest forms of irrational self-obsession. Indeed Goethe goes so far as to link the two types of false bildung (the Canoness's and the Italians') linguistically through variations on the word *Ungeheuer* (monster). The conclusion of the Canoness's narrative reads: "I will never be tempted to pride myself on my own ability and powers, having so clearly recognized the monster [*Ungeheuer*] that grows and feeds in every human breast, if some higher power does not preserve us" (256). Likewise the physician reports that before coming under his care, the Harper had not "taken the slightest interest in anything outside himself. . . . all he looked at was his own hollow and empty self, which was a bottomless pit for him"; the "specters" of friendship and love are most horrifying of all because, he laments, they would rob him "finally of my own precious consciousness of my monstrous existence [*ungeheuren Daseins*]" (267).

It appears, then, that a state of health is a necessary dimension of sane (that is, socially acceptable) self-formation in the novel, and its antithesis is a "monstrous existence." Of the three conflicting and alternately compelling forms of bildung with which Goethe presents the reader, its religious and romantic extremes are both fundamentally incompatible with "healthy," rational bildung and must finally, in the process of necessary self-limitation, be subsumed by it.[27]

Altogether in *Wilhelm Meisters Lehrjahre,* Goethe was searching for a new model of self-formation that would serve as the balancing point between the irrational extremes of romantic and religious subjectivity. He accomplished this in part through a synthesis of contemporary Enlightenment thought and the affective interiority that was the spiritual legacy of Count Zinzendorf and the German Pietist tradition. Though as I hope to have made clear, Goethe's rejection of religious and romantic extremes is by no means neatly categorical: the gravitational poetic force of Mignon and the Harper as well as the Canoness's introspective

Francisco de Goya, *El sueño de la razón produce monstruos* (1797–98), Metropolitan Museum of Art, New York

sensibility and serious-mindedness are in themselves qualities that in various ways impress themselves deeply into Wilhelm's malleable character. As such they significantly help to define the kind of person Wilhelm becomes and indeed make it possible for him, in Schiller's words, to move from "an empty and vague ideal into a definite and active life, but without thereby losing his idealizing power."[28] In this way Goethe presented to the dawning nineteenth century what would become an enduring model for the novel as it evolved into an increasingly complex genre in Germany and beyond.

The superseding of the Canoness's intensely private notions of moral self-culture and the Italians' romantic self-obsession by the uncle's emphasis on development through activity and world-experience is just one way by which self-formation as a religious exercise underwent major changes as it filtered through the artistic medium of the bildungsroman. On both sides of the Atlantic, in England and America, these changes took on different but related casts. It is with *Jane Eyre* that I commence my exploration of English and American literary transpositions of the ideas presented in part 1 because of the four novels under consideration, in its engagement with extreme romantic and religious natures, it shares most distinctly some of the principal concerns in common with *Wilhelm Meister.*[29] At the same time, it draws significantly on uniquely English eighteenth-century religious understandings of the natural affections, conversion, and their bearing upon spiritual self-formation. In *David Copperfield* Dickens similarly faces his protagonist with "fascinating" religious and romantic figures as well as engages certain Wesleyan ideals such as the importance of progressive growth in time and, of course, moral conversion. But whereas Wesley optimistically upholds God's grace as applicable to anyone, Dickens instead focuses his particular version of Arminianism on the meet rewards or punishments an individual encounters here on earth.

While Melville's *Pierre* also demonstrates a certain awareness of Goethe's *Wilhelm Meister's Apprenticeship* as a predecessor, at the same time, Melville dramatizes the Edwardsian inheritance by subjecting Pierre to the same antinomian conflict with which his spiritual predecessors were centrally concerned: that is, how shall one strive toward conversion and grace when actions inherently possess no ontological significance? If the metaphysical paradox proves to be insupportable for a protagonist living beyond the confines of scriptural authority, Melville engages the Calvinist framework to make this point vivid. While Henry James was, in turn, certainly aware of Goethe's legacy, Goethe's influence is arguably the least apparent in *The Portrait of a Lady* than in all other bildungsromans under discussion. *Portrait* still, however, remains preoccupied with the antinomian paradox but presents it as the ethical question of whether or not good faith is its own justification. For Isabel Archer conversion does not instantaneously provide the answer, but it does retain a distinctly antinomian character and permits her to remain at a far remove from the sordid world of "works."

Part II

The inexperienced heart that enters into the world, the optimistic spirit who is yet unacquainted with the shoals of human nature and rushes cheerfully to meet the future, but the world is against him—what more need I say?—the epic of our individualistic epoch bases itself upon this contrast. It is our *Iliad* and *Odyssey.*

Wilhelm Dilthey, "The Imagination of the Poet"

4

"TO ENJOY MY OWN FACULTIES AS WELL AS TO CULTIVATE THOSE OF OTHER PEOPLE"

The Affective Bildung of Jane Eyre

Well, propensities and principles must be reconciled by some means.

Jane Eyre, chap. 30

Brontë and the Eighteenth Century

Just as Goethe in *Wilhelm Meister's Apprenticeship* sought in Wilhelm a balance somewhere between the extreme models of religious and romantic self-formation, so also does Charlotte Brontë in *Jane Eyre* establish Jane as a midpoint between Rochester's anarchic romantic nature and St. John Rivers's Evangelical austerity.[1] By balancing these two forces in Jane's psyche, Brontë suggests the optimistic position that integrity, or wholeness, is a resolution to the project of self-formation in the face of fractured experience. And insofar as Brontë emphasizes in Jane's character the experiences of irregular yet progressive patterns of growth, rigorous self-examination, doubt, and the idea that experience need not be strictly empirical, Brontë's concept of self-formation in *Jane Eyre* exhibits definite affinities with Wesley's Arminian spiritual empiricism.[2] Furthermore alongside other influential thinkers of the eighteenth century, Wesley's understanding of the natural affections significantly contributes toward shaping Jane's path toward self-formation.

The primary difference between Brontë's and Wesley's approaches to spiritual self-formation involves the way each interprets the pivotal conversion experience or, in Wesley's words, the "renewal of the heart in the whole image of God, the full likeness of him that created it" (*Works* 11:444). Heart-renewal is equally valuable to Brontë, but with the significant difference that whatever portion of the conversion Wesley necessarily allots to the biblically based transcendental "other" Brontë replaces with the profoundly *affective*, singular, yet no less religious experience. Heart-renewal leads Jane not to "self-annihilation" (if it did, perhaps she would indeed have gone to India with St. John!) but rather culminates in the freedom, as Jane describes it herself, "to enjoy my own faculties as well as to cultivate those of other people" (chap. 34, 400).[3]

To be sure by the time *Jane Eyre* was written, the idea of spiritual empiricism had significantly altered from, while at the same time still significantly engaged, its eighteenth-century contexts. In this fictional autobiography, set in the first decade of the nineteenth century, Brontë preserves the Arminian dimensions of experience but broadens the concept of creating the self in the image of God into a wider framework of creating the self-in-the-world in relation to other human beings. Brontë's dramatic version of spiritual empiricism appears in the novel as an extended meditation on the "natural affections," a motif central to the Moor House chapters. Her treatment of the cleric St. John Rivers—a polarizing character whose Calvinist tendencies align him with the Evangelical wing of the Church of England—is operative in this context.[4]

The connection of Methodism in particular and evangelicalism generally with the Brontë family is well known to Brontë scholars. The following overview of work in this area is not so much to restate Charlotte's engagement with Methodism in *Jane Eyre* per se but to indicate the scope of Valentine Cunningham's telling remark that "the Brontë novels are effectively rooted in the eighteenth-century Evangelical Revival" (113). This, in turn, allows us better to see the ways in which Wesleyan ideas of spiritual self-formation inflect the status of *Jane Eyre* as an English bildungsroman.

It may be useful to begin the discussion by distinguishing briefly between Wesleyan Methodism in Wesley's time (as a part of the Church of England) and in Brontë's own time (mostly Dissenters but with some Low Church sympathizers). Owen Chadwick distinguishes between conservative Methodists—or those sympathetic with Anglican decorum—and radical Methodists, groups who objected vigorously to the concept of a state-sponsored church (*Victorian* 1: 371). Like many Dissenters, Methodists tended to be working-class. Those with more conservative views sought to distance themselves from the yet lower social orders of Primitive Methodists or "Ranters" (386–87). Primitives typically held camp meetings, some of them disorderly, and preached and sang in the streets.

From this small segment of the complex state of Dissent, it is not surprising that, as Emily Griesinger points out, by 1851 English Methodists had already splintered into six or seven distinct sects (34). Further the overlap between Methodism and Church of England Evangelicalism during the first half of the nineteenth century was significant enough that many critics discuss them in conjunction.[5] Accounts of evangelicalism at the time range from rigid legalism to enthusiastic supernaturalism. Perhaps most significant, between Wesley's and Brontë's time, evangelical piety underwent a "hardening" and experienced "a gradual shift from 'vital religion' to a kind of legalism that today we might call 'fundamentalism'" (Griesinger, "Charlotte" 44).

This "hardening" within the religious power structure of England was in part due to conservative reaction to the French and American revolutions. Susan VanZanten Gallagher argues that many English in the nineteenth century gravitated toward the mainstream Church of England Evangelicalism as a counter to Methodism's "threatening anti-authoritarian, leveling philosophy" ("*Jane*" 62). Methodism's long-standing association with enthusiasm (a problem that harassed Wesley virtually from the beginning) probably intensified these views as did the issue of supernaturalism, in some ways reinforced by publications such as the *Methodist Magazine*.[6] Earlier Samuel Pickering Jr. had argued similarly that evangelicalism's growing emphasis on the letter over the spirit coincided with a general cultural "decline in sensibility," which pointed toward a "secular ethics outside the restraints of religious dogma" (10). Elizabeth Jay, on the contrary, contends that evangelicalism did not so much preclude sensibility but rather for many balanced sensibility with practicality, a combination she terms "practical piety" (7). As such evangelicalism offered a viable alternative for many to the overwhelmingly secular Utilitarian movement of the early nineteenth century.

It is important to recall, however, that both Evangelicals and Dissenters held competing Calvinist and Arminian factions within each tradition. In this respect the Brontë family occupied a position that uniquely reflected this complex network of Victorian Protestant thought in the sense that to various degrees they partook simultaneously in these conflicting theological and cultural trends. Recently critics have begun to dispute the received notion (originating with Elizabeth Gaskell's biography) that Patrick Brontë raised his children in a religiously oppressive environment. In *The Brontës and Religion*, for instance, Marianne Thormählen cites Patrick's toleration for his children's early literary and theatrical pastimes as evidence for his relative liberality in addition to his emphasis on God as love over the fear of hell (7).[7] Thormählen further notes that the two most significant religious influences on Patrick Brontë were Wesleyan Methodism and Church of England Evangelicalism (13). In her monumental biography of the Brontë family, Juliet Barker writes that Patrick was at home with the Methodists, particularly

Wesleyans, even after "it was no longer fashionable or even really acceptable to support them" (28). Of course he had many personal reasons to do so, not the least of which was the fact that his wife, Maria née Branwell, was a Methodist, as was her sister Elizabeth Branwell and even his housekeeper, Tabitha Aykroyd. Some speculate that as a youth Brontë may have heard Wesley himself preach in his Irish birthplace, and we know that Wesley had once preached at Patrick's own pulpit at Haworth (Griesinger, "Charlotte" 40). Further during his Cambridge years, Patrick had befriended many Methodist sympathizers.[8]

Each of Patrick's children variously assimilated this complex network of theological forces into their work. As for Charlotte particularly—though many feminist critics emphasize her personal and fictional forms of self-formation in rebellion (antipatriarchy, anti-Christian, etc.)—another, if comparatively marginal, perspective has begun to surface in the critical discussions surrounding Brontë's treatment of spirituality and its bearing on self-formation in her fiction. To this end Thormählen makes a basic point that is crucial because it is so often overlooked: for the believer faith and doubt are inseparable (*Brontës* 7).[9] It is fallacious, then, simply to equate doubt with anti-Christian sentiment in Brontë's novels, because such critiques "imply that spiritual searching beyond the notions prevalent in one's religious community is at odds with the foundations of faith."[10] This opinion, Thormählen argues, is one the Brontës did not support, for "the most striking quality in their exploration of religious subject matter is its essential liberty." On this point I agree with Thormählen as I do with her general contention that Brontë's handling of religious themes in her novels expresses more often the "heroism of the pilgrim rather than the wrath of the rebel" (8). This is not to say that rebellion does not exist in *Jane Eyre,* but it rarely appears as an end in itself and instead repeatedly aims toward some form of reconciliation between the self, the world, and God.

Similarly both Griesinger and Talley contend that in spite of doubt and unconventional spirituality, Charlotte remained, in Griesinger's words, a "loyal supporter of the Church of England" while at the same time she "leaned toward Arminianism" (46). This position clearly placed her in opposition to the Calvinist factions within and outside the Church of England.[11] In a letter to Margaret Wooler, dated February 12, 1850, she writes that she is "sorry the Clergy do not like the doctrine of Universal Salvation; I think it a great pity for their sakes, but surely they are not so unreasonable as to expect me to deny or suppress what I believe the truth!" (2:343). Imlay interprets these comments to reveal Charlotte's open rejection of Calvinism (a rejection repeatedly dramatized in *Jane Eyre*) in addition to a repudiation of "any form of Christianity which admitted the eternal condemnation of any being" (102). In the same letter, Brontë notes that certain clerics had been "bitter" about *Jane Eyre* but dismisses them boldly as "men in whom the animal obviously predominates over the intellectual. I smile inwardly when I hear of their disapprobation." An earlier letter to W. S. Williams (November 1, 1849) reveals a sharper position against negative clerical reaction to the novel: "When I confronted one or two large-made priests," she writes, "I longed for the battle to come on—I wish they would speak out plainly" (2:272).

Marion J. Phillips further not only demonstrates Charlotte's willingness to entertain perspectives on Christianity apart from Church of England orthodoxy, but also implicitly argues against her isolation at Haworth with respect to current theological thought. This is evident in the fact that Brontë read many contemporary religious tracts and actively, sometimes enthusiastically, corresponded with some of their authors. For instance she called Nonconformist Alexander Harris's *Testimony to the Truth: or, The Autobiography of an Atheist* (1848) "a book after my own heart. . . . No matter whether or not I can agree in all his views, it is the principles, the feelings, the heart of the man I admire" (2:175). One of the passages in *Testimony* Phillips highlights is perhaps one that the two authors (Harris and Brontë) had in common: experience alongside rational thought is important in the trajectory of spiritual development. Harris writes, "the senses thus acting to the development of mind, the mind in like manner goes on to develop *spirit*" (qtd. in Phillips, "Priesthood" 150). The influence of the diverse group of thinkers, from Francis Newman to Harris, manifests itself in *Jane Eyre* through Jane's "extraordinary spiritual authority." The novel itself indeed entertains worldviews as diverse as these, but Brontë shapes them continually to serve her own ethical and aesthetic ends.

Personal Happiness or Philanthropy?
The Reconciling Power of the Natural Affections

If the goal of spiritual self-formation in *Jane Eyre* is the healthy reconciliation of propensity with principle, which I believe it is, and the "natural affections" are the key to reconciling these often contrary qualities, much rests upon how the natural affections are understood and, more important, acted upon in life. The word *propensity* is significant in this context not simply because it indicates favorable inclination or predisposition to some person or idea, but also for its emphasis on the active, Arminian dimensions of these things. St. John insists on forcing the "germ" of natural affection to grow via religion into the abstract category of philanthropy, whereas Jane seeks to cultivate it on the intimate terms of living with another human being as an equal in mind and affections. Jane says, "I *will* be happy"; St. John says, "I *will* overcome" (34, 402; 31, 372).

Of all that has been written on *Jane Eyre*, many memorable interpretations (particularly in the last three decades) have explored the Jane-Rochester-Bertha triangle.[12] In consequence, however, comparatively little has been written about

St. John Rivers's influence on Jane's development. Apart from the fact that his personality contains many attributes either distasteful, incomprehensible, or even repellent to modern readers, his presence in the novel also appears to present a structural problem. As Elizabeth Imlay facetiously remarks, St. John "intrudes into events like a chilled fish pâté between a main course and a sweet" (66). It is true that many readers would rather skim the Moor House chapters (which in fact take up a substantial quarter of the novel) in order to find out what really matters—whether Jane will, finally, reunite with Rochester. The objection is not new: even Thackeray, to whom the novel was eventually dedicated, made the oft-repeated remark that Rivers "is a failure I think but a good failure there are parts excellent" (318–19). Some early reviewers, such as Elizabeth Rigby (Lady Eastlake) for the *Quarterly Review*, skipped over the Moor House chapters entirely in their synopsis of the novel.[13]

And yet Imlay also suggests that Rivers contributes significantly to the novel's overall argument that "it is to love that we owe ultimate allegiance" (66). In my tendency to agree with Imlay on this point, and among those few who have dedicated chapters to St. John Rivers, I would show how the Moor House experience is an indispensible part of Jane's ongoing process of self-formation toward spiritual maturity. Significantly these chapters exemplify the novel's most nuanced engagement with, and critique of, eighteenth-century Evangelical ideas of self-formation. The Moor House chapters are crucial also in part because they tap into themes M. M. Bakhtin has identified to be elemental to the novel: both Jane and St. John struggle with the "inadequacy of a hero's fate and situation to the hero himself" ("Bildungsroman" 37). For Jane this amounts to missing a shared existence with an intellectual and emotional equal; St. John prefers almost anything to the monotonous duties of an obscure ministry, something that would lead him to the "active life of the world" (31, 371).

In relation to the novel as a whole, St. John represents a fuller, more human rendering of the qualities Reverend Brocklehurst exhibits throughout Jane's early ordeal at Lowood. This is due largely to Jane's evolving point of view. Restricted in experience and limited in the exercise of compassion, young Jane's view invests the wicked Brocklehurst with a flatness characteristic of caricature. Similarly her childish conversations about religion with Helen Burns will later modulate into mature judgment upon the same themes. Indeed from the beginning *Jane Eyre* is filled with references, direct and indirect, to evangelical themes. For instance among the books in the opening description of Jane's reading is *Henry, Earl of Moreland* by Henry Brooke. This work is one of the few novels Wesley included among his many abridgments and recommended to his followers, for it "perpetually aims at inspiring and increasing every right affection, at the instilling gratitude to God, and benevolence to man."[14] The concepts of the affections and

Wesleyan benevolence will also become increasingly vivid as Jane continues her self-formative process.

The central quality that draws Jane and St John together and holds them so for a time—apart from the providential plot and familial ties—is that they are equals in force of mind. It is this unmistakable likeness that makes it difficult to dismiss St. John out of hand no matter how unappealing his character may otherwise appear. Perhaps for this reason some commentators have seen in St. John an externalization of intellectual qualities commensurate with Jane's own.[15]

It is entirely fitting, then, that the most important lesson that St. John has to teach Jane, owing less to his conscious intention and more to Jane's growing powers of perception, is an epistemological one. It is that there is a difference between ratiocinative and affective ways of knowing and that the second way comes closer to truth. Before Jane arrives at Moor House, she frequently erred on the side of the first, for example, most dramatically in her categorical rejection of Rochester and exodus from Thornfield. Indeed up to that time, she shows little progress from her behavior as the child who was absolutely unable to forgive those who had offended her. The insight Jane gradually gains into St. John's character allows her to make the epistemological distinction she had up to that point been unable to make (and one that he appears altogether incapable of making). Only once she has crossed this threshold is she able to undergo her own "conversion" experience and to hear with spiritual clarity her own calling. If any renunciation be involved in this formative process, it is that she sacrifice some of her sharpness of mind in exchange for a rounding out of the heart.

The remark with which I began this chapter is spoken by St. John Rivers in an uncharacteristically off-handed way. It appears in chapter 30 as a conclusion to his explanation of his unhappy situation in Morton—a place totally unsuited to his ambitions and one that forces him into self-contradiction. For St. John as much as it would be for Jane, remaining in such a place would equal spiritual death (emphasis on *mort*). With this revelation Jane finds common ground with the young cleric through the painful sense of her own physical, emotional, and spiritual exile at Morton.[16] Describing himself in fittingly distant third-person language, St. John "considers himself an alien from his native country—not only for life, but in death" (30, 363). Similarly St. John is aware that by Jane's accepting his proposal to become a rural schoolmistress—the only proposal from him she will ever be prepared to accept—she would be neglecting the "largest portion" of her mind in addition to her "sentiments" and "tastes" (30, 365). The critical resolution to their mutual problem of exile consists in the way in which each reconciles conflicting propensities and principles by way of the "natural affections." In order fully to appreciate the significance and extent of their differences on this subject, it is necessary first to consider what Brontë means by the phrase itself.

The eighteenth century again provides rich precedent from which Brontë might have drawn, for the "natural affections," or the passions and their regulation, was an important topic not only for theologians such as Wesley but also for the ethical philosophers of the period.[17] One of the most influential writers on the subject was Lord Shaftesbury, whose work, as we recall, informed the Germans' own eighteenth-century concept of bildung; others include Francis Hutcheson and Isaac Watts. This pool of knowledge would have been available to St. John as he studied at Cambridge around the turn of the century (the time coincident with Patrick Brontë's studies at St. John's College).

In "An Inquiry Concerning Virtue, or Merit," included in *Characteristics of Men, Manners, Opinions, Times* (1711), Lord Shaftesbury uses *affections* and *passions* interchangeably and defines the *natural affections* as those "which lead to the good of the public" over and against the *self-affections,* which relate to private good (177–78). As such it is central to the natural affections that they be disinterested.[18] Shaftesbury emphasizes moderation in the exercise of both natural affections and self-affections and indicates that too much or too little of one or the other leads to "vice and imperfection" (180). He further insists on their inseparability: "the natural affections duly established in a rational creature, being the only means which can procure him a constant series or succession of the mental enjoyments, they are the only means which can procure him a certain and solid *happiness*" (182). Included under the heading of the natural affections are the "social pleasures" such as "love, gratitude, bounty" between the sexes, family, and so on.[19]

From a theological perspective, Nonconformist Isaac Watts addressed the subject in his 1739 treatise *The Doctrine of the Passions Explain'd and Improv'd: or, A brief and comprehensive Scheme of the Natural Affections.* Watts uses the phrase "natural affections" less distinctly than Shaftesbury by equating it with the passions such as love, hate, and joy (3). Watts defines the passions as an uncertain mixture between mind and matter, or "those sensible Commotions of our whole nature, both Soul and Body," which react to objects with desire or aversion (5). They are valuable to virtuous actions under the condition that they be curbed, like a steed, by wisdom and reason.[20] Some of the practical means toward self-government include the practice of self-denial, and the exhortation that the individual "get a general Benevolence to Mankind rooted in your Heart" (160); the first religious "direction" Watts lists is that the self-government begin in youth in order to hasten the "universal Change" of conversion: "If you would have the Fruit good, 'tis in vain to labour in breaking off every irregular Bud, or lopping the Branches; but the *Tree* itself *must be made good*" (166).

Wesley apparently valued the ideas in Watts's treatise enough to excerpt as many as eleven portions of it in the *Arminian Magazine* (from April 1782 through February 1783), including the final chapter on "universal Directions" for moral and religious regulation of the passions. Further in his own remarks on the subject, in *A Plain Account of Genuine Christianity* (1753), Wesley appears to be largely in line with Shaftesbury's view of the natural affections as geared toward the public good, even if Shaftesbury was concerned primarily with the secular, civic dimensions of conduct. For Wesley the individual's major contribution to the public good is the approximation of God's love of mankind: a Christian should, therefore, cultivate a habit of disinterested "universal benevolence." Ever concerned with the application of religious principles to practical conduct, and consistent with his doctrine of Christian Perfection, Wesley is moved to stipulate that this disinterested benevolence shall neither interfere with "a peculiar regard for his relations, friends, and benefactors" nor with "a fervent love for his country." Again, very much like Shaftesbury, Wesley considers that well-regulated *social love* and *self-love* shall "give additional force to the other, 'till they mix together never to be divided" (5).

These perspectives should begin to shed some light on Brontë's appropriation of the "natural affections" to her own ends as the primary reconciler between "propensities and principles" in *Jane Eyre*. St. John proves himself to be very much a student of the eighteenth century in his rigid equivocation between the natural affections and public duty but falls short of fulfilling the "self-affections." On the other hand, Jane demonstrates the ability at least temporarily to conform to a balance of self-love (preservation of principles) with "social love" (willingness to work to improve the community), but these eighteenth-century imperatives prove inadequate to the fullness of her vision of life and happiness—to satisfy propensity she *exceeds* these models to conform to her own understanding of the natural affections.

St. John's Will to Overcome

In the novel the phrase "natural affection" appears three times, first as Diana uses it to refer to her brother, and twice by St. John himself. Diana interprets the impulse to indicate filial ties: initially she warns Jane that St. John is willing to sacrifice this, and "feelings more potent still," to his vocation as a missionary (30, 366). In this interpretation St. John's motives coincide with Wesley's in their disinterestedness and emphasis on "public" over "private" good.

But St. John appears to interpret the concept differently, not as a sacrifice but as a realization of his nature as religion has shaped it. St. John discusses it in the pivotal speech in which he most clearly delineates his own cleft character (stoic/Christian—hence his Greek appearance/Evangelical bearing): "I am simply, in my natural state—stripped of that blood-bleached robe with which Christianity covers human deformity—a cold, hard, ambitious man. Natural affection only, of all the sentiments, has permanent power over me" (32, 385). He proceeds to inform

Jane that religion has cultivated in him the "minute germ, natural affection" into the "over-shadowing tree, philanthropy." In many ways this declaration from a minister of the Church of England appears to be conventional insofar as it describes the innate depravity of "natural" man. Yet one of the first observations Jane makes about St. John's character is that he appears *not* to have exchanged the "cold, hard, ambitious" dimensions of his character for the "mental serenity" and "inward content, which should be the reward of every sincere Christian and practical philanthropist" (30, 360). If anything the former qualities only become more pronounced as the narrative develops. Philanthropy provides St. John the safest means for reconciling propensities and principles in the sense that it fulfills the Christian imperative of brotherly love while at the same time avoiding the embarrassments of passionate individual attachment.

In St. John's uniform pursuit of "universal benevolence," he sacrifices his regard for both personal relations and country, ties that Wesley insisted the Christian preserve and cultivate on the path toward perfection. St. John appears to align himself with other Christian thinkers along the lines of Isaac Watts in his government of the passions by reason, his self-denial, and "general benevolence to mankind." But on the question of the "universal change," the basis for all other evangelical Christian virtues, St. John's status appears to be less clear. His gloomy Calvinism—as repelling to Jane as it was to the author of the novel—and unhappy personal state are curiously interwoven in the text, as if the two are on some level inseparable. The effect of the sermon Jane hears him preach, full of "stern allusions to Calvinistic doctrines," leaves her only with the vague impression that his eloquence "had sprung from a depth where lay turbid dregs of disappointment—where moved troubling impulses of insatiate yearnings and disquieting aspirations" (30, 361). She concludes that "pure-lived, conscientious, zealous as he was—[he] had not yet found that peace of God which passeth all understanding: he had no more found it, I thought, than had I." Since the reader knows for certain that Jane has not yet experienced conversion, the implications that a cleric in the same state, determined nevertheless to practice philanthropy without its complement of the Shaftesburian "social pleasures" or Wesleyan "self-love," is bound to act in God's name not from his whole being but only from a part of it.

Yet St. John proves himself not to be as Calvinistic in his beliefs as his sermon had indicated. He tells Jane that "God has given us, in a measure, the power to make our own fate" and proceeds to tell her about his calling as a missionary (31, 371). But the language with which he describes it indicates further the suspiciously incomplete experience of his "conversion." He wishes only to "control" natural inclination by seeking other "nourishment for the mind" apart from his desire (presumably for Rosamond); his "powers," not his heart or spirit, responded to the call from God to become a missionary.[21] Rather than further describing this moment as altering his entire being, he reports only that his "state of mind" had changed. He does not appear to relish the calling for its own sake but rather because in his mind it requites his ambition by combining the glory of the worldly callings of soldier, statesman, and orator.

As many commentators have noticed, St. John is sensibly aware that the "minute germ" of philanthropy is capable of growing into many forms apart from his preferred species of tree.[22] This is most evident in the scene—rare in its comic tone—in which St. John consults his pocket watch and indulges in a fifteen-minute imagining of earthly love with Rosamond.[23] Throughout Brontë again substitutes language of the "mind" for "heart": St. John asks Jane to imagine "human love rising like a freshly opened fountain in my mind and overflowing with sweet inundation all the field I have so carefully, and with such labour prepared—so assiduously sown with the seeds of good intentions, of self-denying plans. And now it is deluged with a nectarous flood—the young germs swamped—delicious poison cankering them" (32, 383). Images of water suggest at once sexual love as well as recall his patronymic, which together provide yet another dimension of St. John's deeply conflicted nature. But this form of earthly love "swamps," poisons, and renders inert the philanthropic impulse. By stating the case in this extreme fashion, it is easy for his will to choose the seed from which his life shall take its form.

Jane imagines the consequences of a relationship with Rochester on the Continent in a similar tone, using language of drowsiness, delirium, delusion, and suffocation, which suggests that she recognizes in St. John an ethos of moral rigor similar to her own (31, 369). They both describe themselves as "hard"—he, "difficult to persuade"; she, "impossible to put off" (33, 394). Further qualities that St. John names that both value include "endurance, perseverance, industry, talent"; Jane is "a specimen of a diligent, orderly, energetic woman" (32, 385). And yet Jane discovers that St. John, on principle, names only those qualities of Jane's that, neatly parallel to his own, fall under the same heading of "philanthropy."

St. John's dedication to his philanthropic calling makes him, as Diana correctly observes, "inexorable as death" (30, 366). His understanding of natural affection, his way of reconciling propensities and principles, casts a shadow across every value he and Jane share. In Shaftesbury's terms the above scene reveals the radical imbalance in St. John's character of the natural affections and the self-affections. Jane recognizes the "imperfection," if not the "vice," of this condition. Moreover the extent to which he undervalues the related "social pleasures"—in Jane's words, the "humanities and amenities of life"—is further evident in his nonreaction to Moor House after its Christmastime "cleaning down." Jane reflects: "Literally, he lived only to aspire—after what was good and great, certainly: but still he would never rest, nor approve of others resting around him. . . . I saw he was of the material from which nature hews her heroes—Christian and Pagan—her lawgivers, her statesmen, her conquerors: a steadfast bulwark for great interests to rest upon, but, at the fireside, too often a cold cumbrous column, gloomy and out of place" (34, 403–4). The descriptive language, here and elsewhere, points to his constant disinterestedness—a heroic quality—paired with a lack of heart. St. John's artificial separation of public and private interests can only lead to unhappiness, his own and that of those around him; Jane apprehends this as clearly as did the moralists of the previous century. At the same time, St. John's urging Jane to develop her powers beyond the domestic sphere makes her own attitude toward domesticity, evident in the disappointment registered in the above scene, appear to be absolutely conventional in comparison.

In spite of the deep contradictions in his nature, St. John's forbearance—particularly in his dealings with Rosamond as he passes the time before embarking for India—is at once "heroic" and "martyr-like." A remark made from the perspective of the mature narrator indicates that Jane remains an admirer of certain aspects of his character and indeed perceives in it a tortured, passionate superabundance: "he could not bound all that he had in his nature—the rover, the aspirant, the poet, the priest—in the limits of a single passion" (32, 378). And for this reason, quite apart from any spiritual necessity, it is fitting that he become a missionary.

Jane's Will to Happiness

Beyond the fact that Jane recognizes without any doubt that her own spirit will not conform to the same mold as her cousin's, it remains for her to discover a fitting alternative. While she is at Morton, natural affection has come for her to mean the joys of kinship, or "full fellow-feeling" (33, 398). As such Jane conforms closely with the Wesleyan model of disinterested benevolence, which, as schoolmistress for the poor, works in tandem with her devotion to her newly discovered family and her love of country. And yet while this situation, set "in a breezy mountain nook in the healthy heart of England," satisfies her principles, her propensities remain unfulfilled: she remains, in the most vital sense, in exile. Only through the crisis that St. John precipitates is Jane able to reach a way of knowing unprecedented in her life—one that enables her to move beyond mere principle or inclination and *act* from her whole being. It is at once a moving out and a returning.

The crisis does not come all at once but beautifully modulates through the series of marriage proposal scenes, beginning where "the mountain shook off turf and flower" in exchange for the austere solitude of heath—an image representing Jane's present and possible future with St. John. The ensuing argument is important primarily not because it is about marriage per se as much as it is about conflicting views of what it means to have a "calling." Jane's articulate self-defense serves as an indirect means of active self-formation: her impulse is to protect her work, which "had appeared so vague, so hopelessly diffuse," from assuming a false but "definite form under his shaping hand" (34, 415).[24]

Their general discussion of missionary work quickly converges into the present—immediately St. John presents himself in the powerful position of a priestly figure who offers, "direct from God, a place in the ranks of His chosen" to those whom he believes capable (34, 413). Jane immediately responds in a typically Protestant manner: "If they are really qualified for the task, will not their own hearts be the first to inform them of it?" That her own heart is "mute" on this question does not indicate that he has silenced it, but only that the sensible experience that would allow it to recognize the missionary vocation is absent. In the face of St. John's persistence, Jane next appeals to the mind: she cannot think like him because, she says, "I do not understand a missionary life" (34, 414). And finally, as she reasons to herself, not the least is the condition of her body, for going to India would amount to "premature death." In this way Jane clearly demonstrates that such a "calling" would be antithetical to her being in its entirety; St. John's perseverance in the face of these insurmountable objections and weak imperative to "simplify your complicated interests, feelings," into a single principle becomes perverse. This is not to say, however, that the missionary calling is something Jane—or Brontë for that matter—universally condemns. What makes her resistance painful is her recognition (whether we agree or no) that it is a noble calling: "is not the occupation he now offers me truly the most glorious man can adopt or God assign? . . . I believe I must say, Yes—and yet I shudder" (34, 416).

Further this scene uncovers marriage as the point upon which St. John's extreme understanding of philanthropic "natural affections" seems most egregious when he informs her that he "wants a wife" not fitted to him as the "insignificant private individual—the mere man, with the man's selfish senses"—but as fitted only to his purpose or vocation (34, 417).[25] Here Brontë aligns herself implicitly again with Wesley in her criticism that religious motives must include the personal alongside the public. She seems to imply that without full conversion (including the dimensions of sensible experience), any subsequent actions in religion's name are bound to be incomplete.

These incidents together contribute to Jane's deepest insight into St. John's character and, indirectly, signal the beginnings of a new stage in her own self-formation:

> I had silently feared St. John till now, because I had not understood him. He had held me in awe, because he had held me in doubt. How much of him was saint, how much mortal, I could not heretofore tell: but revelations were being made in this conference: the analysis of his nature was proceeding before my eyes. I saw his fallibilities: I comprehended them. I understood that, sitting . . . on the bank of

> heath, and with that handsome form before me, I sat at the feet of a man, erring as I. The veil fell from his hardness and despotism. Having felt in him the presence of these qualities, I felt his imperfection, and took courage. I was with an equal—one with whom I might argue—one whom, if I saw good, I might resist. (34, 418)

This passage catalogs the transformation in ways of knowing that is pivotal to Jane's ever-modulating growth: it begins with the objective language of analysis and transposes into a kind of wisdom based on intuition (sight) and affective ways of knowing that approach the truth. This affective insight into St. John's imperfections further allows Jane to relate to St. John with compassion: she momentarily faces him as one flawed human being faces another. And with these new powers of perception, his power over her dissolves. Before she could not "discriminate the Christian from the man," but now that she has, she is moved to "profoundly esteem the one, and freely forgive the other" (34, 419).

With this insight Jane reveals how much she has changed from her sharp and unforgiving habits of mind as a child. Jane's experience with Helen Burns and Helen's abstract "lesson," which at the time was virtually meaningless to the young Jane, suddenly takes on the weight of reality. As a Christian, Helen "can so clearly distinguish between the criminal and his crime; I can so sincerely forgive the first while I abhor the last" (6, 55). Helen's abstract negation has developed over the years in Jane's mind into mature, compassionate judgment that is at once as discriminating as it is affirmative.

The third and final proposal and quasi-conversion scene in which Jane receives her calling requires that she put into action her new way of knowing in order to leave Morton and begin to form her life after its new pattern. It is fitting that St. John choose the twenty-first chapter of Revelation, for it ostensibly provides scriptural justification for his intention to wed only for the sake of his office. The second verse reads, "And I John saw the holy city, new Jerusalem, coming down from God out of heaven, prepared as a bride adorned for her husband." Unwittingly these words serve not his purposes but rather Jane's own. At this crucial moment, the mature narrator intervenes to inform the reader that she was as close to accepting St. John as she once had been to accepting Rochester: "I was a fool both times. To have yielded then would have been an error of principle, to have yielded now would have been an error of judgment" (35, 430). In the first instance, Jane upheld principle, and in the second she is now prepared to exercise (if spontaneously) her newly acquired capacity for judgment. This judgment, however, does not work independently but in tandem with Providence. Both coincide during the "mysterious summons" scene.

From the novel's publication, critics have been puzzled by the scene in which Jane hears Rochester calling to her over many miles. Elizabeth Gaskell reports that Brontë confided to her and a friend that "it is a true thing; it really happened" (337). Certainly the text is ambiguous in its direct appeal to the reader to judge for himself or herself, and so it shall remain. But it is composed in such a way to accommodate readings that Jane undergoes a conversion strikingly similar to the traditional conversion met with in spiritual narratives that are often, as we have seen in the case of Wesley, sensible experiences inspired by a reading of scripture. The type of conversion it describes is as unconventional as the combination of images that accompany it—moonlight, candlelight, nature, scripture, the love of God and of man are all wrapped into the moment. And the language with which she describes it blends the sensible and spiritual so ingeniously that it is difficult to tell them apart: "My heart beat fast and thick: I heard its throb. Suddenly it stood still to an inexpressible feeling that thrilled it through, and passed at once to my head and extremities. The feeling was not like an electric shock; but it was quite as sharp, as strange, as startling: it acted on my senses as if their utmost activity hitherto had been but torpor; from which they were now summoned, and forced to wake. They rose expectant: eye and ear waited, while the flesh quivered on my bones" (35, 431). It is tempting to read the description as a symbolic sexual initiation, as have some commentators.[26] These readings, however, tend to suppress the overall spiritual framework in which the moment is set. Further the fact that the original feeling originates in the heart and passes in turn into the mind and then into the rest of the body suggests that the conversion Brontë describes is spiritual in its essence but, far from denigrating the flesh, enables her to reconcile the spirit and flesh in her final and most decisive and integrative act of spiritual formation: to return to live with the man whom she loves.[27] I agree with Jerome Beaty insofar as he points to Jane's description of the moment the following day as an "inspiration," which in his view "refers specifically to the divine influence on human beings" (206). But Beaty's conclusion that the inspiration "is an experience of the soul . . . not the body (nature)" is incomplete when the full context is taken into consideration (the descriptions of the moment itself, Jane's reflection on it the day afterward, and Rochester's side of the story). Jane does seem to dismiss mere biological causes and alludes directly to the soul—that the "wondrous shock of feeling . . . had opened the doors of the soul's cell . . . whence it sprang trembling, listening, aghast," and most explicitly, that her spirit "exulted as if in joy over the success of one effort it had been privileged to make independent of the cumbrous body" (36, 434). Finally, reunited with Rochester, Jane refers to the experience as "supernatural." From this wider perspective, the text invokes both spirit and flesh to have played a part in her transformation: the scene embodies a spiritual empiricism that is uniquely Brontë's own.

And of course since it is Rochester who is calling her, it is essential to treat his and her experience as one. From Rochester's perspective—for he describes, after all, his own quasi-conversion experience—the separating line between spirit and body becomes even more indistinct: he tells Jane that he "longed for thee both with soul and flesh" and proceeds with the idolatrous confession that he called out to Jane as the "alpha and omega of [his] heart's wishes" (37, 460).

Jane's return to Rochester is not in the capacity of servant to her master but as an equal: in the image of a "green and vigorous tree," he shall serve as a "prop" to a "budding woodbine"; in turn Jane serves as his "prop and guide" as he recovers from his blindness (37, 458, 462). And this return to completion is not simply a complacent affirmation of conventional domestic values. Rather Brontë makes that radical assertion that propensity and principle, spirit and flesh, may be reconciled through a superlative and compassionate form of the "natural affections." Consequently it is possible that this bond exist as the reciprocity between equals, and that each continue toward integration into the other's image and likeness.

Heart is, throughout, the operative force of the novel; it is what pervades and moves all events to their conclusion. Jane and Rochester's "unspeakably strange" call and response is emblematic of this elemental motion. Early in the novel, Rochester imagines their connection as a cord "somewhere under my left ribs, tightly and inextricably knotted to a similar string situated in the corresponding quarter of your little frame," though at the time he fears that the "boisterous channel" would be snapped should they separate (23, 257). Their final reconciliation is an amelioration of this fear, owing as much to Jane's developing affective intelligence as it does to Providence.

Most readers are dissatisfied with or puzzled by the novel's concluding not with the reunited lovers, but with St. John's expected reuniting with Christ. Perhaps Thormählen puts it best when she calls it a "balancing of the book, which leaves the reader to contemplate two very dissimilar patterns of human endeavour under the Heaven to which both assign ultimate power" (*Brontës* 219). As such Thormählen argues that Brontë does not privilege one over the other. But Brontë's extended critique of St. John's incomplete activation of the natural affections lingers as his exile becomes complete. Because the high endeavor of one who loves mankind with a consuming disinterestedness comes to a close in a premature death among strangers, it is difficult not to register some faint overtones of irony in the conclusion. The irony is of the most delicate material, a mixture of approval, admiration, and dread. As Diana reflects, St. John's calling "is right, noble, Christian: yet it breaks my heart" (30, 366).

Charlotte Brontë's connections to Methodism and Church of England Evangelicalism through her father and mother, in addition to her intimate familiarity with Dissent based in part upon her family's Yorkshire residence, all clearly inform her ways of thinking about spiritual self-formation. These influences invest Brontë's work—with the exception, perhaps, of *Villette*—with a brisk Arminian emphasis on the importance of action. On the other hand, Charles Dickens grew into artistic maturity largely without religious influences parallel to those of Brontë's. But because he lived in London at a time during which the Evangelical presence was everywhere apparent, from the Seventh Earl of Shaftesbury's projects for orphans to the theatrics at Exeter Hall, Dickens absorbed, and criticized, much of it. Similarly to Brontë, Dickens reveals a lasting preoccupation with the importance of work, of finding a calling—that is, of Arminian imperatives that have ceased trailing behind them a cloud of eternal rewards. Nowhere is this preoccupation more evident than in his best-known bildungsroman, *David Copperfield.*

5

"FAITH IN THE IMMANENCE OF SPIRIT"

Arminian Self-Formation in David Copperfield

These higher optimists, of whom Dickens was one, do not approve of the universe; they do not even admire the universe; they fall in love with it.

G. K. Chesterton, *Charles Dickens*

Dickens, the Church of England, and Dissent

Through its emphasis on concrete moral qualities that the reader may readily see and "feel" as opposed to theological or philosophical broodings, it is tempting to entertain the notion that, in comparison to its German counterpart *Wilhelm Meister, David Copperfield* is more of an anti-bildungsroman than the "paradigmatic" example of the genre in the English language, particularly if we recall Martin Swales's characterization of the genre as a "rarefied epic of inwardness" ("Irony" 52).[1] In relation to the Goethean tradition this very well may be the case; but within the English tradition of spiritual self-formation, *David Copperfield* finds its place alongside Brontë's *Jane Eyre.* To this end several commentators have suggested Brontë's novel to be a direct precursor to *Copperfield.*[2] Both works clearly document the progressive formation of the protagonist's selfhood by drawing significantly on moral qualities that carry noticeable Arminian overtones. Many commentators have on the one hand explored Dickens's complex attitude toward the many forms of evangelicalism in his novels and private life, and on the other, debated *David Copperfield*'s status as an English bildungsroman.[3] But few have sought to characterize the one in light of the other. This chapter reads *David Copperfield* in terms of its contribution to the "Englishness" of the English novel of spiritual self-formation. While the work Dickens famously named his "favourite child" generally replaces "moral" for "spiritual" empiricism as its central concern, at the same time it argues that (virtually in spite of the author) its particular expression of morality bears residual traces of the eighteenth-century Evangelical tradition of self-formation. Largely due to the author's troubled relationship with both the Established Church and Dissent, many commentators have argued that the "moral" over "spiritual" emphasis in Dickens derives from his concern with the good an individual may accomplish in this life apart from the hopes of any hereafter. In *The Dickens World,* Humphry House puts it most succinctly: for Dickens "religion is emphatically one of works, not faith; but there is no dwelling on any religious merit works may win" (111).

House's remark is especially relevant when applied to Dickens's contentious attitude toward evangelicalism, including Methodism, because it pinpoints both a central affinity as well as marks a teleological irreconcilability: Dickens would not, for instance, find fault with Wesley's basic Arminian belief in the practical experiential value of works. But for each the telos of "works" central to self-formation is radically different. Dickens's characters, such as David Copperfield, do good predominantly to improve their own conditions and those of their friends and loved ones, not expressly to gain an abstract theological merit that will ensure salvation. That is, Dickens stretches Arminianism to its empirical limits, beyond which loom purely utilitarian modes of conduct.

Dickens's biographical connections with Dissent in its myriad forms are well known. When Charles was a child, the Dickens family—whom Robert Newsom describes as "Broad Anglicans" who were "irregular . . . in their observations"—briefly attended a Baptist chapel (42). Charles's beloved sister Fanny eventually underwent evangelical conversion.[4] John Forster, Dickens's first biographer and a Unitarian himself, gives some attention to Dickens's brief foray into Unitarianism. In a letter to Forster, Dickens explains that his decision to "take sittings" in the Little Portland-Street Unitarian Chapel for two to three years resulted in part from his disagreement with the Established Church's catechism for enforcing "mere formalities and subtleties" on the "young and ignorant" (1:324). Apart from these details, Forster generally seeks to minimize the controversial aspects of Dickens's religious views, evident, for instance, in his contention that "upon essential points he [Dickens] had never any sympathy so strong as with the leading doctrines of the Church of England; to these, as time went on, he found himself able to accommodate all minor differences"; he had an "unswerving faith in Christianity itself, apart from all sects and schisms, which never failed him at any period of his life" (1:325).

Whether or not Dickens's "differences" with evangelicalism, either within or apart from the Established Church, were "minor" is certainly debatable; in either case traces of evangelical influence do surface in Dickens's work. This is due in part to its widespread cultural impact: scholars such as Owen Chadwick, Ian Bradley, and Norris Pope have shown evangelicalism to be, in Bradley's words, "one of the most important forces at work in shaping the character of the Victorians."[5] Certain identifiable qualities in Dickens's ethical outlook do indeed bear some resemblance to eighteenth-century Evangelical ideas of self-formation. In addition to the importance of "works," both Dickens and Wesley share an energetic optimism, belief in uneven and yet progressive growth, the value of time, moral conversion, and the power of the affections as a character-shaping force.[6] Throughout *David Copperfield* Dickens seeks to assert the empirical value of these qualities while at the same time retaining their Arminian, process-based ethos. He is, however, anything but rigorous in application. Dickens's rejection of the doctrine of original sin, for instance, is apparent in his treatment of children, but it is something he appears to uphold in certain adults such as the Murdstones.[7] His further indifference to the Wesleyan "renewal of the heart in the whole image of God, the full likeness of him that created it," is evident in his satire of Uriah Heep's fraudulent Evangelical conversion at the novel's conclusion (Wesley, *Works* 11:444). Yet moral conversion remains a central experience for David's own development, most apparent in David's Alpine experience of affective self-renewal toward the novel's conclusion.

Perhaps most important, by upholding the importance of the affections—particularly their external, visceral qualities above their theological or philosophical attributes—Dickens's approach to self-formation in this respect aligns itself, oddly enough, with the sense in which many Victorian critics had come to understand Dissenters' attitudes toward the same. Depending on the critic, this is not always a positive affinity. As discussed in chapter 4, the character of nineteenth-century English Evangelicalism and Dissent had altered significantly from its eighteenth-century origins. By the middle of the century, the increasing influence of Exeter Hall and the Evangelical Alliance of 1846 contributed toward the rise of England's Second Evangelical Revival, circa 1858 (Bradley, *Call* 17). Bradley characterizes the adherents of this new revivalism as "more fanatical, more bigoted and more introverted" than earlier Evangelicals. Dickens clearly saved his satire for precisely those characters displaying these pseudo-Christian traits, including the Murdstones, and joined others such as Leslie Stephen, Matthew Arnold, and John Stuart Mill in a print campaign against them. Stephen's *History of English Thought in the Eighteenth Century,* for example, presents Wesley's Evangelicalism as overly emotional (a negative quality often attributed to religious enthusiasm), effective in the "sphere of practice" but lacking proper philosophical foundation: it is all "heat without light."[8] Similarly David A. Ward remarks on the widely held perception of mid-century Dissenters as limited in intelligence with a "divisive temper of mind" that posed a serious threat to national order ("Transformed" 100–101).[9] Indeed Arnold perceived that the influence of Dissent was causing British culture to move increasingly more toward America and away from the Continent, thereby "toward ever-increasing parochialism and complacency" (103).

Others have been quick to point out that some of the prejudice, including Dickens's own, against Dissent was class-based. Valentine Cunningham remarks on the contradiction between Dickens as a radical sympathizer with the working classes and his antagonism toward "just those sorts of Dissent that in fact constituted the religious sphere of the poor" (*Everywhere* 195).[10] At the same time, Cunningham reminds us of the further distinction that Dickens's personal engagement with Unitarian Dissent indicates the "great gulf fixed between revivalist/fundamentalist and the decorous/learned/liberal wing of Dissent."

It is not surprising, then, that Dissenters themselves enjoyed their Dickens warily. While a reviewer for the *Wesleyan-Methodist Magazine* in 1853 appreciated Dickens's affectional, visceral appeal, he deplored the absence of high religious (above merely moral) themes in his fiction. The reviewer writes, "Pictorial powers, with humour, and loving prattle, is his Samson-lock. When he aims at anything higher, he sinks not only much beneath himself, but even lower than others, and gropes his way like a blinded giant. In his own province he more than makes his readers see what he means—you *feel* it too" ("Charles" 950). Both Victorian skeptics and Methodists, then, appreciated Dickens's familiar emotional appeal, but both were troubled by his apparent antipathy toward all forms of abstraction—either by the lack of philosophical or of theological "light" in his work.

Probably in line with the majority of Dickens's readers, those who located themselves somewhere between these extreme points of view, John Forster counts Dickens's lack of speculation rather to be a positive attribute in *David Copperfield.* Forster's comments on autobiography serve as representative of this moderate position. Autobiography "has too often led to the indulgence of mental analysis, metaphysics, and sentiment, all in excess: but Dickens was carried safely over these allurements by a healthy judgment and sleepless creative fancy"; in the novel "the crowds of external images always rising so vividly before him are more within control" (2:129).

Given, then, Dickens's complex relationship to the religious thought of his time, some preliminary discussion of critical approaches to Dickensian Christianity as well as an overview of overlapping concerns between evangelical interests and Dickens's own is useful. Together these provide the background in order to make the generic connection between *David Copperfield* and spiritual self-formation concrete.

The Dickensian "Christian spirit"

In 1904 Leo Tolstoy wrote the following single-sentence letter: "I think that Charles Dickens is the greatest novel writer of the 19th century, and that his works, impressed with the true Christian spirit, have done and will continue to do a great deal of good to mankind" (637). Precisely what constitutes the "true Christian spirit" in Dickens's work has been a matter of widespread debate, but the general consensus seems to be that the "spirit" in Dickens's work finds its source not in doctrine or sect but in a practical and affective ethics suitable for shaping conduct in time.

Dickens himself provides many instances demonstrating his distaste for the theological "letter" as harmful to the "spirit" of Christianity. In Forster's biography, he records a letter Dickens wrote to a clergyman to this effect: "There cannot be many men, I believe, who have a more humble veneration for the New Testament, or a more profound conviction of its all-sufficiency, than I have. If I am ever . . . mistaken on the subject, it is because I discountenance all obtrusive professions of and tradings in religion, as one of the main reasons why real Christianity has been retarded in this world; and because my observation of life induces me to hold in unspeakable dread and horror, those unseemly squabbles about the letter which drive the spirit out of hundreds of thousands" (2:469).

Due to Dickens's general refusal to trouble himself with the "unseemly squabbles" of the contemporary Church and maintain instead a working code of ethics, and beyond the basic agreement that Dickens's Christianity falls somewhere within the Broad Church tradition, most recent critics approach religion in his fiction from three main perspectives: those who view Dickens's fiction as endorsing the ever-increasing dialectical incompatibility between the natural world and the moral order; those, the majority, who perceive a dialogical interplay between religious and secular themes; and finally a minority who argue that through satire Dickens reveals evangelicalism to be a significant shaping influence on his fiction.[11] Because this work premises spiritual activity as an intrinsic part of the novel of self-formation, while in Dickens's particular case it recognizes that the activity of self-formation aims less toward the transcendental and more toward a particular ethical outlook, it holds most in common with the second group of theorists. Even if *David Copperfield* generally suppresses metaphysical influences, the tradition informing such influences remains intact.

Dickens shared with his contemporary evangelicals the belief in far-reaching correspondences between individual and social improvement. Both were therefore interested in the myriad issues surrounding social reform such as education and philanthropy; in addition they mutually recognized the importance of individual conversion.[12] Including the followers of Church of England Evangelicals such as

William Wilberforce and Anthony Ashley Cooper, Seventh Earl of Shaftesbury, "England's leading Evangelical," many Victorians had become preoccupied with—and disturbed by—the possibility that environmental conditions might well be just as influential a factor in sin as man's original fallen condition (Pope ix). In the following remarks to philanthropist Miss Coutts regarding the Ragged schools, while Dickens shows that the education of the poor is a shared concern, he emphasizes the importance of improving the physical environment over advancing religious agendas: "I took pains to show her," Dickens writes, "that religious mysteries and difficult creeds wouldn't do for such pupils. I told her, too, that it was of immense importance they should be *washed*" (1:324).[13]

As we have already witnessed in *Jane Eyre* the seriousness of Evangelical philanthropic enterprise, and in spite of the fact that Dickens views certain forms of charity as essential to social improvement, he seems nevertheless to let no opportunity pass to satirize the plentiful instances of its counterfeit versions. An early instance of this appears in "The Ladies' Societies" from *Sketches by Boz* (1833–39). In this piece the "ladies" form societies that look more like hostile factions than benevolent groups organized for the relief of their fellows. The "distribution society" combats the "child's examination society"; Dissent is associated with an absurd speaker on the missionary enterprise; Exeter Hall is a place for orators to give affecting speeches utterly diffuse in meaning and purpose (36).

Finally while Pope and others often indicate Dickens's affinity with the eighteenth-century anti-Methodists and anti-enthusiast tradition in his ridicule of the insincere "New Birth," Jerome Buckley, Barbara Hardy, and others make the more convincing case that a "pattern of conversion" is in fact a serious part of Dickens's conception of successful self-formation.[14] I recall Buckley's definition of conversion from *The Victorian Temper* because it still provides the best general description of the kind I have in mind; it is particularly suitable to Dickens in the sense that it describes a dual allegiance to both humanist and spiritual impulses: "The process of Spiritual New-birth involved the crucial insight into a reality, human or divine, beyond the old self-absorbed life. . . . All conversion . . . depended ultimately upon some faith in the immanence of spirit, whether the fullness of realization lay in 'one far-off event' or in the 'imperishable dignity of man.' Such faith, born of awakened feeling, directed and controlled the active reason towards social or religious ends which the unaided intellect could neither perceive nor justify" (105–6). This "faith in the immanence of spirit" is especially crucial to David's own sense of renewal on the trajectory toward self-formation. Indeed Buckley is one of the few to link directly this experience with the English bildungsroman: later in the *Season of Youth,* he describes David as moving through the "pattern of conversion." What Buckley seems to avoid, however, is the uncomfortable sense of compromise such a conversion entails as it necessarily applies to the hero's day-to-day existence. Carl Dawson articulates this discomfort best when he asks, "Can there be a middle-class hero? An industrious and hard-working hero? A hero who plays it safe? A hero whose life in embroiled in trifles?" (*Victorian* 130).[15]

David's Via Media

One advantage of emboldening the religious traditions with secular content is that such a literary act allows Dickens's bildungsroman to reach the broadest possible audience. At the same time, it in some ways obscures the outlines of the new kind of hero who is supposed to emerge from the experience. This type of hero neither assumes the perfection of a saint nor realizes the sublimity of a romantic figure. Applied to *David Copperfield,* the David who issues forth from his trials is not a purified version of the Murdstones' Evangelical hypocrisy any more than he is an innocent embodiment of Steerforth's worldly panache. His character exists as an amalgam of these states, somewhere between heaven and earth.

Accordingly Dickens does not go about presenting David's character directly, based on an increasing set of positive achievements; rather he envisions David's growth as a gradated emergence from a series of "fascinating" enthrallments.[16] This form of presentation dwells more on what David *shall not* be as what he shall become—in this respect his formative process resembles Wilhelm Meister's. During his childhood the Murdstones forcibly exert an enthrallment over both David's intellect and his affections; in young adulthood David remains affectionately attached to Steerforth even as his judgment is undeceived; finally Agnes provides the crowning release of David's affections[17] and enables him, as a product of these shaping forces, to assume his peculiar heroic status.

The crushing discipline of the Murdstone Evangelicalism would most likely have appalled Wesley as much as it does Dickens: their attitudes toward the affections and personal conduct, work, and education present the obstacles from which David must free himself. Steerforth's utter lack of discipline in the form of indifference to the value of time and to finding a calling presents a more formidable obstacle because his aristocratic vision of life is in many ways appealing to David. Occupying opposing ends of the spectrum of right conduct, David must confront and finally, with the help of Agnes, move beyond each before realizing his own moral *via media* of spiritual self-formation.

In sum David discovers that he should be firm, but *not* in Mr. Murdstone's sense of the word; he should be energetic but *not* disperse his energies after Steerforth's wild manner; finally he should undergo a moral conversion in which spirit is immanent—not in order to secure a heavenly station but, as a cumulative result of this particular pattern of growth, to become a new kind of hero. All of these values certainly bear the imprint of Arminian activity if not the stamp of evangelical dogma itself.

The Murdstone Dark Blood

Just as the autobiographical narrative voice in *Jane Eyre* expresses the development of multiple points of view over time, *David Copperfield* follows a similar pattern that reflects the process of self-formation toward a sense of maturity. Both compose narratives retrospectively reflecting upon their preconversion states. But whereas the difference between young Jane's vituperative caricature of Reverend Brocklehurst's Evangelicalism modulates into a nuanced portrait of St. John Rivers, the fixed depictions of the Murdstones suffer no such changes to accompany David's own maturing perspective. Some critics have been sensitive to this unevenness. Valentine Cunningham, for instance, complains that there is in Dickens's work "such an unflagging insistence of the child's view of religious behaviour and language that one wonders whether Dickens was capable of sustaining any other" (*Everywhere* 190).[18] *Jane Eyre* is a superior work in the sense that it convincingly and organically integrates spiritual insight with self-formation. But *David Copperfield*'s presentation of the Murdstones does have this to offer: not only do they provide clear negative models for spiritual conduct—their fraudulent spirituality has rather a cleaving than an integrative effect—but they also embody the reality if not the weight of original sin. That they remain at large at the novel's conclusion further suggests the insidious power of counterfeit spirituality and makes its conclusion less tranquil than is usually assumed.

Further it is important to notice the way in which Dickens chooses to make this critique. By representing spiritual misconduct from either a childlike point of view or by second- and third-hand reports, Dickens's careful deflection from David's mature consciousness functions as a comparatively facile substitute for the manifold (and unavoidably psychological and philosophical) difficulties attending mature consideration of the problems they represent—namely the nature of original sin.[19]

In the Evangelical Murdstones, David appears to affirm the existence of original sin through the visceral language of dark blood and humors, which highlights his general preference for physical demonstration of original sin over theological meditation on the subject: "The gloomy taint that was in the Murdstone blood, darkened the Murdstone religion, which was austere and wrathful" (4, 62).[20] The mature narrator further posits that their religion takes on this cast as "a necessary consequence" of Mr. Murdstone's "firmness." Even as a child, David understands this to be another word for "tyranny; and for a certain gloomy, arrogant, devil's humour, that was in them both" (4, 60).

The funereal churchgoing scene provides evidence, especially fitted to a child's perspective, of material aversion to tranquil religious practices turned torturous: David and his mother are separated by Mr. and Miss Murdstone; Jane dresses in pall-like black velvet, and David hears her "mumbling the responses, and emphasising all the dread words with a cruel relish. Again, I see her dark eyes roll round the church when she says 'miserable sinners,' as if she were calling the congregation names" (4, 63). They momentarily cause David to worry that "our good old clergyman can be wrong, and Mr. and Miss Murdstone right, and that all the angels in heaven can be destroying angels."

Further the Murdstone "gloomy creed" and their Evangelical obsession with work (itself a perversion of Arminian self-betterment), as applied to David's early education, forces a split between gratuitously cruel parlor sessions and the education through novels David creates on his own. With the focus on original sin to the neglect of Christ's example, the Murdstones do not suffer David to associate with other neighborhood children because children are "a swarm of little vipers" who only "contaminated one another" (4, 66). On the rare days David successfully completes his lessons, he reports that Miss Murdstone "never could endure to see me untasked" and inflicts labor merely for another excuse to exercise her cruel power over him. Bildung in the sense of education fails completely under their rule, which only leads David to become "sullen, dull, and dogged . . . almost stupefied."

The single remedy for the pseudo-religious isolation the Murdstone character inflicts upon David is, not unexpectedly, novel reading—the same remedy young Jane Eyre finds to counter her own similar experiences of domestic cruelty and isolation. David's father's library provides him the decidedly secular "glorious host" of *Tom Jones, Robinson Crusoe, Don Quixote,* and others (4, 66–67). These and similar works in turn function for David in a way that the Bible would for others: he reads "as if for life"; the novels encourage his "hope of something beyond that place and time." Dickens is nevertheless careful to qualify these statements by emphasizing David's childish apprehension of the books—"I have been Tom Jones (a child's Tom Jones, a harmless creature)"—thereby to sidestep any charges of moral miseducation. Dickens further makes clear that this private form of early education, a remedy for debilitating isolation, nevertheless does not lead him to live life only through abstract fancy. It is rather a sign of David's early intelligence that he instinctively perceives a continuity between what he reads and the world outside his window: "Every barn in the neighbourhood, every stone in the church, and every foot of the churchyard, had some association of its own, in my mind, connected with these books, and stood for some locality made famous in them." Also as with Jane, the particular frame of mind generated by this early painful situation proves to be germinal to his authorial calling later in life.

In the later wish-fulfillment scene of chapter 14, Aunt Betsey articulates every accusation against the Murdstones David would have wished to make himself had he not been still a boy. Though Betsey does not directly mention their religion, the most damning accusation she makes regarding the Murdstones' treatment of David's mother reflects indirectly upon it: Mr. Murdstone was "a tyrant to the simple baby, and you broke her heart . . . and through the best part of her weakness you gave her the wounds she died of" (14, 224). Here Betsey refers to the systematic way in which the Murdstones perverted David's mother's natural affections through their doctrine of withering seriousness and self-restraint.

Though this scene signals David's legal release from the Murdstones, they persist in casting their small dark shadows throughout the novel. When Jane Murdstone, for instance, appears in the almost improbable situation of Dora's "confidential friend," David honors her request that they keep the details of their shared history to themselves (26, 397).[21] David's generosity in this respect serves as evidence of his own growing confidence in self-formation, but still he perceives Miss Murdstone and her "little fetters" to remain unchanged from when he knew her before; these tokens, in typical Dickensian shorthand, remind him "of the fetters over a jail-door; suggesting on the outside, to all beholders, what was to be expected within" (26, 401).

David had been further chilled by meeting Mr. Murdstone as he procured a new marriage license from Mr. Spenlow's office, and later, upon David's returning from the Continent, the strange Dr. Chillip informs him of the outcome in what is probably the novel's most acerbic criticism of Evangelical extremism. Again Dickens carefully deflects the criticism from David's consciousness by several removes: throughout the conversation he mostly listens to and agrees with the doctor, many of whose sharpest remarks he attributes to his absent wife. In what amounts to spiritual vampirism, the Murdstones appear to be repeating precisely the destruction of David's mother (including her fortune) with the current Mrs. Murdstone: "she was," Dr. Chillip reports, "a lively young woman, sir, before marriage, and their gloom and austerity destroyed her." Chillip recalls his wife's words that Mr. Murdstone's doctrine is "ferocious"; that their sense of self-formation is antithetical to the spirit, for "Mr. Murdstone sets up an image of himself, and calls it the Divine Nature." Finally their unhealthy inwardness represents a complete reversal of introspection as a positive means toward spiritual self-formation—for the Murdstones it becomes its own punishment and an exercise in self-destruction, "for they are turned inward, to feed upon their own hearts, and their own hearts are very bad feeding" (59, 839).

Though the Murdstones' power over David sensibly diminishes as he continues in his own self-formative processes, it is never fully extinguished in the novel beyond Chillip's observation that their actions constitute an intrinsic punishment. Indeed the fact that Dickens associates spiritual sterility with material sterility (we presume Jane will never marry and that Mr. Murdstone's wives will not flourish) further contributes to this judgment. Beyond the above exchange, Dickens is silent. He would thus appear to be arguing *in favor of* original sin, at the very least as it manifests itself in religious curmudgeons and frauds, and its destructive power as a continuing reality in David's and in Dickens's own world.

Steerforth's Fascinating "Bad Apprenticeship"

The Murdstones' deepest sin against themselves and others, and what makes their religious creed a perversion of constructive spiritual development, involves the basic violence they commit against the human affectional impulse—their attitude toward work, education, personal conduct, and all else derives from this. Nevertheless David acknowledges their degree of power by likening their influence upon him to "the fascination of two snakes on a wretched young bird" (4, 65–66). David uses the same word to describe Steerforth's powers over him, but to an alternate effect. Once David discovers Steerforth's role in Emily's downfall, in a wistful subjunctive mood he reflects, "I should have loved him so well still—though he fascinated me no longer—I should have held in so much tenderness the memory of my affection for him, that I think I should have been as weak as a spirit-wounded child, in all but the entertainment of a thought that we could ever be reunited. That thought I never had. I felt . . . that all was at an end between us" (32, 461–62).

Just as David marks the death of his own childhood with the interment of his mother and her infant son, this moment marks David's passage between adolescence and young adulthood. While the Murdstone fascination constitutes an intellectual and affectional paralysis over the young David, his fascination with Steerforth is more dangerous because, unlike the Murdstones', it appears to be attractive in its lightness and in its aristocratic sense that the world is a wide place indeed. David's eventual recognition of the speciousness of this vague romantic vision of unchecked freedom—that Steerforth's "bad apprenticeship" of lawless self-indulgence has the power actually to destroy people—reveals that while Steerforth continues to exert a fascination over David's affections, David is no longer intellectually enthralled. Nor is he a "spirit-wounded child," but a young man whose maturing judgment is beginning to test its own range and powers. He learns from Steerforth's negative example (his aristocratic levity and his indifference to finding a calling) the value of time and a sense of seriousness about his own work.

Both the virtues of seriousness and a strong sense of the value of time are certainly integral to the legacy of Arminian spiritual self-formation; they comprise necessary steps toward Agnes, though at this moment in David's development they still tend to point in an outward rather than heavenward direction. By affirming these values, David begins to define his own middle-class-based heroism over and against Steerforth's aristocratic model.[22] The placement in the text of David's break with Steerforth attests to its high significance in David's growth: it appears in chapter 32, halfway through the narrative. To see how David's judgment gradually recovers from its fascination is to trace his vision of Steerforth as he moves from being "theguidingstarofmyexistence" to the living memory of "a cherished friend, who was dead."[23]

An important aspect of Steerforth's heroism that troubles David is the same one that disturbs Jane in St. John Rivers: neither Steerforth nor St. John gives any real thought to the "little people" of the world. Steerforth's damning remark to Mr. Mell—"I don't give myself the trouble of thinking at all about you"—is early evidence of arrogant dismissal of his social inferiors (7, 107). Of course for St. John personal regard for such people was lost in his consuming disinterestedness; Steerforth forgets them from the opposite impulse of radical aristocratic selfishness. This tendency of Steerforth's appears from the beginning of their acquaintance and sets up the ongoing conflict that he presents to David's fragile but slowly developing sense of judgment.

Well in keeping with an ancient aristocratic ethos, Steerforth's sense of being above the law of Mr. Creakle's school eventually extends into a sense of exemption from the moral code of the lower classes. Steerforth's attitude is particularly insidious during his visit to the Peggoty household, for he has since become subtler in the exercise of his powers. After the first meeting with the Peggotys, David is shocked by and misunderstands the meaning of Steerforth's abrupt remark that Emily's fiancé is "rather a chuckle-headed fellow for the girl" (21, 326). David mistakes Steerforth's genial hypocrisy for genuine artistic empathetic power—something, of the two boys, only David is capable of feeling.

During their visit to Yarmouth, the time David and Steerforth spend together—and apart—magnifies their growing differences. As Steerforth is learning to sail with Peggoty as well as succeeding in his seduction of Emily, Copperfield haunts Blunderstone with a seriousness of purpose foreign to his friend: "My reflections at these times were always associated with the figure I was to make in life, and the distinguished things I would do. My echoing footsteps went to no other tune" (22, 327).

The evening conversation between the two when David surprises his friend alone in Peggoty's house indicates a complex skirmish, an advancing and retreating, between David's judgment and his sympathetic feeling for his friend's conduct. Steerforth's continual association with the fire in a bark so close to the sea embodies his elemental incompatibility with his present surroundings. Steerforth's "passionate dejection," his gloom and moody demeanor all indicate romantic struggles of conscience that cause David's confusion to deepen (329).[24] David's unintentionally ironic remark upon seeing his friend brooding before the fire—"Have I called you down from the stars?"—sets the tone for the rest of the conversation, apparently filled with double entendres to everyone's ears but David's.

They discuss, for instance, how Steerforth has become a "nautical phenomenon," whose interest in the sea persists "as long as the novelty should last" (22, 331). The unease of the conversation portends the ill consequences of the trip, though David can only as yet feel these things darkly.[25] Much later, of course, when he pronounces judgment on his friend, David admits his "unconscious part in his pollution of an honest home"—Steerforth's enacting of David's own unlawful impulses, his unchaste appropriation of Emily's affections, allow David's character to remain chaste, free of the libertine's "experience," but just how to define "experience" in this situation makes David himself rather uncomfortable (32, 461).

The havoc that results from this visit evidences the dangerous consequences of Steerforth's refusal to pursue a serious calling.[26] This is especially grievous to David, long an admirer of his friend's energetic brilliance and native talent. Why, he asks, is Steerforth contented with "such fitful uses of your powers"? (22, 331). "Contented?" he answers. "I am never contented, except with your freshness, my gentle Daisy. As to fitfulness, I have never learnt the art of binding myself to any of the wheels on which the Ixions of these days are turning round and round. I missed it somehow in a bad apprenticeship, and now don't care about it." Steerforth's "bad apprenticeship," based upon the insubstantial foundations of caprice and romantic freedom of movement, reveals his incommensurability to the essentially Arminian virtues of industry, application, perseverance, and "firmness." These all are, finally, moral qualities David himself is destined to assume as he fashions himself into a new hero of the *via media.*

At once beautiful, arrogant, intractable, selfish, and unsusceptible to positive or constructive forms of self-formation, Steerforth can have no lasting place in the new universe the novel creates. The replacement of David-as-hero focuses on the bildung of someone infinitely more good, more conscientious, and finally, more—average. From the onset of their acquaintance at Mr. Creakle's school, the reader is forewarned of the insubstantiality of his example: David admires his friend's beauty when all have gone to sleep, yet "no veiled future dimly glanced upon him in the moonbeams. There was no shadowy picture of his footsteps, in the garden that I dreamed of walking in all night" (6, 99).

David's "Faith in the Immanence of Spirit"

Agnes brings about the final refining of David's affective nature that he needs in order to realize spiritual maturity. Even before his mournful but decisive change in attitude toward Steerforth appears, Agnes in the guise of David's "good Angel" gives him judicious warning against his "bad Angel" (25, 374). With a tactful indirection suitable to her angelic station, she says to David, "I feel as if it were some one else speaking to you, and not I when I caution you that you have made a dangerous friend." She is here, as elsewhere, Advice personified. Only her words have the power to stir David's affectionate nature at its deepest levels—their effect is that Steerforth's "image, though it was still fixed in my heart, darkened."

In combination with the fallible but morally sound Aunt Betsey, the normative voices for successful self-formation come largely from the good women of the novel. Betsey provides the practical ethics, and Agnes sanctifies them. Betsey's vision of "firmness" provides the positive antidote to Murdstone tyranny—it circumscribes the virtues of generosity, truthfulness and kindness, diligence, and self-reliance and, of course, earnestness.[27] David is always well-disposed to these virtues, but as long as his affections remain in the image of the brilliant but insubstantial Steerforth, they are of limited effect on his character.

As Robert R. Garnett argues, "the impulse that created Agnes was essentially religious, or as close to religious as Dickens ever came" ("Why" 226). In Garnett's view *David Copperfield* is "not so much about David becoming David, as about David achieving Agnes," and his vocation is not to become a novelist but to marry Agnes, for "as a religious vocation, this is naturally of more importance than his secular career" (214). This reading seeks to answer the many critics of Agnes's lack of psychological or even physiological realism—as an "emblem of spiritual serenity," her presence and influence takes on allegorical dimensions (226).[28]

In order to reach this serene state, however, David must undergo a moral conversion that bears more than passing resemblance to its religious counterpart. Dennis Walder notices that in the 1840s, the decade in which Dickens composed *David Copperfield,* he had become increasingly interested in the theme of conversion, or "a sudden inner enlightenment perceived as the product of external action, not necessarily divine in origin, but tending to carry a burden of religious implication" (*Dickens* 113). Barbara Hardy, in her classic work on moral conversion in Dickens, provides a similar definition, but one that eclipses religious conversion with its secular versions. For Hardy the best Victorian novels feature conversion not as a divine intervention but as "a turning from self-regard to love and social responsibility" (*Moral* 27).[29] Even if David's conversion experience is lacking in the precise substance of religious conversion, by closely engaging its forms, Dickens reveals a serious commitment to the idea that a basic spiritual change is the necessary crowning moment in constructive self-formation.

Chapter 58, "Absence," reads like a spiritual autobiography in miniature and shows Dickens at his most introspective, at work in uncovering the truth of David's inner condition.[30] David calls his Alpine travels "my pilgrimage"; it is largely retrospective and set in a foreign place, perfectly suitable to the activity of memory because it lacks the immediate associations of a teeming London (58, 820). The conversion David undergoes is gradual and affectional, and his opening description of his state of mind sounds very much like the point in which the penitent is struck low with the full weight of consciousness of sin. But in place of sin, though still in keeping with a dark night of the soul, David is oppressed by a sense of loss and impermanence: "By imperceptible degrees," his desolation "became a hopeless consciousness of all that I had lost—love, friendship, interest; of all that had been shattered—my first trust, my first affection, the whole airy castle of my life; of all that remained—a ruined blank and waste, lying wide around me, unbroken to the dark horizon" (58, 819). The language he uses to describe the accumulated weight of mourning and sadness takes on biblical overtones—"I said in my heart that it could never be lightened"—and he feels that death is imminent. His wanderings are directionless, purposeless, and he "had no sustaining soul within me, anywhere."

David takes a path opposite from William Wordsworth's as he moves from Italy into Switzerland, and his experience of Alpine sublimity is markedly different from the Romantic poets' experiences.[31] "Those awful solitudes" do not have the power to speak to his heart—their influence is indifferent because it is amoral and because the landscape's presence exceeds all proportion; it cannot provide the concrete instruction or guidance David wants. Rather than inciting an expansion of spirit, issuing a challenge to the individual consciousness to match its majesty, the sublime landscape has a peculiar contracting effect on David's spirit. That his "conversion" moment appears while in an inhabited valley, then, is more suitable to his condition. By looking down into a valley at the tiny hamlet—its "softening influence" bespeaks of "beauty and tranquility"—he is reminded of the existence of civilization, human order, work, and comprehensibility of scale. He begins to feel that "some better change was possible within me" (58, 821).

Whereas Jane Eyre's conversion experience—the recognition of her "calling"—involves more direct parallels to traditional religious conversion, including the reading of the Bible and instantaneous and metaphysical effects, Dickens's portrayal of conversion is less ecstatic, decidedly earthbound—a mixture of religious, romantic, and pastoral elements: "In the quiet air, there was a sound of distant singing—shepherd's voices; but, as one bright evening cloud floated midway along the mountain's-side, I could almost have believed it came from there, and was not earthly music. All at once, in this serenity, great Nature spoke to me; and soothed me to lay down my weary head upon the grass, and wept as I had not wept yet, since Dora died!" (58, 821). The "almost" stands out in this description—though David takes on an exulted mood, his eye does not move as Shakespeare's poet. Instead the description begins firmly planted on earth, in the village, wanders up to the "crowning snows" above and drifts back to the turf immediately below him. While the experience lacks transcendence, it does suggest a momentary but decisive fulfillment of a long-sought reconciliation between his own life and the world.

Nature itself has become the substitute for scripture—God's word transfers from the Bible to the word as it expresses itself in nature. At the same time, an additional replacement for the scripture appears in the form of handwritten script from the woman David loves. The letter provides nothing in the way of a direct calling—David remarks that it contains neither advice nor imperatives to duty—but its effect nevertheless permeates him: "When I heard the voices die away, and saw the quiet evening cloud grow dim . . . yet felt that the night was passing from my mind, and all its shadows clearing, there was no name for the love I bore her, dearer to me, henceforward, than ever until then" (58, 822). His resolution from this point does not dwell on turning away from sin, but under Agnes's guiding confidence, involves a returning to his work with renewed feeling and a greater sense of experience.

As if to drive home the difference between David's change and its glaringly hypocritical version (clothed in appropriate Evangelical language), three chapters later during David's tour of a London prison, he meets again with Uriah Heep, now "this converted Number Twenty Seven" (61, 857). Heep impresses his philanthropic interlocutors with a "celestial state of mind" he has assumed since his incarceration. To prove the soundness of his conversion, he insists, "'I was given to follies; but now I am sensible of my follies. There's a deal of sin outside. There's a deal of sin in mother. There's nothing but sin everywhere—except here.' 'You are quite changed?' said Mr. Creakle. 'Oh dear, yes, sir!' cried this hopeful penitent" (859). Similar to the Murdstones' fraudulent holiness at the beginning of the novel, Heep presents the perfectly fraudulent version of spiritual conversion at its conclusion. Though he is to be exiled from England, sentenced to "transportation for life"—perhaps to join the Micawbers in Australia—the way the novel takes its leave of Heep as well as of the Murdstones compounds the uneasiness upon its conclusion. Both remain at large in England and abroad, and though they no longer have the power to harm David, their presences, or specters, remain as a reminder of the ongoing cultural irritant of ungodly Dissent.

Finally the successful undergoing of the ordeal that comprises "Absence" serves as an affirmative answer to the novel's opening question. David has earned the title of hero of his own life, and the immanence of spirit he feels emanates from the person of Agnes and extends into the world through his work. The virtues he has gained from his cumulative experience have set him apart from the Murdstones' tyrannical "firmness" as well as from Steerforth's glamorous heroism. David summarizes the latter from his mature perspective: "I have never believed it possible that any natural or improved ability can claim immunity from the companionship of the steady, plain, hardworking qualities, and hope to gain its end. There is no such thing as such fulfilment on this earth" (42, 613). The staccato assurance of the words "on this earth" expresses confidence in a concrete surface from which David is safe to look upward.

Melville's *Pierre,* published just two years after *David Copperfield* in 1852, provides a remarkable contrast to David's successful Arminian ethic. The contrast between the two young heroes speaks to the elemental division between their respective theological traditions. While David is able to grow beyond religious tyranny and romantic idolatry by focusing on the value of work and his calling, Pierre's distrust of the significance of any decisive action pushes him into fatal static isolation. Indeed *Pierre* takes the antinomian incommensurability between one's formative experience and predetermined condition to anarchic limits.

6

PIERRE, OR MELVILLE'S ANARCHIC CALVINIST BILDUNGSROMAN

When the substance is gone, men cling to the shadow. Places once set apart to lofty purposes, still retain the name of that loftiness, even when converted to the meanest uses.

Pierre, book 19

Ah, if man were wholly made in heaven, why catch we hell-glimpses?

Pierre, book 5

Suppression and Continuation: The Second Great Awakening

Altogether by the nineteenth century, the centuries-long debate between Arminianism on the one hand and antinomianism on the other, between works and faith, change and stasis, between John Wesley and Jonathan Edwards began to incline dramatically in the direction of agency-based, socially oriented Arminianism. The division of influences in Melville's own childhood reflect this larger cultural shift: while Melville's father, Allan, was a Unitarian (as was the family of Elizabeth Shaw), Maria Gansevoort Melville was raised in the Dutch Reformed Church, one of the oldest stalwarts of austere Calvinist orthodoxy.[1] In this sense, then, neither in his thought nor in his work did Melville stand above or outside the religious culture of his contemporaries, but rather he engaged it headlong. In *Pierre* particularly Brian Higgins and Hershel Parker confirm Melville's conflicted engagement with this culture in their collection of *Pierre*'s critical reception. The central objection most contemporary reviewers had—if indeed they could see beyond the lurid intimations of multiple incestuous or otherwise illicit relationships—involves the "slough of metaphysical speculation, which constitutes the largest portion of the work."[2] The nature of this speculation combined with what Newton Arvin has called Melville's "saturation in orthodox Calvinism" together work tellingly to define this peculiar and difficult book as an American bildungsroman. Because *Pierre* appears to promise a traditional bildungsroman but delivers a complete defiance of the genre's traditional goal of healthy spiritual self-formation, some further explanation must be sought as to why this is the case. The intense American legacy of Calvinist spiritual self-formation contributes, in my view, significantly to this generic reconfiguration. Namely the grim Calvinist determinism built into the novel's shaky framework and the concurrent antinomian struggle between necessity and agency together hew a path leading from the country to the city that is altogether divergent from the one taken by the likes of David Copperfield and the heroes of other English and Continental bildungsromans.[3] First some background on the Second Great Awakening serves to contextualize the condition of nineteenth-century Calvinism as Melville and his contemporaries inherited it from Edwards.

The following observation, which opens the chapter titled "Causes of Fanatical Enthusiasm in Some Americans" in Alexis de Tocqueville's *Democracy in America*, comprehends the ongoing problem of the Edwardsian legacy in antebellum America: "Although the desire of acquiring the good things of this world is the prevailing passion of the American people, certain momentary outbreaks occur, when their souls seem suddenly to burst the bonds of matter by which they are restrained, and to soar impetuously towards Heaven."[4] It epitomizes the complex interchanges between materialism, expansion, Protestant revivalist culture, and what Charles Sellers calls the "market revolution" culture of Jacksonian America. Amid the confusion of shifting approaches to Protestant belief and the ways in which these engaged or failed to engage antebellum culture—particularly its burgeoning industrialism and capitalism—it is important to notice how commentators have used the terms *Arminian* and *antinomian* increasingly less to describe theological outlooks and more to reflect the comparatively secure material conditions of early nineteenth-century Protestant America.[5]

Similarly readers concerned with the impact of the Second Great Awakening on antebellum culture in general almost uniformly interpret the movement from antinomianism to Arminianism as a theological parallel to the political shift from monarchical/aristocratic culture to democratic culture. The hard-line Calvinism of the eighteenth century could not compete with the more optimistic and democratically compatible Arminianism. As David Reynolds most simply states, "If politics was embracing average people, so salvation was no longer reserved for a chosen elect. Anyone could attain it" (*Waking* 127). Indeed the church membership statistics of the period would appear to make this position difficult to contest: Reynolds reports that before the Revolution, Congregational and Presbyterian churches claimed the largest portion (one third) of the American churchgoing population (126). By 1850 the number of Congregationalists had dwindled dramatically to a mere 4 percent. Methodism, in turn, enjoyed a virtual reversal of these numbers.[6]

Coincident with the fermenting elements of Methodism, Republicanism, revivalism, and reform, the Second Great Awakening additionally saw the flowering of popular religious (often anti-Calvinist) journalism (Underwood, "Awash" 98). Elias Smith, founder of the significantly titled *Herald of Gospel Liberty* in 1808, used this publication as one such anti-Calvinist platform. To take one instance, I cite verses excerpted from Smith's poem "On Predestination," published in 1809 in the *Herald:*

> If this be the way,
> As some preachers say,
> That all things were ordered by fate;
> I'll not spend my pence,
> To pay for nonsense,
> If nothing will alter my state.
>
> If preachers were wise,
> Their int'rest they'd prize,
> And lay aside predestination;
> And they'd live by their art,
> And not preach to a part,
> But preach up a free proclamation.
>
> (qtd. in Hatch, *Democratization* 228)

Clearly these pro-Arminian lines are geared toward luring ministers toward the lucrative possibilities of "democratizing" their congregations. By the 1840s this change appeared to be irreversible. Timothy L. Smith notes that Arminianism was "noticeable everywhere" and that the idea of "personal predestination could hardly survive amidst the evangelists' earnest entreaties to 'come to Jesus'" (*Revivalism* 89).

The special case of millenarianism during the Second Great Awakening merits separate mention because it provides an important link between the two awakenings in the sense that it highlights the different ways in which the Protestant cultures of both periods chose to understand cosmic change. This, in turn, had a major impact upon the way they thought about themselves as individuals and their formative purpose or "calling" in the world. Donald C. Swift argues that during the Second Great Awakening, there was more interest in the millennium than in any preceding period in American history (*Religion* 92). The 1830s witnessed, along with the establishment of other controversial sects such as Mormonism, the genesis of Adventism, whose founder, William Miller, infamously predicted the Second Coming in 1843.

John F. Wilson maintains an important distinction in his contention that the intervening Enlightenment between awakenings fundamentally altered the idea of millenarianism and in turn made a decisive impact on the ways in which Edwards's legacy was received. Wilson indicates that Thomas Paine's Deism was significantly responsible for "literalizing" religious thought: "the great, rich, internally complex Christian tradition of the West" was consequently "either reduced to propositional form and thus believed to be concerned only with the mundane world, or held to be essentially unintelligible" ("History" 135). Perhaps the most significant consequence of this reduction, Wilson continues, is the suppression or dismissal of the poetic, symbolic, and mystical dimensions of religious experience. These are the very qualities of religious experience, as I have shown in part 1, that Edwards insists are indispensible to spiritual self-formation. What this suppression meant for the nineteenth-century Protestant culture at large was a widespread, literal-minded millenarianism split between whether Christ would appear on earth before the millennium (premillennialism) or after it (postmillennialism).[7] Pre-Enlightenment Christianity, including the thought of Jonathan Edwards, did not make the distinction as sharply. Instead it embraced a comparatively metaphysical millenarianism in which Christ is present in the past, present, and future all at once (138).

Wilson's article provides a plausible reason why the theological Edwards appropriated by the nineteenth century appears shorn of the qualities that constitute his original identity. Qualities such as quietism, the poetic, the mystical, and the antinomian paradox of stasis immersed in unremitting change, so the argument goes, were abandoned as outdated, unsettling, and unsynchronized with the new values the citizens of antebellum America were supposed to hold most dear. On the one hand, a newly "Methodized" religious culture was deployed and dedicated to reforming major issues of social injustice; on the other expansion and commerce looked confidently into the future.[8] In the face of these powerful social forces, Edwards's torturous philosophical paradoxes became inconsequential to the individual concerned with self-improvement, with the direction of American culture, and finally with the fate of the cosmos itself.

It is *this* spectral Edwards that Mark A. Noll most certainly had in mind when he complained about the air of "occult influence" with which Edwards always seems to be shrouded in discussions involving his impact on nineteenth-century American letters ("Jonathan" 228). Yet it seems, given these conditions, seeking the antinomian Edwards and his inexorable mysticism in the nineteenth century was, if not exactly an occult activity, one that required considerable diving below and to large extent moving against the dominant cultural currents of the period. To be sure, figures such as Edwards's grandson Timothy Dwight and his circle at Yale reintroduced Edwards's ideas (with appropriate modifications) to new generations of parishioners. By their efforts and the efforts of others, according to George M. Marsden, from about 1800 until 1850, "Edwards was the polestar of the most formidable and influential American theology" (499). The few outside this exclusive clergy still troubled by what they perceived to be unresolved metaphysical questions in the nation's short history were artists, namely Hawthorne, Melville, and Dickinson; before them Emerson and Thoreau; after them Henry James and Mark Twain. Each still wrestled with the legacy of antinomianism and the troubling paradoxes it contains and how these manifested themselves in their own changing narratives of individual self-formation. Haroutunian concludes *Piety vs. Moralism* with the admission that in spite of everything, Calvinism in nineteenth-century America "continued to live without reason" (281). Above all others Herman Melville took the presence of this weighty specter most personally.

Once Bereft of Scriptural Authority

The plot of *Pierre* is, on the surface, simple and melodramatic. Pierre Glendinning is born the sole heir to his family's ancestral grounds: he lives with a domineering mother who worships their position among the American aristoi. The young hero, a successful writer, is engaged to marry the equally spotless Lucy, with whom he enjoys idyllic rides through the countryside. But when Pierre meets Isabel, a dark girl with a dreamlike presence who claims to be his half-sister, he is forced to reevaluate the moral standards by which his world is constructed. Rather than reveal her identity and destroy his family's name, he deserts his mother and Lucy and "elopes" to the city with Isabel. There they seek help from, and are spurned by, Pierre's well-connected cousin Glen. They come to reside in an ancient church with a community of misfits living under the eye of the mysterious philosopher Plotinus Plinlimmon; Lucy rejoins them there to form a miserable ménage à trois; Pierre attempts, and fails, to write what was to have been his best novel. The philosopher's ultimate lack of guidance proves to be fatal to all involved.

Bruce L. Grenberg locates *Pierre* as the novel linking Melville's "two careers" as a writer: "It is on the one hand the post mortem and epitaph to Melville's heroic vision, and on the other it is the first chapter to Melville's extended anatomy of a nightmare world devoid of certainty, justice, and truth, a world lit not by light, but by darkness visible" (*Some* 121). Speculations abound concerning the biographical reasons behind this general shift in tone. Some emphasize the psychological effect of Hawthorne's departure from Lenox in November 1851, the time during which Melville was writing *Pierre;* others highlight the oppressive domestic situation at Arrowhead farm; still others see the change as resulting from Melville's increasingly strained relationship with his publishers and his growing disgust with the contemporary "Young America" literary culture.[9]

Beyond biographical influences *Pierre* can also be read as a painful literary enactment of the very metaphysical problem that Edwards spent his intellectual life trying to elucidate: how the ever-inviolate Puritan soul reconciles itself with the experience of being in constant forced contact with the world. What makes this conundrum most potent in the nineteenth century is the knowledge that it was once a theological problem that capable theologians such as Edwards had the proper framework (reason, intuition, and revelation) within which to address it. But in the nineteenth century, the antinomian paradox was taken up by artists such as Melville, unsystematic but deeply intuitive thinkers, who no longer attribute absolute authority to the Bible. In this new context, the same problem opens into abyssal regions. It is indeed a pregnant coincidence that Melville composed the majority of *Pierre* in the Berkshires in close proximity to the place in which, exactly one hundred years before in 1751, Edwards settled into his exile to compose his last major works. Nor was Melville unaware of this fact.[10]

Edwards answered the all-important question for Calvinists—how shall I know the condition of my soul?—through the intensive, lifelong activity of self-examination that culminated in a visionary mystical annihilation of the self into the image of God. Christ's all-conciliating presence provides the saint a glimpse, however partial and temporary, of the saint's eternal condition. This conversion experience encompasses the crowning moment of spiritual self-formation. Sermons and treatises provide suitable means for abstract meditations on these and other related matters; placed in fictional contexts, their urgency becomes sharper most immediately due to the demands of character and plot. In *Pierre* Melville epitomizes the antinomian paradox on the eve of Pierre's departure from Saddle Meadows in two successive questions: "Did he, or did he not vitally mean to do this thing?" followed by the agonizing "Whence then this utter nothing of his acts?" (bk. 9, chap. 4, 170).[11]

Some readers have rightly questioned whether the actual plot of the novel—a young man discovers the identity of a hidden half-sister and wishes to legitimize her position to the world without damaging his family's reputation—is powerful enough to sustain its metaphysical concerns.[12] With respect to the plot itself, I am inclined to agree but at the same time would insist on the distinction between the novel's failure on this level and its crushing success in demonstrating the metaphysical insupportableness of Calvinist antinomianism once bereft of scriptural authority. To use H. Bruce Franklin's terms, the "symbolic action" overwhelms the "physical action" of the novel because this is the very paradox of living in a Calvinist world in which action does not signify in the face of God's sovereignty. In the novel this conflict is embodied in the single act, committed by Pierre's father before Pierre had come into existence, that eventually accomplishes Pierre's destruction. The ensuing struggle unfolds Pierre's paradoxical urge to act but reveals the futility of action in the face of impersonal forces that are by necessity out of his control. Whereas for Edwards the telos of spiritual self-formation culminates in the experience of being "emptied and annihilated" and filled with Christ's image, Pierre, Melville's latter-day antinomian, also courts annihilation but with the thought that it may be complete.

A Rural Idyll, Interrupted

Commentators such as Clark Davis have remarked on the artificial and static quality of the landscape with which *Pierre* opens; its lack of physical weight mirrors Pierre's immaturity.[13] The weightless stasis of Saddle Meadows may in addition be read as an externalization of the Calvinist stasis of being, something that constitutes "the deepest element" of Pierre's "culture" as well as links him directly to his Puritan ancestors: "as he now stood heir to their forests and farms; so by the same insensible sliding process, he seemed to have inherited their docile homage to a venerable Faith, which the first Glendinning had brought over sea, from beneath the shadow of an English minister. Thus in Pierre was the complete polished steel of a gentleman, girded with Religion's silken sash" (1, 2, 6–7). Pierre complacently views the property of Saddle Meadows, girded with noble tradition, as "sanctified"; the forests and meadows themselves are his protective "talisman" (1, 2, 8). Books are the second contributor to young Pierre's culture. Like David Copperfield, he is early nourished by his late father's library. But while David read to escape his present conditions, the "fastidiously picked and decorous library" of Pierre's father appears merely to serve his son's present complacency by evoking "soft, imaginative flames in his heart." The third and least token of Pierre's cultivation comes from his annual visits to the city with his mother in which he mingled with "a large and polished society"—this last is the world of Glendinning Stanly.

By all such indicators, *Pierre* appears prepared to become a traditional bildungsroman of all-around formation with spirituality at its apex. We know that Melville had borrowed and read *Wilhelm Meister's Apprenticeship* in 1850; Goethe's prototype of the genre would therefore have been fresh in his mind as he began composing *Pierre* just a year later.[14] Indeed as we shall see, the parallels between the texts are extensive. The most glaring difference between the works is that Wilhelm and Pierre come to completely opposite ends—the first in maturity and social success; the second in madness and annihilation. And yet in many ways *Pierre* bears more resemblance to this bildungsroman than to its English counterparts. Most important, Melville shows a marked affinity for the metaphysical ambiguities for which the German bildungsroman is well known. Both Wilhelm and Pierre are would-be artists who read and provide commentary on *Hamlet* and who eventually abandon their art; both are accompanied in their wanderings by ethereal, romantic figures whom each protagonist must give up (Mignon, the Harper, and Isabel are all musicians haunted by ambiguous pasts and associated with incest); both recognize but finally move past evangelical forms of spirituality; both come under the influence of a mysterious society (both of which are associated with towers) that decisively affects their careers.

Of course as many differences may be noted based on each of the above points of correspondence. With the significantly lifelong involvement of the Tower Society (symbolic of the inescapably *social* nature of successful individual self-formation), Wilhelm abandons the theater for a productive and socially integrative calling; his claiming of his paternity coincides with his assuming this higher social responsibility. The Omega Order of the Apostles led by the Grand Master, Plotinus Plinlimmon, provides Pierre refuge but finally no coherent direction for his art, philosophy, or life. The romantic figures haunting Wilhelm dissolve either of their own accord or through the machinations of the society so that he may emerge fully healthy; Isabel never liberates Pierre with her death but rather accompanies him in self-annihilation.

These differences are due to no small extent to the individual temperaments of the authors.[15] Goethe's searching optimism both touches and provokes Melville—probably in ways similar to his impression of Emerson. In *Pierre* Goethe is mentioned twice, and both times he is the object of sharp satire. In the first instance, Goethe is lumped together with Plato and Spinoza, or "the guild of self-impostors" who have claimed to have found the "Talismanic Secret" (14, 2, 208). Goethe later appears in a fragment of Pierre's incoherent new "novel": "Explain this darkness, exorcise this devil, ye can not. Tell me not, thou inevitable coxcomb of a Goethe, that the universe can not spare thee and thy immortality, so long as—like a hired waiter—thou makest thyself 'generally useful'" (22, 3, 302). Of course as I hope to have made clear in the third chapter, Goethe no more claims ownership to the Talismanic Secret than he dismisses the problem of evil.[16]

Few critics have failed to remark upon Pierre's association with absolute (chronometrical) values and their underlying incommensurability with the relativist (horological) world.[17] The following takes this basic conflict for granted but further seeks to understand the prior conditions that determine Pierre's absolutism (and thereby his trajectory of self-formation) and the dramatic power with which these conditions pervade the "action" of the novel as a whole. By locating the source of these conditions in the Absolute itself, *Pierre* presents a philosophical continuation of Melville's concerns in *Moby-Dick*. Of course the immense sublimity of the whale's countenance would appear to lend itself more easily to speculation on first causes than would the comparatively familiar countenance of a fellow human being. And yet in *Pierre* Melville appears to be making, and asking readers to make, this connection. As I show below, the countenance of Isabel and the countenance of Plinlimmon together make up a complementary and ubiquitous vision of the Absolute. Isabel's countenance is significantly associated with the romantic Absolute as embodied in natural forces—with lightning, electricity, water, and trees—and thereby belongs most immediately to the rural environment of Saddle Meadows; Plinlimmon's countenance appears in the city, fixed in the tower to the Church of the Apostles. While his presence persists in an absolute ubiquity, it provides Pierre with no corresponding means with which to reconcile the world with his own soul but only magnifies his isolation from it. Taken together the countenances of Isabel and Plinlimmon offer a dangerously paradoxical both/and vision of the Absolute: it is both as impersonal, arbitrary, omnipresent, and terrible as the God of Jonathan Edwards and indistinguishable from the blankness of annihilation.

God's Ambiguity I: The Countenance of Isabel

After hearing the first part of Isabel's story, Pierre gradually begins to feel the scope of Isabel exceeding all the normal boundaries of existence he has known to date: "Is it possible then, thought Pierre, that there lives a human creature in this common world of every-days, whose whole history may be told in little less than two-score words, and yet embody in that smallness a fathomless fountain of ever-welling mystery? Is it possible, after all, that spite of bricks and shaven faces, this world we live in is brimmed with wonders, and I and all mankind, beneath our garbs of common-placeness, conceal enigmas that the stars themselves, and perhaps the highest seraphim can not resolve?" (7, 8, 138–39). This passage is particularly suggestive in the sense that it links the figure of Isabel directly with the values associated with the Absolute. In light of this moment and others, Wendy Stallard Flory's contention that *Pierre* is not a realistic novel but rather a "symbolic romance," and that accordingly Isabel is not so much a woman as a manifestation of Melville's own "creative imagination"—as sinister as it is powerful—is useful ("Melville" 121).[18] Taken in this way, "Pierre's greatest fear is not that Isabel is his sister but that she is not" (134). Should the latter be the case, the absolutes of truth and virtue to which she incites Pierre become illusory.

The above quotation from *Pierre,* however, invests yet a greater significance in the figure of Isabel as another enigmatic manifestation of the Absolute itself. That is, what Melville had begun in contemplating the countenance of the Whale, he contracts in part into the minute visage of a young woman. Chapter 79, "The Prairie," of *Moby-Dick* serves as a point for comparison: "Champollion deciphered the wrinkled granite hieroglyphics. But there is no Champollion to decipher the Egypt of every man's and every being's face. . . . If then, Sir William Jones, who read in thirty languages, could not read the simplest peasant's face in its profounder and more subtle meanings, how may unlettered Ishmael hope to read the awful Chaldee of the Sperm Whale's brow? I but put that brow before you. Read it if you can" (503). The challenge of the last sentence echoes throughout *Pierre*. This is evident, for instance, when Melville describes Pierre's feeling of mystical correspondence with Isabel. As Pierre addresses her imagined countenance, the narrator reflects, "'Explain ye my deeper mystery,' said the shepherd Chaldean king, smiting his breast, lying on his back upon the plain; 'and then, I will bestow all my wonderings upon ye, ye stately stars!' So, in some sort, with Pierre. Explain thou this strange integral feeling in me myself . . . and I will renounce all other wonders, to gaze wonderingly at thee. But thou hast evoked in me profounder spells than the evoking one, thou face! For me, thou hast uncovered one infinite, dumb, beseeching countenance of mystery, underlying all the surfaces of visible time and space" (3, 2, 51–52). Like the Whale, whose silence is a defining feature of its sublimity, Isabel's appeal to Pierre is equally inscrutable and yet also distinctly human. That Isabel is a woman, desired by Pierre in a complicated way, furthers the confusion; yet this addition provides a feeling of correspondence and intimacy that was necessarily remote in Ishmael's obsession with the Whale. Therefore Isabel's symbolic association with the Absolute by no means precludes her physical presence in the novel—Melville most likely would not encourage such a separation. Repeatedly Pierre remarks on her combined spiritual and physical powers of attraction, which Melville epitomizes in the image of the magnetic "buckler" of her brow that simultaneously attracts and repulses.[19]

The countenance of Isabel becomes as ubiquitous in Saddle Meadows as was the Whale in the sea: "Escape the face he could not. Muffling his own in his bedclothes—that did not hide it. Flying from it by sunlight down the meadows, was as vain" (3, 2, 47). Isabel's ubiquity contains both romantic as well as religious elements, evident in prophetic biblical parallels as well as in dreams and visions that Pierre experiences in addition to seeing Isabel in her "mortal lineaments of mournfulness." To complicate matters the narrative presents these experiences with a conscious indifference to chronology. The effect of this indifference casts the plot further into a sense of stillness, into a world in which cause and effect are foregone conclusions and actions are an afterthought of being itself.

We are told that Pierre has in fact met Isabel first "some weeks previous" to his ride with Lucy into the hills of Saddle Meadows (3, 1, 43). By arranging his initial meeting with Isabel amid the pious work of the society for the relief of emigrants (if rather unimaginatively couched in a portrait of the unmarried, hard-of-hearing, foolishly gossiping Miss Pennies), Melville's irony strikes on several levels. He suggests that the deepest problems of the most vulnerable emigrants of all, Isabel and by extension her mother, even in the very midst of the society's earnest efforts, remain unaddressed and, more problematically, unrecognized.[20]

Subsequent to this meeting, Lucy's reference to the "mysterious, haunting face, which thou once told'st me, thou didst thrice vainly try to shun" shows that while the average inhabitants of Saddle Meadows are certainly aware of the existence of suffering, most, including Lucy, are incapable of facing the host of ambiguities with which suffering is inevitably accompanied (2, 5, 37). Further her allusion to Christ's prophecy that Peter would deny him three times unconsciously parallels Pierre's three denials of Isabel.[21] In addition to seeing and in effect denying Isabel at the Miss Pennies' and seeking to banish her presence from himself and Lucy during their pastoral idyll, Pierre encounters the phantom countenance for a third time, alone, under an ancient pine tree. In this location Isabel's presence is more completely presaged through the tree's Eolean boughs of "melodious mournfulness," which confound grief and pleasure (2, 7, 40). As Pierre sits looking upward from amid the exposed roots, his demands show how deeply his values remain assimilated with those of Saddle Meadows—of Lucy and his mother—and their intolerance of everything ambiguous: "If thou hast a secret in thy eyes of mournful mystery, out with it. . . . what is it that thou has veiled in thee so imperfectly, that I seem to see its motion, but not its form?"

These visionary presentiments culminate in Isabel's letter to Pierre and together constitute an overturning of his moral being. Again, taken on the bare surface, these experiences hardly seem powerful enough to cause this foundational shift in Pierre's heretofore unstrained process of self-formation. But the way in which Pierre *experiences* the intelligence supports this overturning entirely. He begins to see Isabel not simply as a beautiful young woman but as a ubiquitous presence; he begins to face for the first time the reality that the universe is composed of predetermined ills (the sins of his father) that he himself has no possible chance to rectify in any absolute sense.

In spite of these circumstances, at this point in the narrative, *enthusiast* is the word that Melville most often uses to describe Pierre. This term carries evangelical connotations that recall Edwards's efforts to distinguish between the truly converted and those given to the mere display of a change in state. In his enthusiasm Pierre never doubts *what* to do but only *how* to accomplish it (5, 1, 87). And there is something heroic-minded about his ethical certainty in the face of these powerful forebodings. While the ensuing interviews with Isabel never alter Pierre's basic conviction, they do escalate the problem of "how" he is to accomplish what he knows to be right—and they further hint at the antinomian position of the likely insignificance of his choice. This situation would still accommodate an ensuing Calvinist spiritual conversion experience, for Pierre is overpowered by an awareness of sin and suffers from an "utter pauperism of the spirit" (7, 7, 136). The narrator comments that most people in this condition will comfort themselves by recalling the good deeds they have done. "But," he continues, presumably with reference to Pierre, "with men of self-disdainful spirits; in whose chosen souls heaven itself hath by a primitive persuasion unindoctrinally fixed that most true Christian doctrine of the utter nothingness of good works; the casual remembrance of their benevolent well-doings, does never distill one drop of comfort for them, even as . . . the recalling of their outlived errors and misdeeds, conveys to them no slightest pang or shadow of reproach" (7, 7, 137). The overt Calvinist language of this passage and its implications constitute a nineteenth-century retelling of the position that caused figures such as Anne Hutchinson so much trouble two centuries before. Edwards, in turn, would have agreed with the narrator's remarks on "works" and yet remained oppressed by consciousness of sin throughout his life.

Perhaps in Pierre's place a more orderly Calvinist would next consult the Bible for guidance. Though Pierre does no such thing, he tries, and is disappointed by, the complacent counsel of the Reverend Falsgrave. Pierre is left, then, with *Hamlet* and with the *Inferno.* The late-night conclusions he derives from these texts may evidence a conversion of sorts, and if this is so, its character appears to consist more in a growing sense of reprobation than of grace. The moment is, at the very least, Melville's criticism if not rejection of the nature of the conversion process that Edwards had taken great pains to elucidate a century earlier: "The intensest light of reason and revelation combined, can not shed such blazonings upon the deeper truths of man, as will sometimes proceed from his profoundest gloom" (9, 2, 169).

Among the uniformitarians and the catastrophists, Pierre is surely a catastrophist. But because Melville characterizes his catastrophic "conversion" as occurring without the "light of reason and revelation," its effects are accordingly opposed to the traditional experience. Instead of being "totally wrapt up in the fullness of Christ," Pierre experiences a disconcerting sense of spiritual barrenness. Melville likens this newly desolate state to the image of an Arctic explorer who has lost "the directing compass of his mind; for arrived at the Pole, to whose barrenness only it points, there, the needle indifferently respects all points of the horizon alike" (9, 1, 165). In this state of spiritual suspension, having recognized and claimed Isabel in her full significance, Pierre finds himself ironically further removed from the Talismanic Secret than ever before. In his move from the country to the city, he must seek Isabel's urban counterpart: Plotinus Plinlimmon.

God's Ambiguity II: The Countenance of Plinlimmon

Most readers who have taken on the ambiguities of *Pierre* acknowledge the tantamount importance of that tattered pamphlet "Ei," bereft of its conclusion, which Pierre finds during the transitional carriage ride between the country (as silent and still as the novel's opening scene) and the city.[22] Readings of Melville's intentions behind Plotinus Plinlimmon's pamphlet range from satirical to, as Herbert W. Schneider has claimed, "the nearest Melville ever came to making a technical, academic formulation of what might be called his philosophy" (*History* 257).[23] In my view Schneider (due perhaps in part to his position outside the field of literary studies), alongside Floyd C. Watkins, contributes the most accurate appraisal of the pamphlet's relevance to Pierre's struggles with spiritual self-formation. Their findings serve as a background to the main focus of this section: the Church of the Apostles and, most important, the countenance of Plinlimmon himself.

As a pragmatist philosopher, Schneider sensibly recognizes that Melville's "chief transcendental insight consisted precisely in his realization that absolute and relative standards are necessary to each other, neither being intelligible in itself" (257). Plinlimmon's doctrine is, then, Melville's "reformulation of the Calvinistic distinction between saving faith and good works" that necessarily accommodates two distinct readings: it is both an ironic commentary on the failures of Calvinist orthodoxy as well as a "tragic revision of the transcendentalist doctrine of correspondence" (260). Watkins comes to a similar conclusion that the pamphlet supports two separate readings that indeed make up the novel's central ambiguity: on the one hand, Melville's emotionalism and skepticism are in alignment with Pierre's absolutist rebellion, whereas philosophically Melville somehow comes to terms with the horological, relativistic reality he associates with living in the world ("Melville's" 51).[24]

The narrative structure of book 14, "The Journey and the Pamphlet," supports these dual readings and emphasizes a tone of urgency. The layered effect of the three short chapters it comprises comes across as variations on the same theme, which the first chapter articulates as the essential disjunction between abstract truth and its enactment in the world. The second chapter provides the next layer, in which the narrator articulates his own version of Plinlimmon's theory of "Chronometricals and Horologicals." The narrator names the "Talismanic Secret" as the solution to the disjunction, something that will "reconcile this world with his own soul" (14, 2, 208). That the pamphlet itself is cleft constitutes the final layers. Its first section provides the theory itself, and the second section advances the provisional solution of "virtuous expediency."

To Pierre's credit his reaction to the pamphlet's latter portion is of a distinctly *non*enthusiastic character: the doctrine of "virtuous expedience" teaches him nothing that he does not already know—it is the world of his mother and of Reverend Falsgrave and one that he has consciously rejected as false.[25] On the other hand, the first section torments him with the possibility that the doctrine of irreconcilable separation between the world and the individual soul is only apparent and that a "contradictory" yet "meridianal correspondence" exists between the two. Pierre's inability to apprehend the pamphlet's "central conceit" is due not to his absolutism but because the center is not geometric: it drifts elusively among these many layers.

Others, such as Emerson, have assigned to poetry the reconciling talismanic office; for Edwards it is the mystical-intuitive experience of Christ that provides the ultimate reconciliation between the world and the soul. Edwards would likely appreciate the idea behind Plinlimmon's chronometricals and horologicals and, like Pierre, reject Arminian expediency in favor of searching out visionary correspondences. But whereas Edwards was, finally, able to give his ultimate consent to being and thereby realize spiritual self-formation to the extent possible while living, Pierre continues on into the city to search out the promised correspondences in vain.[26]

Melville's choice of domicile for Pierre in the city could not be more symbolically fitting to his inner condition as well as representative of larger cultural shifts in antebellum America at the time. The Church of the Apostles is a hotchpotch of the old and the new, of art and commerce, a visible relic of virtue's devolution into expediency. The original tower, "a singular and ancient edifice," appears first to have been a colonial fortress, the sides of which were "pierced with small and narrow apertures" (19, 1, 265). In its second incarnation and new additions, it grew into its namesake; it enjoyed "its days of sanctification and grace; but the tide of change and progress had rolled clean through its broad-aisle and side-aisles, and swept by far the greater part of its congregation two or three miles up town" (268). And neither does Melville appear to show any nostalgia for this portion of its history: he describes the clergyman of a "half-palsied form" as pathetically continuing to pound his "worm-eaten pulpit" until he, too, passed away. Now surrounded by warehouses and the trafficking of merchants and clerks, the merchants decided on the most expedient option for the structure's future: the church "must be divided into stores; cut into offices; and given for a roost to the gregarious lawyers." Subsequent additions to accommodate the new tenants grew seven stories high, "almost to a level with the top of the sacred tower." As the city continued to shift and amplify, the Church of the Apostles became increasingly isolated, commerce ebbed, and it became, finally, tenanted by the very people most marginalized by and isolated from the interests of the majority—the artists, the philosophers, students and teachers of the humanities, and writers.

With their idealism and their poverty in common, these self-elect theorists, reformers, propagandists, and artists form a society that demonstrates Melville's sharp awareness of the business of cultural reform, particularly as it distortedly reflects the evangelical idealism of the Second Great Awakening. Like many contemporary evangelicals obsessed with utopian experiments, reform societies, and millenarianism, the narrator describes the Apostles' society as "secretly suspected to have some mysterious ulterior object, vaguely connected with the absolute overturning of the Church and State, and the hasty and premature advance of some unknown great political and religious Millennium" (269). The Apostles, then, may be described as anarchic postmillennialists—protected and represented by the vaguely menacing image of the fortress-tower in their midst.

The effect of this setting on Pierre's continued efforts to salvage a sense of creative self-formation is accordingly symbolic. In his new quarters in the Church of the Apostles, he worries that the camp-bedstead of his renowned grandfather is too large for his own stature. The violence of actual war that distinguished his ancestor's heroism is still with him but in an unsatisfactorily abstract way: "Pierre is a warrior too; Life is his campaign, and three fierce allies, Woe and Scorn and Want, his foes. The world is banded against him; for lo you! he holds up the standard of Right, and swears by the Eternal and True!" (19, 2, 270). Hyperbolically the narrator emphasizes how Pierre's insistence on absolute ideals in the world does anything but change it and only contributes to his further isolation. The setting, then, projects rather grimly yet another variation of the antinomian predicament: no matter his heroism, no matter his painstaking work, isolation begins to engulf him completely.

It bears remarking at this point how differently in the prototypal bildungsroman Goethe conceived the socializing role of the Tower Society in comparison with Melville's American version. While both appear vaguely to associate each society with Freemasonry, the most significant difference between the two is that in *Wilhelm Meister*, the Tower Society is composed of the most influential people in Germany—the aristocrats, the landowners, the politicians. They are aristocrats in the traditional sense—the "best" in wealth, beauty, birth, virtue, and talents—and therefore best suited to wield power. In addition to governing, they are also concerned with expanding their power by controlling (or rather shaping) certain promising individuals within the culture that they may eventually join their ranks, as in the case of Wilhelm himself. As discussed in chapter 3, the premier objective of the Tower Society is to *prevent* individual isolation, evident in their contention that the source of isolation originates within excessive self-absorption, either of a religious or of a romantic character, and that its inevitable conclusion is madness. An individual such as Wilhelm must shed these unhealthy aspects of his personality (embodied in the poetic figures of the Harper and Mignon and the mystical Canoness) in order to realize a rational, balanced, healthy-minded, socially productive bildung. As the physician, a member of the society and indicative of its approach to rational self-formation, summarizes his program for "curing" madness to Wilhelm: "nothing maintains common sense more than living in a normal way with many people" (210).

Pierre, on the other hand, brutally inverts the cultural role of the "mystic Society" of the Apostles (21, 3, 290). The Apostles could not be further socially removed from the American aristoi: they consist rather of the disinherited, the exiles, the unemployed. The Apostles' social, political, philosophical, economic and, in short, complete estrangement from the powers responsible for shaping American culture can consequently have little integrative effect upon the individuals constituting the society. Indeed the very cultural insubstantiality of the Church of the Apostles mirrors each individual's growing sense of personal insubstantiality and isolation. Though Melville's satire of the adherents to the "Flesh Brush Philosophy" (whose ranks Pierre naturally joins) is apparently unsparing, it is not without some sympathy for their condition.[27] From a letter to Hawthorne in the summer of 1851, Melville indicates some degree of affinity with the Jeffersonian idea of a "natural aristocracy," among whom the self-elect Apostles would certainly count themselves, though to what extent it is unclear.[28] At any rate, however absurdly Melville paints the obscure activities of the Apostles—he flatly states in the same letter that "Truth is ridiculous to men"—it is clear that both the lack of material compensation and cultural recognition for those interested in ideas is unjust and reflects poorly upon the culture extending beyond the tower's walls.

Further Pierre's unusual domestic situation in the church certainly does not encourage the rational "common sense" of a Goethean physician but rather its opposite. Indeed no physician is present to pluck Isabel from Pierre's presence because such an act is impossible in Pierre's Calvinist world of immutable facts. Isabel's continuing ubiquity is emblematic of Pierre's commitment to truth and his deepening descent into antinomian stasis. The question of whether Pierre and Isabel at this time consummate their incestuous union is rather a foregone conclusion—their "marriage" and metaphysical consummation, if it may so be called, occurs in Saddle Meadows the moment Pierre ceases to deny and recognizes Isabel in her widest significance.

The problems that the Apostles embody as a society culminate in the characteristics of their "Grand Master," Plotinus Plinlimmon (20, 2, 280). Accordingly the effect of Plinlimmon's countenance on Pierre is anything but conciliating; it amplifies and eventually eclipses Isabel's. Plinlimmon's presence intensifies what was always latently tyrannical and threatening in Isabel's influence over Pierre. F. O. Matthiessen's association of Plinlimmon with Emerson has influenced many subsequent readings of this character (*American* 471). While Melville hardly conceals the association, evident in chapter headings such as "Some Remarks on the Transcendental Flesh-Brush Philosophy," beyond these satirical criticisms, he is simultaneously attempting to rearticulate the mystery in the character of Plinlimmon as an extension of the mystery he expresses in the character of Isabel and how each, in turn, reflects increasingly impersonal, isolated, and isolating aspects of the Absolute itself that culminates in a sense of terrible stillness.[29]

Like the church itself, Plinlimmon's countenance expresses both youth (the Apollonian eye) and age (the saturnine brow); like Isabel his demeanor is both "winning" and repellant, enveloped in an atmosphere of "Inscrutableness" (21, 1, 290). As Isabel's countenance permeated the landscape of Saddle Meadows, Plinlimmon's haunts the Church of the Apostles. While at work on his new manuscript, Pierre "had been struck by a steady observant blue-eyed countenance at one of the loftiest windows of the old gray tower, which on the opposite side of the quadrangular space, rose prominently before his own chamber. Only through two panes of glass—his own and the stranger's—had Pierre hitherto beheld that remarkable face of repose,—repose neither divine nor human, nor any thing made up of either or both—both a repose separate and apart—a repose of a face by itself. . . . Now as to the mild sun, glass is no hindrance at all, but he transmits his light and life through the glass; even so through Pierre's panes did the tower face transmit its strange mystery" (21, 3, 291). So described, Plinlimmon's face is the epitome of isolation, of a repose no longer benign. Similar to the God of Edwards, which also perhaps wears an expression of "non-Benevolence," Plinlimmon's mysterious countenance exists in a world of ever-present impersonal necessity. But because in Pierre's case, Plinlimmon's incoherent philosophy has replaced the truth of the Gospels, Pierre finds little upon which to support his devotion to the transcendent presence, and it begins to take on an increasingly sinister expression. Like Isabel at her worst, Plinlimmon's face from on high begins to "domineer in a very remarkable manner" over Pierre. As he formerly in Saddle Meadows sought in vain to conceal himself from Isabel's presence, Pierre presently covers his window with muslin, and Plinlimmon's "face became curtained like any portrait. But this did not mend the leer. Pierre knew that still the face leered behind the muslin" (21, 3, 293).

A key feature, if it may so be called, of the blank repose of Plinlimmon's countenance is its unresponsiveness. As such it is the perfect image of complete antinomian stillness that follows the inexorable antinomian logic in counting each action of affirmation or of denial of an individual soul to be a fundamental violation of its metaphysical character. This vision of the Absolute is understandably terrible, because it suggests to Pierre that if any action he commits, whether affirming or denying, registers no significance within the Chronometer itself, it could not possibly have any meaning in the horological world. Needless to say, this apprehension likewise suspends what was left of Pierre's dwindling will to spiritual self-formation through heroically affirmative actions and artistic creation.

The moment in which Pierre needs consolation most—having just received notice of his mother's death, his disinheritance, and his cousin's pursuit of Lucy—is the only time he meets Plinlimmon in person. Compared with Pierre's hurrying, overwrought state, Plinlimmon advances toward him as "a very plain, composed, manly figure, with a countenance rather pale if any thing, but quite clear and without wrinkle" (21, 1, 289). He lifts his hat, bows, smiles, and continues on without a word. Whereas Wilhelm had the leader of the Tower Society, the Abbé, to remind him that "a young man always has cause to seek the company of other people," Plinlimmon in no way provides any clues, philosophical or material, indicating how Pierre should proceed. His presence instead magnifies Pierre's sense of isolation and mocks him with the thought that any direction in which he chooses to proceed is equally insignificant.

While in his largest dimensions Plinlimmon looks backward to the God of Jonathan Edwards, in his human character he looks ahead to the character of Bartleby. In his plainness, his composed but pale and smooth brow, he resembles Bartleby physically. In his changeless passivity and his nonbenevolence, he resembles Bartleby's blank neutrality. Like Bartleby, "whence he came, no one could tell"; he has no known family ties and, most significant, he refuses to write anything down (21, 1, 290).[30]

The experience of being cornered in virtually all senses by the countenances of Plinlimmon (from on high) and of Isabel (in the adjoining room) ultimately proves to be too much for Pierre; their combined effect is to intensify his isolation to its highest pitch. In this almost complete state of introversion, his attempts at self-examination conclude, finally, in defiant and consciously futile acts of melodramatic revenge that lead to his suicide. Faced with much the same metaphysical problem of the disjunction between the individual soul and the world, Edwards courted annihilation in Christ with the ultimate aim of reconciling his soul into the image of God. The character of Pierre's annihilation seems, rather, to comprise a final fragmentation, the falling away of a soul from its final ties to the world.

The nature of Pierre's end comprehends the greatest unresolved ambiguity of the novel: it is the paradox of the individual soul sensing at once God's teeming omnipresence alongside an abyssal blankness.[31] Melville best communicates this ambiguity in the following sequence of images: he likens Pierre's development to a traveler into the Alps who faces "their overawing extent of peak crowded on peak"; he has not reached "his Mont Blanc" and has yet to hear about the Rockies and the Andes (22, 1, 284). Melville's traveler then moves on to Egypt, where the "old mummy lies buried in cloth on cloth. . . . By vast pains we mine the pyramid; by horrible gropings we come to the central room, with joy we espy the sarcophagus; but we lift the lid—and no body is there!—appallingly vacant as vast is the soul of a man!"

Pierre represents, finally, an almost complete inversion of the Goethean bildungsroman model by utilizing many of the same conventions to point toward opposing conclusions. With respect to the Edwardsian antinomian tradition, *Pierre* becomes the embodiment of that tradition taken to its furthermost reaches. Insofar as Pierre's core struggles are the struggles of his more doctrinally minded forebears, *Pierre* is an American bildungsroman. But in the cultural environment of mid-century America, these metaphysical impasses have an air of the anomaly about them. This fact does not, however, contribute any further toward making the ambiguities they raise, particularly as they relate to the question of spiritual self-formation, go the way of Calvinist dogma itself.

In the following generation of American letters, the next author to combine with the same level of intensity urgent introspection alongside an ambivalence toward formative experience is Henry James. James domesticates Melville's metaphysical imponderables; he occupies himself with many of the same themes that invest *The Portrait of a Lady* with the ever-evolving shape of the American bildungsroman as it appears in the late nineteenth century. Unlike Melville's near portrait of a reprobate in Pierre (lines 9–10), Isabel Archer survives and perseveres. Whereas Pierre chooses death over ethical compromise, Isabel finds at the end of the novel that she may continue to survive in a physically deadening environment, provided that she preserve a particular antinomian cast of mind that at once apprehends and remains distinctly apart from her surroundings.

7

"AN IMPULSE MORE TENDER AND MORE PURELY EXPECTANT"

The Ardent Good Faith of Isabel Archer

And what is a Henry James young woman?
T. S. Eliot, letter, July 9, 1919

Melville's connection with the James family was more than passing. Henry James Sr.'s biographer, Alfred Habegger, notes a series of provocative intersections in the lives of the two men. Though no solid evidence exists that the two were direct acquaintances, Melville was a neighbor of the James family in Albany; he attended the same school as two of James Sr.'s brothers and was a clerk at the bank the elder James's father helped to run (298). Later both were in Manhattan over the winter of 1848 and, at that time, became members of the New York Society Library. But beyond circumstantial connections, however remarkable, Melville and James Sr. shared the experience of a strenuous Calvinist background that colored their respective worldviews long after each had freed himself from the dogmatic constraints of the faith. This legacy, in turn, left its impression upon James's novelist son primarily in the ways in which he understood the inner processes of his characters' self-formation.

A Generation Once Removed

"If the general love of women," Melville reflects in *Pierre,* "had in Pierre sensibly modified his particular sentiment toward Glen; neither had the thousand nameless fascinations of the then brilliant paradises of France and Italy, failed to exert their seductive influence on many of the previous feelings of Glen." In describing the cousins' disintegrating "love-friendship," Melville continues, "it is among the evils of enlarged foreign travel, that in young and unsolid minds, it dislodges some of the finest feelings of the home-born nature; replacing them with a fastidious superciliousness, which like the alledged bigoted Federalism of old times would not—according to a political legend—grind its daily coffee in any mill save of European manufacture, and was satirically said to have thought of importing European air for domestic consumption" (15, 1, 218). Though Melville's critical portrait in *Pierre* of the Europeanized American is only one in a long line, it foretells with a great degree of accuracy the very real criticisms with which Henry James, just eight years old at the time of *Pierre*'s publication, would find himself confronted as he struggled to establish his own artistic identity.

Nearly thirty years, later in November 1879, the influential Unitarian and social activist Thomas Wentworth Higginson wrote a review, "Henry James, Jr.," in the *Literary World* in which he evaluated the whole of James's works to date. Among other things Higginson predictably criticized James's apparent contempt for a republican aesthetics of fiction. In ways reminiscent of Pierre's cultured cousin Glen, James has "kept a little too good company: we do not find in his books such refreshing types of hearty and robust manhood"; further "Mr. James's life has been so far transatlantic, that one hardly knows whether he would wish to be accounted an American writer, after all" (Higginson, "Henry" 582).

This representative review arrived at a critical transitional period in James's own career, over which he had already accomplished a considerable body of short fiction, travel writing, reviews, and a handful of novels. In 1879 he was traveling on the Continent, during which time he "did a good deal of work"—including the short monograph on Hawthorne, *Confidence,* and *Washington Square* (*Notebooks* 219). Shortly before he began working in earnest on *The Portrait of a Lady,* James was "badly stung" by Higginson's review and asked William Dean Howells, then editor of the *Atlantic Monthly,* to protect him in the future from the "Higginsonian Fangs" (Howard N. Meyer, *Magnificent* 486). Perhaps what had offended James most in the article was, apart from the usual admonishments, the fact that Higginson counted James among the delicate and perceptive but still essentially immature writers of the time who lack "symmetry of structure, and steadiness of hand" (Higginson, "Henry" 582). That James would continue on to become a master of both points strongly suggests that *The Portrait of a Lady* indeed inaugurates, in Philip Horne's words, "a new, more technically conscious phase in James's writing" (*Henry* 197).

Higginson's criticism may have startled further due to the fact that it appeared from close quarters—he was a friend of Henry Sr., and both belonged to the Radical Club of Chestnut Street in Boston, whose other members included Emerson,

John Greenleaf Whittier, Oliver Wendell Holmes, Julia Ward Howe, and Elizabeth Peabody (Meyer, *Magnificent* 485). While Higginson's liberal democratic activism represented a part of the club's core interests (religion, theology, education, philosophy) that James would continue to engage in his fiction—Henrietta Stackpole is, for instance, a daughter of Higginsonian ideals—the character of his father's influence cast a shadow of a darker hue and a different texture.

"More than perhaps any other family in American literature and philosophy (that of Jonathan Edwards excepted)," Habegger writes, "the James family was founded on the *Word*" (172). From his infancy Henry Jr.'s religious education represented the first generation of leisure-class Protestant Americans to experience the legacy of Calvinism indirectly, through observation rather than through participation, through the experiences of his father. Mary Robertson Walsh, the elder James's wife, also came from a family "as stoutly Presbyterian as the Albany Jameses" but was in time persuaded to accept her husband's increasingly liberal philosophy (Edel, *Untried Years* 40). In *A Small Boy and Others,* James reflects ruefully on the family's "pewless state" and the social confusion this caused (133). While James the elder provided his children with "plenty . . . of the most charming and familiar" forms of religious instruction, Henry Jr. was struck by a vague sense of "a certain sophistry" in his father's proclamation that his children "could plead nothing less than the whole privilege of Christendom and that there was no communion, even that of the Catholics, even that of the Jews, even that of the Swedenborgians, from which we need find ourselves excluded" (133). The background that culminated in the elder James's radical approach to the religious education of his children is important, because it is informed in large part by his life-changing experiences with the dogmatic Calvinism of his own youth.

Not only did the elder James's lifelong preoccupation with Calvinist ideas tinge the atmosphere in which his children were raised, but it is my contention that Henry Jr.'s nuanced engagement with this tradition in *The Portrait of a Lady* distinguishes the transitional character of this novel, marks an intensification of his aesthetics of fiction, and most important, shapes its status as a distinctly American bildungsroman. Though they are proportionally few, commentators such as Fritz Oehlschlaeger, James Duban, John Owen King III, and James G. Moseley Jr. have over the past thirty years variously considered this much studied and debated novel in relation to Henry James Sr.'s complex theology. These critics predominantly focus on Henry James's engagement with his father's universalist, disinterested social vision. Oehlschlaeger and Duban (in *The Nature of True Virtue*) variously read *The Portrait of a Lady* as a critique of this vision; Moseley argues that Isabel Archer enacts a self-transcendence that is more closely aligned with his father's ideas. I discuss King in detail below.

The rich intensity of Henry Sr.'s long struggle with Calvinism merits further attention particularly because it persists in repeating the experiences that his Calvinist predecessors such as Edwards underwent: according to Habegger the elder James insisted continually throughout his life upon the fact that "individual human agency is a pernicious lie" (168). Further Henry Sr. was directly familiar with Edwards's thought. Though he did not complete his studies at the Princeton Theological Seminary, it was there that he "assiduously studied" its former president's works.[1] Habegger goes so far as to state that during this period, James Sr. "turned into a kind of fanatic" who would become more orthodox than his professors on the point of justification by faith (135). A comment that James makes in the preface to his *Lectures and Miscellanies* (1852) concisely demonstrates his connection to Edwards: just as Edwards demanded a theology that is compatible with reason as much as it touches the affections, James's new theology (here characterized in the feminine) looks forward to "a career of unexampled brilliancy, because every position she takes henceforward will be fortified by science, and so claim the equal approval of the heart and the head" (x).

In another instance in *Notes of a Son and Brother,* James quotes his father's 1842 letter to Emerson in which he rather boldly calls Emerson "philosophically infirm" because he does not "look upon Calvinism as a fact at all" (346). The elder James further speculates that "I believe Jonathan Edwards redivivus in true blue would, after an honest study of the philosophy that has grown up since his day, make the best possible reconciler and critic of this philosophy" (347).[2]

Nineteenth-Century Autobiography of Puritan Terror

According to Giles Gunn, certain members of the elder Henry James's family "had been after him for years" to distill his religious philosophy (*Henry* 33). The result is a personal narrative in the Edwardsian tradition but with marked generic changes both to structure and content. The following section briefly considers the autobiography's driving ideas as well as the elder James's account of his notorious "vastation" experience as it later appears in *Society the Redeemed Form of Man* (1879). The ideas that arise from these texts face both forward and backward—back by reengaging the Calvinist paradoxes with which Edwards contended in the eighteenth century and forward by providing substantial meaning to the religious "atmosphere" that James's novelist son internalized from his youth and later confronted in his own work.

One particularly marked feature of the autobiography is that it is incomplete—a feature that echoes James's reflection on the conclusion of his own *The Portrait of a Lady,* that "the *whole* of anything is never told" (*Notebooks* 18). Further the elaborate fictionalizing frame in which the elder James situates his narrative demonstrates his sensitivity to the interdependency of its aesthetic and spiritual elements: its full title reads "*Immortal Life: Illustrated in a Brief Autobiographic Sketch of the Late Stephen Dewhurst,* edited, with an introduction by Henry James." Dewhurst is a fictional character whom James claims to have known at seminary and whose manuscript he discovered posthumously and edited for publication. William James, who finally published the work in *The Literary Remains of the Late Henry James* (1884), directly cut through these screens and provided annotations with historically accurate details ("Autobiographical Sketch" 34).[3]

As for its theological qualities, James's narrative differs dramatically from its American Calvinist predecessors: whereas Edwards's narrative clearly follows a teleological trajectory that culminates in an affirmation of God's sovereignty, James explicitly rejects Calvinist theology as an "insane terror" that has deadened his natural moral sense and instead establishes a this-worldly utopian socialistic vision in its place ("AS" 39).[4] Elsewhere in the autobiography, the elder James aims further vitriol at Calvinism's doctrine of innate depravity, which he pronounces to be a "puerile and disgusting caricature of the gospel" (51). On the other hand, while James would continue the Edwardsian tradition of abhorring individual pride, its character changes significantly in the autobiography. Edwards's burdensome sense of sin and selfhood is released through mystical unification into the image of Christ; James's individual self ideally realizes instead "the social sentiment" in which "man is destined to experience the broadest conceivable unity with his kind" (39).

The following quotation captures the magnitude of the elder James's attempted transition from the religion of his father into his own idiosyncratic worldview; at the same time, it points forward to concerns that later engaged his sons William and Henry. The "enforced" faith of the elder James's youth amounted to this: "that a profound natural enmity existed from the beginning between man and God, which however Christ had finally allayed, and that I ought therefore gratefully submit myself to the law of Christ. I never had a misgiving about my absolute duty in the premises, but practically the thing was impossible. For this law of Christ . . . revolted instead of conciliating my allegiance, inasmuch as it put me at internecine odds with my own nature, or obliged me to maintain an ascetic instead of a spontaneous relation to it" ("AS" 49). The psychic carnage implied by physical and spiritual nature being at "internecine odds" clearly preserves the centuries-old Calvinist dichotomy but shifts the reaction from troubled perseverance into conscious revolt. If the otherworldliness of Calvinist Christianity proves to be too much for the elder James, his rejection of it is tempered by his immediately replacing the God of Edwards with what he optimistically calls "the serene immaculate divinity of the social spirit" ("AS" 47). The language is hardly removed from the tradition he is presently rejecting, and many have commented on James's shifting terms for what remains a postmillennial utopianism.[5]

Furthermore it is useful to recall that the basis of what James describes as his "religious conscience" remains private and preserves a distinctly antinomian quality—a point that his novelist son continued into his fiction. The early establishment of his religious conscience, James Sr. writes, "practically disowned a moral or outward genesis, and took on a free, inward, or spiritual evolution. Not any literal thing I did, so much as the temper of mind with which it was done, had power to humble me before God or degrade me in my own conceit" ("AS" 45). This description happens also to be commensurate with his new social paradigm, which counts among the greatest sins not outward offenses but rather those against the "vital self respect" of another human being.

For Henry James the elder, within this pastiche of influences that made up his spiritual sense, conversion continued to play a central part. But interestingly he did not record his conversion experience in his spiritual autobiography.[6] It appears instead, again under revised Swedenborgian terminology, as what has come to be known as his "vastation" experience. But the thread that ties this experience to the Edwardsian tradition appears in the insistence that conversion be a self-destructive process. Psychohistorian John Owen King has noted that the Swedenborgian term expresses "a purification, emptying the self of all its natural filth," which closely corresponds with Edwards's imperative that the experience cause the spirit to separate from its corporeal bonds (*Iron* 91). In this sense, then, "the word . . . bridged the sacred and the profane, the Puritans' conversion and mental collapse."

At the time of his vastation, James had moved his family to England; Henry Jr. was just six months old, and, as Leon Edel reports, his father was busy with the Book of Genesis trying to solve the essential Calvinist problem of reconciling "physical well-being and Calvinistic spiritual well-being" (*Untried* 31). In addition to its spiritual dimensions, this problem took on a personal character to the elder James due to his having lost a leg at the commencement of an energetic youth; for him it "seemed indeed that Divine punishment had finally been visited upon him for all his sins" (25).[7] This set of circumstances would appear to support an ensuing traditional conversion. But after a peaceful meal, James found himself alone by the fire "when suddenly—in a lightning-flash as it were—'fear came upon me, and trembling, which made all my bones to shake.' To all appearance it was a perfectly insane and abject terror, without ostensible cause, and only to be accounted for, to my perplexed imagination, by some damnèd shape squatting invisible to me within the precincts of the room, and raying out from his fetid personality influences fatal to life" (*Society* 55–56). Based on this pivotal moment, scholars commonly associate James the elder's thought with an acute sense of the palpable presence of evil.[8] Further this moment marks probably the greatest difference between James the elder and the Edwardsian tradition that, for the latter, culminates in a confirming and reconciling vision of Christ's superlative perfection. But whereas Edwards was working wholeheartedly within a known and accepted tradition, the elder James, like Melville, was no longer (King, *Iron* 85).

Thus King has most cogently described the elder James's thought as forming a bridge between the familiar Puritan "pattern of crisis" leading to conversion and the psychology of religious conversion that his son William later studied at length (94). That is, both the elder James and William wrestled with relocating conversion into an unknown territory that existed somewhere between spiritual experience and actual mental or psychic derangement (91).[9]

But what, from his father's and elder brother's treacherous engagements with the long tradition of American Calvinism, does Henry James inherit? F. O. Matthiessen's standard contention is that while the elder James faced his life crisis by committing himself to an idiosyncratic spiritualism, and William "found his way out through philosophy," Henry Jr. went on to complete the humanist trinity through his devotion to the aesthetic (*Henry* 142). Henry the elder's "religious consciousness," in other words, transforms itself into James's "religion of consciousness"—a world in which good and evil are indeed realities but are gauged not by dogma but by the intensity of individual moral awareness (146).[10] As for conversion James employs the term in his preface to *The Portrait of a Lady* to indicate, through an unusual combination of religious and scientific language, the turning of "adventure" and "action" away from physical and toward psychic realities (11–12). While this new sense of conversion has its explicitly aesthetic purposes, applied to individual characters it supports the long-standing tradition that the most significant and formative individual experiences are the ones unseen. For Isabel Archer particularly, change or conversion is distinctly uniformitarian or gradualist in nature.

"A matter of faith, not of experience"

Based on the above discussion, I hope to show more particularly that certain questions involving spiritual self-formation that concerned the father continued to occupy the son: namely the antinomian emphasis on inner condition over physical action, the pronounced importance of self-examination, and, of course, the powerful sense of evil. With respect to the last point, it is useful to recall the elder James's vision of the artist's relation to morality. In his early lecture "The Principle of Universality in Art," the elder James sees the artist not as the "perfect man" who transcends the moral dialectic altogether, but rather as one who takes on a quasi-religious character in his approximation of this perfection: artists in the broadest sense of the term "may therefore be called truly Providential men, men to whom the Lord has accommodated His stature in the past. They are not the Lord" but "harbingers of the perfect man" to come (127, 135). This is not to say that James's novelist son saw himself precisely in this role, but these exalted terms do hover somewhere in the background and inform the exceptional seriousness with which he approaches the art of fiction.

Isabel Archer is a remarkable heroine of the American bildungsroman because she preserves the tensions of her spiritual predecessors and somehow manages to survive beyond their dogmatic ends. In this way Isabel is indeed an aberrant daughter of the Puritans as Pierre is an aberrant son. Though the "social sentiment," to use the elder James's phrase, is to be sure more carefully developed and ultimately carries greater significance in James than in Melville, both Pierre and Isabel eventually must contend with numbing isolation—the one on the ragged fringes of American culture and the other in the very heart of Europeanized American eminence and propriety.

As for James's engagement with Goethe's prototypal bildungsroman, we know he read *Wilhelm Meister* (in Carlyle's translation) and wrote an early unexceptional review of it in the *North American Review.* James also referenced characters from the novel in the early short story "Professor Fargo" (1874).[11] It has been established that generally James did not appreciate German fiction on the same level that he did the English, French, and Italian writers. As Evelyn A. Hovanec in *Henry James and Germany* summarily observes: for James "the Germanic often lacked beauty and gracefulness; it was often ugly. It was at best homely. Often it was grotesque. And Henry James could accept the grotesqueness only if it were covered and ensconced in form, ritual, and manners. He had no taste for the rawness, the starkness of the German perception of the human condition" (42). Indeed the same observations could equally apply to James's attitude toward America and the majority of its inhabitants.

With respect to his English predecessors, much later James mentions Brontë's *Jane Eyre* and *David Copperfield* together in a letter to H. G. Wells. James's comments reveal the degree to which he had come to perceive the limitations of the first-person point of view, the "accursed autobiographic form" that "puts a premium on the loose, the improvised, the cheap & the easy. Save in the fantastic & the romantic (Copperfield, Jane Eyre . . .) it has no authority, no persuasive or convincing force—its grasp of reality & truth isn't strong and disinterested" (*Life* 500). Even granting the qualification James places upon Brontë's and Dickens's "fantastic" and "romantic" works, the author may much more convincingly reach the "truth" of a character's formative inner life by removing himself or herself from it. This stance in fact brings James back to the detached narrative technique of *Wilhelm Meister.*

Architecturally James's *The Portrait of a Lady* falls within the bounds of the American bildungsroman tradition if we read the novel's two volumes as a late nineteenth-century magnification of the old Calvinist ambivalence toward experience: the first volume of the novel occupies itself with uncovering the nature of Isabel's "ideas"; the second subjects those ideas to, in James G. Moseley's words, "life as it really is" (*Complex* 50).[12]

This basic division is not revelatory in itself (indeed it might be read as a refined version of Melville's metaphysical chronometricals and horologicals). Few Jamesians will dispute that one of James's central objects in the novel is to reveal the painful disparity between his heroine's vision of how the world ought to be and the way it actually operates.[13] Beyond this, however, great difference of opinion exists about the nature of Isabel's reaction to this basic disparity once she becomes aware of its full extent. Recently the emphasis seems to fall upon Isabel's foolhardy imagination, to take Isabel to task for the vague, woefully unexamined, and naive quality of her "ideas." Her mistake, so the argument goes, is that her self-complacency, her own willful ignorance, makes her complicit in her own disastrous errors of judgment that determine her fate.[14]

The vital point that seems to be overlooked by such readings, and one that James takes some trouble to emphasize, is that Isabel loves and commits her deepest errors always, as Ralph observes, in "ardent good faith" (chap. 34, 398).[15] Rather than dismissing this as yet another weakness in Isabel's character, the following explores to what extent James develops this idea into a central ethical question of the novel: if one makes an error in judgment based upon the impulse of good faith, is it possible, finally, to be damaged by the consequences of that judgment?

The question is itself antinomian: some of Isabel's noteworthy ancestors would likely have answered in the negative. Although neither Isabel nor James shares precisely their biblical sense of sin nor finds reconciliation in the atonement, the consequences remain pressing. To the extent that James emphasizes the value of Isabel's inner condition over any outward action she may commit or that others may commit against her, and to the extent that he maintains the central importance of self-examination to her self-formation, Isabel continues the rigorous tradition of antinomian inviolability, including its attendant paradoxes. These qualities, in turn, inform *The Portrait of a Lady*'s status as an American bildungsroman. This is not to overlook the many readings that emphasize James's far-reaching sense of evil—indeed this constitutes a large portion of his inheritance from his father—but rather to try to attain a more substantial sense of his comparatively obscured idea of the good in relation to it.

Isabel Archer's Ideas

James's opening account of his young heroine from Albany both invites and engages in the kind of "scientific criticism" that perceives and judges the quality of her thoughts, which he observes to be "a tangle of vague outlines which had never been corrected by the judgment of people speaking with authority" (6, 104). Isabel is someone for whom self-doubt is "unnecessary"; she exhibits a quick impatience that "might easily be confounded with superiority"; she is thought to have read classical authors—"in translations." In spite of these manifold imperfections, which amount to a large and perhaps ultimately dangerous measure of self-complacency, James writes that through her presence he wishes "to awaken on the reader's part an impulse more tender and more purely expectant" (105).

Isabel inspires and sustains this form of expectancy through the sense that she ineffably communicates that she "carried within herself a great fund of life, and her deepest enjoyment was to feel the continuity between the movements of her own soul and the agitations of the world" (4, 89). For Isabel, Albany is a world of meridianal correspondences wrought by her active idealism, a subtler domestic version of the state Pierre enjoys in Saddle Meadows before he encounters his own Isabel. As with Melville, James is quick to imply that correspondence is relatively easy to feel with the "agitations of the world" when they still appear across long or obscured distances. Isabel preserves her correspondences by keeping the paper over the windows in the room where she reads: the world outside becomes something new and rare, altogether different from the jostling carriages and sodden stoops that anyone else might have observed from the same vantage point.[16] From the beginning the visionary and the "real," the immaterial and the empirical, are at odds for Isabel.

James's initial analysis also contains a delicate probing of Isabel's moral sense that demonstrates certain connections with the elder James's thoughts on the subject. Whereas the elder James emphasizes the inward genesis of his "religious conscience" and claims that the only real offenses against others are those against their "vital self respect," Isabel similarly emphasizes the importance of psychological over physical actions: she reflects that the "worst thing that could happen to her" was "inflicting a sensible injury upon another person" (6, 104). Furthermore like her religious forebears, Isabel engages in ardent self-examination. But the following description is remarkably different from the outdoor visions of a Jonathan Edwards, for instance, largely because it exudes a prelapsarian atmosphere: "Her nature had, in her conceit, a certain garden-like quality, a suggestion of perfume and murmuring boughs, of shady bowers and lengthening vistas, which made her feel that introspection was, after all, an exercise in the open air, and that a visit to the recesses of one's spirit was harmless when one returned from it with a lapful of roses" (6, 107). In such a state, Isabel has no sense of the reality of sin; the activity of self-examination is harmless, even delightful, because she has no fear that at the bottom of it she may find what the Canoness in *Wilhelm Meister* describes as "the monster that grows and feeds in every human breast." Without the feeling of original sin so central to orthodox Christianity (the doctrine that Henry James the elder also explicitly rejects), the operative reason for repentance and conversion disappears with it.

Isabel's approach to life is deductive: she aims first toward "getting a general impression of life," and only then will she feel qualified to give attention to the special cases of those others whose souls lack the verdure of her own.[17] This predilection for vague abstraction at the expense of the "facts" of everyday experience, for seeing without judging, lies at the heart of those criticisms against Isabel's character because it appears to be an ethically irresponsible outlook. Even if we take into account her extreme youth, it is, for instance, still disturbing to hear that during the Civil War, she was "stirred almost indiscriminately by the valor of either army" (4, 89).

But what Isabel has cultivated from her youth, however capriciously, is a way of seeing that is to some degree its own justification, for it recognizes the integrity of a viewpoint based upon "ardent good faith." In practice, however, this viewpoint has two extremes: on the one side, imagination; on the other, intuition. Imagination leads to error; intuition is immediate and never inaccurate. Both qualities privilege inner over outer experience. As for the first, James writes that Isabel "had a certain nobleness of imagination which rendered her a good many services and played her a great many tricks," which makes it clear that this faculty is liable to deceive her more often than to reveal the truth (6, 104). But at the same time, at her best Isabel shows great capacity—perhaps greater than any other character in the novel—to experience life with a spontaneous immediacy that gives the impression of experience in its most authentic form. Most other characters have in place something that constantly intervenes between themselves and their own experience: Osmond and Merle have their ambition, Henrietta has her democratic gospel, Ralph has his human experiment, and so on. This habit, or predisposition, of Isabel's links back once more to her religious forebears and goes deeper than the faculty of "active imagination" that James makes so much of. As Jonathan Edwards establishes in *A Divine and Supernatural Light*, the most important knowledge of all is that which is acquired independently of all "flesh," and it is imparted to the saint by God through an act of immediate intuition. This experience, in turn, causes the saint to *see* in a new way and behold God's image from within and without.[18] The world of temporal experience cannot compare with, nor indeed affect the ontological status of, this inner experience. While James certainly does not imply the presence of God hovering above Isabel waiting to impart this transcendental knowledge, he does preserve the foundational importance of seeing as a key to authentic experience. In other words however great their differences, for James as for Edwards, the quality of intuition (from *intueri*, to look upon) is of paramount importance to the way each understands the nature of inner experience and the all-important bearing this has on Isabel's self-formation.

This disposition does not prevent terrible things from happening to Isabel, but it permits her to treat these occurrences as a bystander witnesses an accident. It is this combination of imagination and intuition, of fallibility and authenticity, that constitutes the draw of this very Jamesian heroine: these qualities together embody her "ardent good faith." Taken separately the reader might only judge her with admiration or condemnation, but taken together James invites the reader to see her in a more comprehensive way: he asks us to expect something from her. But what? Unlike the traditional heroine of a tragedy who is distinguished by her capacity to suffer, we are told from the beginning that Isabel's great gift springs from her capacity for generosity. To what will she commend herself, such as she is? What will she give? In what way? These are the questions that keep everyone waiting.

A look at the characters of Henrietta Stackpole and Serena Merle highlights what *not* to expect. However much each woman's life and views differ from the other, unlike Isabel, Henrietta and Madame Merle are individuals for whom the activities of seeing and judging are indistinguishable. This quality compels them to different degrees to approach experience through a series of filters that have become ingrained and lacking in intuitive spontaneity. Indeed it is to the eye that James devotes the substance of his remarks upon Henrietta's first appearance in the novel: she looks about with "remarkable fixedness"; her glance "rested without impudence or defiance, but as if in conscientious exercise of a natural right, upon every object it happened to encounter" (10, 138). In reaction to her friend's intention to write about Gardencourt for the American papers, Isabel accuses Henrietta of lacking a sense of privacy. Underlying Henrietta's intentions is the feeling that if everything is as it appears, and if everything is up for debate, there is no need for privacy. It is this distinctly American public impulse and glance that, in a sense, has decided in advance upon interpretation: she looks at Ralph, for instance, and immediately sees "the alienated American" (140).

The difference between Isabel and Henrietta is most apparent in each woman's reaction to Ralph's gallery. Henrietta passes over the pictures in silence and seizes the opportunity to interrogate Ralph, or rather her idea of Ralph as alienated expatriate, and is full of suggestions for how he might rectify his inactivity, make himself "useful," and cultivate his "conscience" (10, 143). Henrietta is, in other words, an activist; her rigorous sense of duty and ceaseless activity is reminiscent, if not in letter, then in spirit, of the socially conscious "Methodized" evangelicals of the previous generation. Isabel, in turn, wanders the gallery with her cousin and engages him in a conversation about the nature of knowledge and the ghost at Gardencourt; the scene dramatizes many of Isabel's qualities that James had already established in the early exposition. Isabel is "very fond" of knowledge—"pleasant knowledge," Ralph corrects her—and declares that people are not made for suffering and that suffering is not necessary to the human condition (5, 102).[19]

To her credit, if Henrietta's sight-judgments are often incomplete, they are for the most part disinterested in the sense that she measures each according to her own rigorous standard of American democracy. Serena Merle, on the other hand, sees and judges according to the ambiguous tangle of standards and qualities that amounts to James's Europeanized social sense that all but obliterates the individual consciousness. Isabel's first meeting with Madame Merle begins what James calls in the preface Isabel's gradual "conversion" into a way of living apart from her more familiar compatriots'. On the surface Merle is the embodiment of late-century superficial European bildung bereft of its key element of spiritual elevation: she is clever, accomplished, graceful, "complete" (18, 230). It is significant that Isabel first sees Serena from behind and from a distance: in painterly terms it is the *Rückenfigur*, a mysterious Caspar David Friedrich model brought away from a sublime landscape and into a Vilhelm Hammershøi interior, permeated with concealed motives.

As with the painting, the viewer may share the present moment but may not directly share the experience of the figure. In the context of the novel, even more might be made of the complex relationship and disjunction between the model and the viewer: once Madame Merle finishes the Schubert piece, she turns around "as if but just aware" of Isabel's presence (18, 225). From the beginning Madame Merle demonstrates the capacity for multiple points of awareness that intensifies Isabel's comparatively inchoate capacities. Merle's expert social observations combine with her judgments to strengthen, through covert indirection, her own position in the social hierarchy. I have always found it a telling detail that no one had invited her to Gardencourt as Isabel's uncle was dying—as if she possesses a supernatural sense for, and is irresistibly drawn to, the event of death as a locus of pecuniary dispersal.

Isabel's reflections on her growing acquaintance with Madame Merle show the high value but also the deep reservations she associates with the idea of friendship that mark a related difference between the two women. Isabel "often wondered indeed if she ever had been, or ever could be, intimate with any one. She had an ideal of friendship as well as of several other sentiments, which it failed to seem to her in this case—it had not seemed to her in other cases—that the actual completely expressed. But she often reminded herself that there were essential

Vilhelm Hammershøi, *Interior with Ida Playing the Piano* (1910), National Museum of Western Art, Tokyo

reasons why one's ideal could never become concrete. It was a thing to believe in, not to see—a matter of faith, not of experience. Experience, however, might supply us with very creditable imitations of it, and the part of wisdom was to make the best of these" (19, 239). This passage is significant because it shows that Isabel intuitively apprehends that there is something elusive about her friend—later she names this quality "unnatural"—that Madame Merle is so completely socialized as to have removed from her composition all traces of the "tonic wildness" that bespeak individuality (19, 244).[20] Already the rationale for Isabel's faint misgiving suggests that experience is useful as long as she recognizes it to be approximate, incapable of affecting her in any fundamental way. Here we see Isabel's antinomianism as it is thrown into relief against her friend's merely expedient point of view. James describes in perversely accurate terms how Isabel gives her new friend "the key to her cabinet of jewels. These spiritual gems were the only ones of any magnitude that Isabel possessed" (19, 239). In a rare direct reference to Isabel's future perspective, James shores the magnitude of this "generous error" with both experiential and spiritual dimensions through the simple statement that Isabel would never regret the giving and that "if Madame Merle had not the merits she attributed to her, so much the worse for Madame Merle." It is certainly a strange moment that lends substance and capaciousness to the idea of Isabel's antinomian "ardent good faith," because it is a judgment she continues to make not as a novice but as one who knows.

Ralph, too, has a "plan" for Isabel, though one of a more experimental, open-ended nature than Osmond's and Merle's. Ralph's own ardent good faith, with which he originally convinced his father to make Isabel an heiress, becomes a self-fulfilling proposition. He describes his intentions to his dying father as "to facilitate the execution of good impulses, what can be a nobler act?" (18, 238). Isabel later fulfills his hopes directly as they speak of her engagement: "Pray," she asks Ralph, "would you wish me to make a mercenary marriage—what they call a marriage of ambition? I've only one ambition—to be free to follow out a good feeling" (34, 397).

The Poisoned Cup

One "jewel" Isabel reveals to Madame Merle at Gardencourt is her definition of success, or "to see some dream of one's youth come true" (19, 252). Merle calls her definition "very pretty, yet frightfully sad. Measured in that way, who had ever succeeded? The dreams of one's youth, why they were enchanting, they were divine! Who had ever seen such things come to pass?" Even though it is evident that such things have come to pass no more for Osmond than they have for Madame Merle, oddly enough Osmond shares the same definition. Just into the second volume of the novel, the author of Isabel's initiation into "life as it really is" reflects that his courtship with Isabel shows real signs of success. The dream of Osmond's youth, we are told, is "to have something or other to show for his 'parts'" (29, 356). Success, then, with Isabel would mean the acquisition of his crowning showpiece, an animated expression of his style, something that allows him to preserve an impression of aristocratic dignity, still and aloof.[21]

The scene in which Osmond makes his most concerted efforts toward achieving this success reveals James's masterful demonstration of the great divide between Isabel's and Osmond's quality of experience. This scene is one of many in which James illustrates that while Isabel's intuition lacks the abstract and absolute clarity of a spiritual insight, it nevertheless continues to operate decisively upon her process of self-formation, though in a much more covert, and in this sense more realistic, manner in a world no longer experienced through religious frames. By reviewing his overarching, preconceived plan, the narrative itself places the filter over Osmond's perspective, whereas in moments Isabel meets the experience with a vital conflict between imagination and authentic immediacy. She reacts viscerally to Osmond's declaration "with the sharpness of a pang that suggested to her somehow the slipping of a fine bolt—backward, forward, she couldn't have said which," just as her imagination sentimentally invests her suitor with the "golden air of early autumn" (29, 360). As the scene continues, however, she begins to feel a dread for "the sense of something within herself, deep down, that she supposed to be inspired and trustful passion. It was there like a large sum stored in a bank—which there was a terror in having to begin to spend. If she touched it, it would all come out." Again, as with Madame Merle, James uses his images to convey the fact that Isabel's imagination is about to be sold; but at the same time he reveals Isabel's sense of foreboding, her imprecise yet marked awareness of the rare magnitude of these reserves. After Osmond departed Isabel's imagination stopped and "hung back: there was a last vague space it couldn't cross—a dusky, uncertain tract which looked ambiguous and even slightly treacherous, like a moorland seen in the winter twilight" (363). Where Isabel's imagination stops, her intuitive awareness continues into ambiguous feelings of upcoming difficulty, and autumn fades into winter.

After Isabel's marriage James chooses to reveal his heroine's progress from a distance through the eyes of young Mr. Rosier.[22] As he sees her framed by a gilded doorway, Rosier observes that Isabel has become "the picture of a gracious lady" (37, 418). She appears like a polished John Singer Sargent model in black velvet, and has apparently suppressed the single flaw Osmond silently detected during their courtship, that of "too precipitate a readiness": she had now, Rosier significantly observes, "the air of being able to wait" (29, 355; 37, 418). That James uses the unlikely Rosier to make the following observation makes its accuracy all the more prominent: he observes in Isabel the primary feeling of a detached inviolability, he recognizes in her "that secret of a 'lustre' beyond any recorded losing or rediscovering" (418).

What James suggests through Rosier's view, he amplifies with Ralph's more intimate meditations on Isabel's change of state. What had once been a love of lightness, freedom, and truth had become replaced by a grotesque sense of "exaggeration" that indicates a muted rebellion against being forced into a nature alien to her own: "There was a kind of violence in some of her impulses; of crudity in some of her experiments," and at her strangest she appeared to be indifferent, urbane, insolent (39, 443). At the center of this change and what makes Isabel appear so unnatural in light of it is her being forced into the position of representing someone completely controlled by conventional opinion. Among the manifold ironies of Osmond's character, the fact that this ideal comes close to his original compatriots' own must be one of the sharpest. Furthermore Isabel's new position is a portrait of false bildung; it exhibits culture lacking (or, in Isabel's case, suppressing) a certain spiritual elevation—it is what makes Madame Merle fit so smoothly into this role and what makes Isabel persist in feelings of maladjustment to it.

Even in the face of these ominous circumstances that together indicate the degree of damage Isabel's choice in partner has done to her future happiness, the narrative continues to indicate that Rosier had indeed perceived some part of the truth about Isabel's character. Her intuitive faculty remains intact; if anything it has become stronger and more accurate, especially in its capacity to detect the sinister. In Isabel's situation, since freeing acts of spiritual insight are absent, she retains in their place a muted but persistently imaginative authenticity. She does not, in other words, simply fall into a caricature of what she once was; this in turn makes her dismal situation all the more at odds with her inner life. Ralph may have been partly mistaken when he rued her loss of concern for "the pure truth" in exchange for exaggeration. Though the question of purity has somewhat fallen away from its formerly direct association with truth, Isabel's concern for the truth only intensifies.

This is evident, for instance, in the scene in which Isabel returns home and encounters her husband and Madame Merle from a distance, through a doorway (indeed the tableau recalls her first encounter with Merle). In all outward gestures, their association appears casual, but Isabel stops because she had "received an impression"—always a potent phrase for James—she "instantly perceived" the seriousness of the moment, and the scene "made an image, lasting only a moment, like a sudden flicker of light" (40, 457–58). And again this all-significant moment occurs as something Isabel witnesses, not through anything she does. Though the intuitive impression does not originate within a supernatural force, it still is something that comes to her from without and reveals instantaneously a flicker of truth—an indication but by no means complete.

From this germinal experience, James develops his authoritative chapter 42, the one to which he brings critics' attention in the preface as "obviously the best thing in the book" (55).[23] It is important to remember also that he pairs it with the scene in which Isabel first encounters Madame Merle, and that both constitute two instances of "mystic conversion" of plot-based discoveries to psychic ones. The conversion is both aesthetic in terms of technique and character-based in terms of its bearing upon the antinomian frame of mind of his heroine. At Gardencourt, Isabel experiences but does not mine a vague insight that she has given something to Madame Merle for which she has received no corresponding return. Chapter 42 attaches the complementary experience with Osmond. But the time that has passed between scenes has positioned Isabel to experience the gradual and full awakening to the fact that the world is not a world of correspondences: correspondences with the divine are out of the picture entirely, and the vital replacement, elemental correspondences and reciprocity with other people, has also become unavailable to her. The romantic, still spacious moorland in the winter twilight that she saw earlier becomes here a prospect "impenetrably black" (42, 474).

The twin facts to which her mind continually returns are her husband's inexplicable and elemental hatred for her, and her inability to reciprocate this hatred. Isabel reflects, "It was as if he had had the evil eye; as if his presence were a blight and his favour a misfortune. Was the fault in himself, or only in the deep mistrust she had conceived for him?" (42, 474). This question is an important one, but the remainder of her reflections tips the balance toward the former option, particularly since feelings of mistrust are not primary but always arise in reaction to something else, in this case in response to her husband's "evil eye." She takes care to show that this perception is not solipsistic delusion, that the blackness is not "an emanation from her own mind," that "she had done her best to be just and temperate, to see only the truth." This moment is one of the most vivid in the scene, and it is perhaps not too much to say that it represents an aesthetic version of the experiences that James's father and his brother encountered in their own lives. More broadly it embodies a key component of Isabel's bildung: her clear apprehension of Osmond's evil presence as an objective reality will become central to the novel's conclusion, to her final "conversion."

Further Osmond's presence comes strikingly close to the malevolent God leering down at Pierre and his work: in her own home, "Osmond's beautiful mind indeed seemed to peep down from a small high window and mock at her" (42, 478).[24] What is most remarkable about her character is that, upon making this synthesis and seeing that the source of her mistake is beyond her control, she does not, like the comparatively precipitous Pierre, commit herself to self-destruction. Instead she taps into almost unreal depths of persistent good faith that under any other circumstances would appear simply naive or even foolish—but Isabel's present circumstances give the position an unusual authority. Though in most ways Isabel does not share Ralph's feelings, his words "I love without hope" best describe her own situation and relationship to the world as she finds it at this time in her life.[25]

To prepare for the actual rupture between husband and wife, James sets up conflicting expectations for the consequences such an action will entail. On the one hand, he seems to indicate that a direct rupture would necessarily lead to some positive action such as divorce. "To break with Osmond once," Isabel reflects before leaving Rome, "would be to break with him for ever; any open acknowledgement of irreconcilable needs would be an admission that their whole attempt had proved a failure" (45, 511). On the other hand, her musings on the train to England are more consonant with her earlier antinomian midnight vigil that privileged sight over anything that she might do. Even now with significantly more knowledge and insight than she possessed at the earlier time, her tone almost seems to return to the tonic note of the early Miss Archer. Her sense of future endurance over renunciation "was a proof of strength—it was a proof she should some day be happy again. It couldn't be she was to live only to suffer; she was still young, after all, and a great many things might happen to her yet. To live only to suffer—only to feel the injury of life to be repeated and enlarged—it seemed to her she was too valuable, too capable, for that. Then she wondered if it were vain and stupid to think so well of herself. When had it even been a guarantee to be valuable? Wasn't history full of the destruction of precious things?" (53, 607). Hints of the old self-complacency are still present, but what is new is Isabel's ability to perceive this complacency and to subject it to scrutiny. The tone of these reflections signifies the further solidification of her enduring good faith and seems to persist in claiming a personal exception to the last question: though she should not "escape," she should last.

A Return to the Source

Surprisingly few critics have discussed parallels between the conclusion of *The Portrait of a Lady* and that of *Jane Eyre:* but they are many and serve further to highlight the differences in self-formative visions between the British and American spiritual traditions.[26] Just as at the end of *Jane Eyre,* Jane finds herself alone in the final of many confrontations with the wrong man, St. John Rivers, Isabel likewise must face the equally persistent Caspar Goodwood. As discussed in chapter 4, so many elements of traditional conversion are apparent in Brontë's novel, including reading of the scripture, a "calling" in the form of Mr. Rochester's voice, and a sensible, Wesleyan "heartwarming" experience: the conversion event in its entirety successfully marries spirit and flesh, impulse and action. While for Isabel the moment is equally decisive, James inverts its effects in such a way that, rather than affirming the value of hearing and accepting a "calling" that leads toward active happiness, Isabel's "revelation" consists in a turning away from action once more toward the antinomian stillness of foregone conclusions.

Both use images of water to describe the heroine's state of confusion. While facing Caspar's unwelcome urgency, Isabel might have used Jane's words to describe her own state of mind: "I was tempted to cease struggling with him—to rush down the torrent of his will into the gulf of his existence, and there lose my own" (*Jane* 35, 430). But the possibility of drowning in Brontë never seems threatening to the degree that it does in James. Like St. John Rivers, Goodwood uses quasi-religious language to present his case ("you can't turn anywhere. . . . turn straight to *me*"; "Here I stand; I'm as firm as a rock"); these words for Isabel invoke an image of the sea, where she floats in "fathomless waters," and Caspar's offer of help catches her "in a rushing torrent" (55, 634–35).

To bring out the full import of these images, particularly Isabel's strange simultaneous participation in them and dissociation from them, I include the immediately following sequence in full. The idea of giving herself over to Caspar

> was a kind of rapture, in which she felt herself sink and sink. In the movement she seemed to beat with her feet, in order to catch herself, to feel something to rest on.
>
> "Ah, be mine as I am yours!" she heard her companion cry. He had suddenly given up argument, and his voice seemed to come, harsh and terrible, through a confusion of vaguer sounds.
>
> This, of course, was but a subjective fact, as the metaphysicians say; the confusion, the noise of the waters, all the rest of it, were in her own swimming head. In an instant she became aware of this. "Do me the greatest kindness of all," she panted, "I beseech you to go away!" (55, 635)

In this sequence James goes as deeply as he was prepared to go with this character and accomplishes several elemental truths about her in his descent. First he exposes once more the pain involved in calling and hearing no answer, in living in a world that lacks the most important kinds of mutual correspondence, but now Isabel finds herself on the other side, unable to respond. It is this dual awareness that creates the effect of being there, with another, but through the confused medium of agitated water.

Another standout quality of this scene is the multivalence of the word *rapture*. At least three distinct meanings of the word resonate at once: Isabel falls into what would come to be called a "rapture of the deep" in which a diver experiences euphoric disorientation.[27] Further the sexual connotations of the word place ecstasy uneasily alongside the suggestion of forced violation or abduction.[28] Lastly the term carries mystical overtones as well, particularly as it refers to the Second Coming in which God's chosen are caught up into the air to join Christ for the coming apocalypse.[29] I do not pretend to say which sense James consciously wished to emphasize but only remark that these meanings cluster together to generate the powerful force of the moment as a conversion in Isabel Archer's life. Finally something further happens when Isabel suddenly—indeed in a crowning intuitive flash—sees her experience from the outside and is able instantaneously to discriminate between objective and subjective facts—what is real and what is not real (those things that are only in her "swimming head"). In her great mistake in marrying Osmond, Isabel was still unable to distinguish knowing from imagination. But now the divisions are much clearer. Seen in the best light, the moment represents her triumph over self-deception. More dimly it is the moment in which Isabel denies the reality of her subjective life.

Isabel's recognition of this "subjective fact" serves as the long-awaited complement to her apprehension in chapter 42 that the evil presence her husband has come to represent is an objective reality. By moving away from Caspar and the garden and into the house, Isabel symbolically accepts this "objective" reality. Her path leads directly opposite to that of Jane Eyre.

The subsequent return to Rome, to the world of "ghastly forms," invites two separate readings.[30] First Isabel returns because she recognizes that these forms constitute its objective reality. The evil in it is as palpable to James as it was to his father or to his brother. On the other hand, Isabel finds herself in a position to return to Rome because she feels the inviolability of persevering in a state of good faith with which she began her career six years before. She has indeed changed in the sense that she no longer confounds imagination with knowledge. On his deathbed Ralph tells Isabel that he doesn't believe that "such a generous mistake as yours can hurt you for more than a little" (54, 623). Isabel suffers but persists in the idea that if one experiences the world always in generous and ardent good faith, it is not, finally, possible to be damaged by the consequences.

Isabel's long-held perception of inviolate personal exceptionalism is psychologically reminiscent of the perseverance of the saints. Her main act in the novel, if it may so be called, is purely internal and thereby antinomian in character: her new capacity to distinguish between imagination and knowing (intuition) ensures psychic protection both from self-complacency and from errors in judgment, howsoever the latter may determine her outward circumstances. As such Isabel Archer as the heroine of this bildungsroman succeeds by a particular kind of withholding. Between *Pierre* and *The Portrait of a Lady,* then, a range exists within which the Edwardsian tradition may manifest itself in the nineteenth-century American bildungsroman. Inherent in this view is the ever-present notion that the world is always something with which the soul will never completely reconcile itself.

CODA

An Old Cornucopia

Three years after Henry James's death in 1916, an ambitious young poet and critic who believed himself to have "far more *influence* on English letters than any other American has ever had, unless it be Henry James," wrote a letter to Charles W. Eliot, former president of Harvard.[1] Charles Eliot, a distant relative of T. S. Eliot's, knew the elder Henry James well and William "very well." Charles had spoken with Henry James on his last visit to America, and his impression was not favorable. It seemed to him that James's "English residence for so many years contributed neither to the happy development of his art nor to his personal happiness." For his part it is well known that T. S. Eliot greatly admired James and called *The American Scene* "wonderfully well written" and "full of acute criticism" (*Letters* 233). Indeed certain themes in *The American Scene* would have appealed to Eliot, particularly regarding the spiritual condition of America at the commencement of the twentieth century, but more generally its implications for later artists and intellectuals on both shores.

In 1904, at sixty-one years of age, James found himself back in America exploring the still vast and barren tracts of the New England countryside in a "wonder-working motor-car."[2] As he passed through the Massachusetts Berkshires, the places in which some of his literary and religious forebears lived and wrote, he found "the heart of New England which makes so pretty a phrase for print and so stern a fact, as yet, for feeling" (*AS* 48). As he continued into the mountains, James remarked on the romantic views and concluded that "again and again the land would do beautifully, if that were all that was wanted." In the midst of the sweeping presence of open landscape, this quality of absence, or blankness, extended for

James not only to the inhabitants of the sparse villages within the landscape but also to their religious institutions.

Perhaps the most difficult and ultimately insurmountable problem for the "restless analyst" in search of an American subject is the impression that the inhabitants of the sweeping landscape are as incapable of profound secrets as are the raw mountains and valleys themselves. For evidence to the contrary, James looked to the churches. Just over the Connecticut border, he observed "the high, thin church, made higher, made highest, and sometimes, as at Farmington, made as pretty as a monstrous Dutch toy, by its steeple of quaint and classic carpentry; but this monument appeared to *testify* scarce more than some large white card, embellished with a stencilled border, on which a message or a sentence, an invitation or a revelation, might still be inscribed" (*AS* 43–44). The once-all-consuming presence of New England Calvinism as embodied in the white church is now reduced to a paper-light grotesque—still, hollow, empty.

The metropolitan churches of New York and Boston, on the other hand, carried greater meaning for James and inspired a nostalgia for the dwindling parts of individual interior life that exist in a stillness apart from the aggressive push and pull of the surrounding commerce. The particular New England churches James chose to commemorate—Park Street Church in Boston and Church of the Ascension in New York City—are especially significant and indeed are, together, emblematic of the theme I have been tracing throughout this book. Both churches were well-known bastions of evangelicalism in the nineteenth century: Park Street, a Congregationalist church situated on "Brimstone Corner," was a Calvinist mainstay throughout the century; the Episcopalian Ascension adhered to Low Church precepts. The one represents the direct legacy of Jonathan Edwards; the other the Low Church legacy of John Wesley; and both found their material existence threatened at the beginning of the twentieth century.

The condition of these American churches assumed an unusual significance for James, not as a believer but as an artist concerned with the development of the interior life. A glimpse at the history of Park Street Church magnifies the importance of James's comment, in July 1904, that the church was, "for the hour, the most interesting mass of brick and mortar and (if I may risk the supposition) timber in America" (*AS* 240).

Park Street Church was founded in 1809, shortly after the first wave of the Second Great Awakening.[3] Several New Divinity ministers of the Second Great Awakening have been associated with the church: Sereno Edwards Dwight, the great-grandson and first biographer of Jonathan Edwards, was ordained as its pastor in 1817.[4] By 1901 church membership had ebbed to an all-time low, and the church was sold to the *Boston Herald* for one million dollars; the *Herald* intended to tear down the edifice and raise an office building in its place (Bendroth,

Fundamentalists 163). By the time James had come to Boston, the predicament of Park Street had come to embody the suspense between the "impudence of private greed" and the intellectual and spiritual past of New England: it helped James "to look at everything in some related state to this proposition of the value of the Puritan residuum" (*AS* 240–42). James unequivocally sided with the preservationists, who eventually were able to raise enough money to save the church from demolition.[5]

But more than the actual outcome of the controversy, it was the symbolic situation that captured James's interest. For James Park Street represented "the question of what the old New England spirit may have still, intellectually, aesthetically, or for that matter even morally, to give; of what may yet remain, for productive scraping, of the formula of the native Puritanism educated, the formula once capacious enough for the 'literary constellation' of the Age of Emerson. Is that cornucopia empty, or does some handful of strong or at least sound fruit lurk to this day, a trifle congested by the keeping, up in the point of the horn?" (*AS* 241). The church further represented a certain intelligence that "flowered formerly . . . from so strong a sap and into so thick and rich a cluster." This vital language seems especially unusual for James to use in relation to an American church—indeed in relation to any American institution—and gives some indication of his conception of what such an institution might mean to a culture.

In New York City, the conflict manifested itself in the Episcopalian Church of the Ascension on Fifth Avenue as it became increasingly oppressed by crops of newly burgeoning skyscrapers. Of this and another nearby church, James remarks that "half the charm of the prospect . . . is in their still being there, and being as they are; this charm, this serenity of escape and survival positively works as a blind on the side of the question of their architectural importance" (*AS* 93). James's preoccupation with these structures clearly extends beyond what they may represent beyond their landmark or civic value. The Ascension was founded in 1827 during the second wave of the Second Great Awakening. It furthered the presence of Low Church Anglican worship in America and, as such, found itself well in line with the increasingly Arminian orientation of American evangelicals. Historian Carolyn Pitts describes the church's reputation from the beginning as "intensely Protestant": its "'evangelical' Episcopalians were militant, passionate, eloquent preachers, vigorous proselytizers, and conspicuous philanthropists" ("Church" §8). Its location, moreover, in Greenwich Village associated the church with the arts in the latter part of the nineteenth century. Pitts notes that the first rector, Rev. Manton Eastburn, quarreled with the architect Richard Upjohn (who also designed the famous High Church Trinity Wall Street) over the chancel, which Eastburn insisted be "very shallow" to ensure that there "would be no room for high church doings" (qtd. in Pitts).

Eastburn had had his way, and by the time James stepped into the Ascension's refuge, the shallow chancel harbored "a great religious picture" by his old friend John La Farge (*AS* 93). James reflects, "the cool shade, within, with the important work of art shining through it, seemed part of some other-world pilgrimage—all the more that the important work of art itself, a thing of the highest distinction, spoke, as soon as one had taken it in, with that authority which makes the difference, ever afterwards, between the remembered and the forgotten quest." Here we are once more on familiar Jamesian ground, a place in which the religious and aesthetic experience are nearly indistinguishable. But the occult language of pilgrimages and quests becomes quickly fraught as he hears once again the "sinister voice of the air" and remembers "the suspended danger, the possibility of the doom" (94). The feeling magnifies as he steps back into the streets and observes "the newest mass of multiplied floors and windows visible" near the church: "*They* . . . were going to bring in money—and was not money the only thing a self-respecting structure could be thought of as bringing in?" (*AS* 94).

The apocalyptic language that James employs to describe the threat against what was just beginning to feel like a historical presence in America is not equally necessary, of course, in England. There the situation is less acute, simply by the grace of history: for individuals raised among "English ancientries" (underwritten by the presence of the parson and the squire), one lives "as in a world toward the furnishing of which religion has done a large part" (*AS* 24). James's observations of institutions representing the different traditions on American soil do, however, serve to show the precariousness each held in common at the commencement of the twentieth century. At present, the situation in both places is perhaps equally fraught. For a contemporary instance based upon an impulse similar to James's, compare Zadie Smith's recent protesting the proposed demolition of London's Willesden Library (1895) to make room for new luxury flats ("North" 10–12).

Though T. S. Eliot's 1934 lecture "Religion and Literature" speaks with a High Anglican rigor, it continues to voice some of the primary concerns that Henry James raises in *The American Scene.* Eliot writes: "There are a very large number of people in the world to-day who believe that all ills are fundamentally economic. Some believe that various specific economic changes alone would be enough to set the world right; others demand more or less drastic changes in the social as well. . . . These changes demanded, and in some places carried out, are alike in one respect, that they hold the assumptions of what I call Secularism: they concern themselves only with changes of a temporal, material, and external nature; they concern themselves with morals only of a collective nature" (111). What is missing from this description is, obviously for Eliot, the presence of an acknowledged metaphysical order that holds precedence over purely secular concerns: this order, in his view, is vital not only to everyday life but also to all works of art created within the culture.

Eliot's general observations lead me to a few final remarks on possible implications for readers and writers of fiction today. What relevance, particularly, does my critical approach have within a field largely committed to cultural studies and its many variations? Such a question quickly brings us to the reasons why we read, enjoy, study, teach, and write novels to begin with. The answer, in my view, always goes back to the ways in which we understand literary value. When critics restrict the novel to its role as a general agent for, or gauge of, cultural change, the result is that the literary text becomes simply another manifestation of culture, that the novel has no more value to the human spirit than, say, the daily newspaper or any other object of cultural production. As such the novel is restricted to being written and read merely as a propaganda tool or as a specialized form of anthropology, sociology, or political science, for instance. But as Heidegger writes, cultural objects of a given period, like shoes, wear out, whereas the work of art, if it has value, does not wear out.

What separates a novel, or any other valuable work of art, from other objects of cultural production is the presence of a self-perpetuating inner life; it is something *made,* and as such it is an object of individual integrity. The novel in its most basic appeal is internal and concerned with *becoming:* by unraveling its own processes of development, it speaks to the individual-in-progress. At the same time, I would not dispute that a good novel is almost always of its own time and as such does hold meaning and value—just not *primary* meaning or value—outside itself as an art object and its influence on the individual.

All authors whom I have discussed in this study intuited that, on some level, aesthetic and religious experience bears an ontological relation to the other. Works of art created upon this premise speak most intimately to the riddle of what constitutes the dimensions of individual experience neither fully quantifiable by nor limited to empirical standards. Throughout this work I hope to have made it clear that the novel—particularly the bildungsroman—is a genre hospitable to these kinds of explorations and that indeed insofar as it concerns itself with the long tradition of self-formation, these elements, however overlooked, are inherent in it.

NOTES

Introduction

1. See McNees, *Development*, for an overview of these issues. McNees's collection provides a useful historical presentation of debates surrounding the novel primarily in England and America by writers as well as by critics, including the contribution of spiritual autobiography to the genre and related long-standing debates such as ethics vs. aesthetics, romance vs. realism, and so on.

2. Rivers describes this international movement as one of "reaction and reform, hostile to the secularist tendency of much contemporary religion and philosophy, and confident of its own ultimate success" (*Reason* 206–7). Rack characterizes widespread revival tendencies as addressing (vis-à-vis contemporary intellectual trends) "worries about materialism in public and social life; a concern for inward rather than merely conventional religion; spirituality rather than mere morality; a desire to remedy defects in official church organization" (*Reasonable* 170).

3. The American connection with German Pietism goes back at least to Quaker William Penn's 1677 invitation to Frankfurt Pietists to come to the New World (Kerry, *Enlightenment* 160). For this summary account I am indebted to Weinlick's useful history "Moravianism," esp. 133–49.

4. As Eugene Taylor in *Shadow Culture* further points out, the Great Awakening did not occur solely in New England nor exclusively among Puritans, but also among other denominations including the Pietists. A splinter group from Zinzendorf's Moravian Brethren, the ascetic Ephrata movement led by Johann Conrad Beissel was one such that traveled as far as Connecticut from Pennsylvania seeking converts (38).

5. Theological interpretations of "image" and "likeness" range from literal physical to symbolic resemblances. See, to start, N. W. Porteous's entry, "Image of God," in the *Interpreter's Dictionary of the Bible*, edited by George Arthur Buttrick et al.

6. As often is the case, it takes a while for popular usage to assimilate what a few have already been thinking and writing about for years—such is the case with Herder, who in 1774 published *Auch eine Philosophie der Geschichte zur Bildung der Menschheit* (Also a Philosophy of the History on the Bildung of Humanity).

7. In addition to the discussion of these thinkers in Cocalis, "Transformation," esp. 402–7, see Kontje, *German*, 2–7, and Argyle, *Germany*, 16–20.

8. Cf. Goozé, *Challenging* 15. I discuss the issue of gender in greater detail below.

9. As late as 1991 in *Reflection and Action*—a collection of bildungsroman essays by eminent critics such as Fritz Martini, Martin Swales, Jeffrey L. Sammons, and Thomas P.

Saine—James Hardin describes the bildungsroman as "a type of novel more talked about than understood" (x).

10. Because each method of interpretation works from different and in some cases contradictory premises, it is not possible by means of comparison to determine which provides a definitive understanding of the genre. Cf. Kontje, *German* 111. Cocalis's argument in "The Transformation of Bildung from an Image to an Ideal" is a good representative of criticism devoted to bildung as a historical concept belonging exclusively in the cultural milieu of Germany in the Age of Goethe. On the other hand, Howe's *Wilhelm* is the first full-length study in English of the bildungsroman as it applies primarily to the Victorian novel. An example of a pair of critics interested in definite generic characteristics vs. comparatively open-ended accounts would be Sammons in "Mystery" and Swales in *German,* respectively. To be sure, some overlap within the main divisions exists as well: Shaffner, for instance, in *Apprenticeship* is willing to include non-German works as bildungsromans but at the same time advances definite criteria by which to identify the genre.

11. Swales argues that "the degree to which the [generic] expectation is or is not fulfilled is not the criterion for participation in the genre construct. As long as the model of the genre is intimated as a sustained and sustaining presence in the work in question, then the genre retains its validity as a structuring principle within the palpable stuff of an individual literary creation" (*German* 12). This approach affirms the historical existence of genres but at the same time validates the autonomy of each creative work. It additionally accounts for the dynamic nature of genre itself, which changes with each new contribution to the form. For these views on genre, Swales acknowledges his debt to Todorov's *Fantastic* (9–10).

12. In 1961 Martini made the major discovery that this distinction belonged not to Dilthey but instead to the comparatively obscure professor Karl Morgenstern of Dorpat, who had used it as early as 1819. Morgenstern created the term primarily to buttress his critical perspective of the novel "as a moral means of education, as opposed to the conception of the novel as mere entertainment, pleasure, fantasy, and as an escape from reality" (Martini, "Bildungsroman: Term and Theory" 24). Still earlier Friedrich von Blanckenburg's germinal *Versuch über den Roman* (1774) describes the novel itself as concerned most essentially with formation and "inner history" (20). Martini detailed these findings in "Der Bildungsroman: Zur Geschichte des Wortes und der Theorie." An English version, "Bildungsroman: Term and Theory," from which I have quoted above, appears in *Reflection and Action,* edited by James Hardin. See also Tennyson, "Bildungsroman," 137; Steinecke, "Novel," 93; Argyle, *Germany,* 25–27.

13. Misattribution in these instances is partly due to the passage of time, partly due to new models upon which to define the genre. Recently, for instance, Maier in "Portraits" misattributes Dilthey's "lengthy, critical consideration" of *Wilhelm Meister* to his 1870 biography of Friedrich Schleiermacher. In fact in that work he only defines the genre in a brief discussion (see *Leben* 1:282). His extended critique of the novel appears instead in *Poetry and Experience,* which I discuss below.

14. Elsewhere, in the essay "Einbildungskraft" (1887), Dilthey explicitly links Charles Dickens to Shakespeare's externally oriented aesthetics: both Shakespeare and Dickens drew their primary inspiration from images and experiences encountered in the world

(*Gesammelte* 6:211). Note on translations: with the exception of individual words or short phrases that, beginning here, I shall translate in the text, I supply English translations of the German sources and provide the original text in notes. Unless otherwise indicated, all translations are my own.

15. "Goethes eigenste Gabe ist, die Zustände des eigenen Gemüts, die Welt der Ideen und Ideale in ihm anzusprechen" (Dilthey, *Erlebnis* 152).

16. "Von dem *Wilhelm Meister* und dem *Hesperus* ab stellen sie alle den Jüngling jener Tage dar; wie er in glücklicher Dämmerung in das Leben eintritt, nach verwandten Seelen sucht, der Freundschaft begegnet und der Liebe, wie er nun aber mit den harten Realitäten der Welt in Kampf gerät und so unter mannigfachen Lebenserfahrungen heranreift, sich selber findet und seiner Aufgabe in der Welt gewiß wird" (Dilthey, *Erlebnis* 272).

17. "Nie ist dieser Optimismus der persönlichen Entwickelung . . . heiterer und lebenssicherer ausgesprochen worden als in Goethes *Wilhelm Meister*: ein unvergänglicher Glanz von Lebensfreude liegt auf diesem Romane" (Dilthey, *Erlebnis* 273).

18. Political and cultural conditions in Germany and America, particularly in the eighteenth century, contribute further to these literary affinities. At least two qualities stand out in this regard: especially in the eighteenth century, both Germany and America were composed of loosely associated "states" under foreign rule (in Germany, under the Vienna-based Habsburg dynasty of the Holy Roman Empire), and both contained a largely uneducated public (in *Wilhelm Meister* and in his letters, for instance, Goethe frequently complains about this latter problem).

19. The author writes, "*Wilhelm Meister* is a work of extraordinary variety, ranging from . . . commonplace realism . . . to . . . poetic romanticism . . . its flashes of intuitive criticism and its weighty apothegms add to its value as a bildungsroman in the best sense of that word" (185).

20. Beginning, of course, with Richard Chase's controversial *American*. For a useful bibliography that traces the debate in American criticism from 1799 to 1996, see Thompson and Link, *Neutral*, 221–47.

21. This connection between America and Germany goes back yet further: Boyle notes that from the late seventeenth and into the early eighteenth century, "religious revival could be said to have taken the place of literature as far as the German middle classes were concerned" (*Goethe* 1:12).

22. Holman cites the young protagonist in Hawthorne's story "My Kinsman, Major Molineux" to exemplify this idea in miniature.

23. Though Fessenden does not write explicitly about the bildungsroman, in Culture she contributes an important study of the influence of Protestant thought on the nineteenth-century American novel, with the emphasis on the ways in which it becomes secularized through the filters of race, gender, and class.

24. Those who also note this discrepancy include Abel, Hirsch, and Langland, *Voyage*, 7, and Maier, "Portraits," 323.

25. Though Bradley's work covers only Evangelicalism as it remained a part of the Established Church (scope 1800–1860), its impact on Dissent has already been established. Throughout this work, when I refer to evangelicalism, I capitalize it to indicate its association

with the Church of England (of which Wesley remained a member unto his death); I use lowercase to indicate its association with organizations apart from the Established Church.

26. See Carwardine's "Second" on the effects of this central difference on the respective British and American cultures: in America revivalism was able to grow unchecked because "there were no institutions of sufficient ecclesiastical and social authority to repel it" (89). In Britain, on the other hand, the Established Church was also the "church of the socially powerful, the nobility and gentry," capable of exerting social as well as financial suppression of English Dissent.

27. Williams locates the Second Awakening as actually a series of geographic unfoldings that occurred throughout antebellum America, beginning at the turn of the century with the "New Divinity," heirs of Edwards (including Joseph Bellamy and Jonathan Edwards Jr.) (*America's* 184).

28. Dickens mercilessly satirized similar evangelical societies in his native London—see the discussion in chapter 5.

29. After William James later social scientists broadened this basic division to contain, in addition to mystical instantaneity, gradual variations of intellectual, experimental, affectional, revivalist, or coercive conversion. Tate provides a useful discussion of the ways in which most of these elements apply to Victorian religious discourse ("Tell" 8).

30. These basic distinctions are further outlined in the *Oxford Dictionary of the Christian Church.*

31. For the critical discourse surrounding Darwinism and Victorian literature, see esp. Levine's work in this area, e.g., *Darwin and the Novelists* and *Realism, Ethics and Secularism.*

32. George Eliot, too, could be readily taken up in this light, although I do not include her here in favor of those texts less often considered in light of evangelical influences.

Chapter 1: John Wesley's Formative "Spiritual Empiricism"

1. Walker marks the beginning of the Evangelical Revival around the turn of the eighteenth century with Scottish pastors Ebenezer and Ralph Erskine; its conclusion occurred in 1779 with the first "formal separations" of denominations from the Church of England (*History* 455–56). For the following overview of English Protestant theology in the seventeenth and eighteenth centuries, I am largely indebted to the first volume of Rivers's intellectual and religious history, *Reason.*

2. Rack implies that the latitudinarian approach to the religious life was in part due to the largely secular duties to which eighteenth-century Church of England clergy were subject: "in a lightly governed society lacking most official social services," clergy served as sources of education, mediation, charity, medical care—even as community leaders and keepers of the order (*Reasonable* 10).

3. According to Hindley enthusiasm in Anglican thought largely derived from Locke's definition of it: the insistence on direct revelation of God independent of reason, the Bible, and the church ("Philosophy" 105–6). Wesley warned his followers against enthusiasm as "that daughter of pride . . . give no place to a heated imagination. . . . You are in danger of enthusiasm every hour, if you depart ever so little from Scripture . . . [or] if you despise or lightly esteem reason, knowledge, or human learning; every one of which is an excellent gift of God, and may serve the noblest purposes" (*Works* 11:429).

4. Indeed Wesley never wished to separate from the Established Church; accordingly Wesleyan Methodists did not do so formally until 1795, four years after his death (Brantley, *Locke* 3n6). American Methodists, however, separated in 1784 (Payne, *Self* 3).

5. See Rivers, *Reason* 1:253. Additionally Rack emphasizes the distinction between two kinds of Wesleyan perfection, one that is attainable while living and one that is not. The attainable kind of perfection offers "experiential attractions" (conscious or unconscious transgression of a known law and the ability to rectify by obeying the law) as opposed to unattainable perfection (perfect alignment with God's law) (*Reasonable* 399).

6. Dreyer notes that beginning with Leslie Stephen's dismissal of Wesley's theology as instinctive and emotionally based ("Faith" 12), many critics have not taken seriously Wesley's thought apart from its emotional appeal. Others in turn have read him in the vague tradition of zealousness, or as a Lutheran, Calvinist, Arminian; finally Methodism has been understood as a pastiche ("Faith" 27–28). Hindley's "Philosophy" arguably provided the germinal alternate discussion comparing, and linking, the epistemologies of Wesley and Locke. Others following along these lines, in addition to those discussed in the text, include Matthews, "Eyes"; and English, "John." Most recently Mealey has attempted to move beyond the discussion relating the two epistemologies, which, in his view, are antithetical. Wesley's credulous misreadings of Locke reveal instead his premodern, quixotic orientation: where he sees giants (Locke's piousness, contradictions to this piousness as "little mistakes"), "we" see windmills (Locke as the harbinger of modern materialist epistemology) ("Tilting" 345).

7. However, Rack cautions against overemphasizing Locke's influence on Wesley's epistemology. Wesley was "rational in form but enthusiast in substance. He supported supernaturalist beliefs with empiricist arguments well beyond what Locke would have allowed in his more limited form of 'rational supernaturalism'" (*Reasonable* 388). Indeed Wesley's decidedly un-Lockean interest and belief in supernatural phenomena was "an integral part of what Methodism . . . meant and help[s] to explain its peculiar appeal" (432).

8. As Clapper aptly states, Wesley "saw that the rough contours of felt experience are where the gospel either grows or dies" ("True" 422).

9. For a useful overview of Catholic mysticism, see Underhill's classic *Mysticism*.

10. The usual account, in Runyon's view, is an anachronistic, nineteenth-century way of understanding conversion before Kant, in whose epistemology "God collapsed into the experiencing subject in order, in turn, to be derived from the subject." This resulted in "the absolutizing and subjectivising of experience in a way which has fundamentally distorted the understanding of religious experience in our own time and leads to a misreading of the intention of pre-nineteenth-century texts" ("Role" 192).

11. The subject of English spiritual autobiography in England and America underwent a critical renaissance in the late 1960s–1970s. Some of the most comprehensive studies of the genre in Britain include works by Delaney (*British*), Ebner (*Autobiography*), and Watkins (*Puritan*).

12. In the context of the mid-century revivals, Rack suggests that attainable perfection had a practical use: for the many new converts faced with everyday living after the initial ecstasy of conversion, it provided an intelligible model for working through and beyond postconversion doubts and fears (*Reasonable* 427). The degree to which Wesley concerned

himself with the religious importance of daily experience is apparent in the following, taken from "Plain Account." Wesley advises those seeking "perfection" to be "exemplary in all things; particularly in outward things, (as in dress,) in little things, in the laying out of your money," etc. (*Works* 11:435).

Chapter 2: The Paradox of Experience in Jonathan Edwards

1. It is remarkable that these are precisely the same grounds upon which Wesley condemns the mystics (*Journal* 1:468–69 §7).

2. Miller, of course, was largely responsible for advancing this particular approach to Edwards—that we should see him not as a "Puritan Platonist" but as "the first and most radical, even though the most tragically misunderstood, of American empiricists" ("Jonathan" 124). Cf. Anderson, "Practical," esp. 406–7, 409. For a corroboration of Dreyer's position from a contemporary of Miller's, see Stewart, *American*, 10.

3. For more on this conundrum and possible ways out of it, see Sharf's article "Experience," esp. 104.

4. In *Varieties of Religious Experience*, William James had already begun to feel a similar uneasiness and expressed it in political terms: the cruel and arbitrary "monarchical type of sovereignty" of Puritan America's God seemed "positively to have been required by their imagination. . . . But to-day we abhor the very notion of eternal suffering inflicted; and that arbitrary dealing-out of salvation and damnation to selected individuals, of which Jonathan Edwards could persuade himself that he had not only a conviction, but 'delightful conviction,' as of a doctrine 'exceeding pleasant, bright, and sweet,' appears to us, if sovereignly anything, sovereignly irrational and mean." He goes on to argue that as a culture we dispense with any belief system whenever it ceases to follow the perceived direction in which the culture is tending—in America's case, of course, the movement from monarchy to democracy (257–58).

5. An early and stirring instance of Edwards's simultaneous awareness of these elements appears in "The 'Spider' Letter," purportedly a scientific study on "flying" spiders but actually a meditation on joy and destruction in the natural world. In a corollary to his observations on the insects, he concludes: "Hence the exuberant goodness of the Creator, who hath not only provided for all the necessities, but also for the pleasure and recreation of all sorts of creatures, even the insects. But yet . . . I am assured that the chief end of this faculty that is given them is not their recreation but their destruction, because their destruction is unavoidably the constant effect of it" (*Works* 6:167).

6. See Stewart, *American*, 11. Stewart further compares Edwards's transcendentalism with Emerson's based on the high value they mutually place on intuition.

7. See, for example, Sharf, "Experience," 104.

8. For Edwards's "astonishing" personal role in the Great Awakening, see Marsden, *Jonathan*, 158.

9. Though Conner does not pretend to solve this paradox, he explains it by making the distinction between the temporal and the eternal: in time progress necessarily coexists with experience of good and evil, but these things all "disappear under the aspect of eternity, where all things are seen to be . . . 'all one'" (*Cosmic* 126).

10. Maclear provides a seventeenth-century precedent for the kind of conflict I am describing in Edwards. He argues that psychological concerns based on geography were one of the motivating factors in the clergy's creating the stern legalist/dogmatic position of the period. The fact that the New England colonies were little more than frontier communities fostered "morbidity and emotional instability in religious life . . . a mentality of desperation, terror, and siege," the cumulative "nightmare" that distinguished American from English Puritanism ("Heart" 634). On this last subject, in *Puritan* Caldwell has contributed a useful study making the case that the geographical fact of America constitutes a major difference between English and American Puritans' attitudes toward spiritual formation and salvation, and that these differences are apparent through a close examination of the conversion narratives of each nation.

11. To take one of many instances, John Cotton's *A Treatise of the Covenant of Grace* (1659) offers many similar arguments contained in Edwards's *Divine and Supernatural Light*. Cotton argues that it would be absurd for the created to use any saving "work" as evidence for salvation since the creator is author of all works. Also the Bible itself is not enough to reveal grace: "there is need of greater light than the word of itself is able to give. . . . neither the word of grace, nor all the works of grace, are able to clear up the grace of God unto the soul. It is the spirit of God that must do it" (150–53). See also Maclear's reading of the mysticism implicit in antinomianism and of mystical tendencies in the controversy's leading figures such as Cotton and Hutchinson.

12. Twelve years later in *A Treatise Concerning Religious Affections*, Edwards defines "a principle of nature" as "that foundation which is laid in nature . . . for any particular manner or kind of exercise of the faculties of the soul. . . . So this new spiritual sense is not a new faculty of understanding, but it is a new foundation laid in the nature of the soul, for a new kind of exercises of the same faculty of understanding" (*Works* 2:206).

13. In his introduction to the "Personal Narrative," Claghorn notes that many literary scholars "consider the document a new and quintessentially American form of self-discovery that builds on the traditional Puritan conversion narrative" (*Works* 16:749). In addition to critics discussed in this section, other commentators who engage early American autobiography include Imbarrato ("Early"); Gordis ("Conversion"); Carton ("What"); Aldrich ("Children"); Bercovitch ("Ritual"); Weddle ("Image"); and Griffith ("Jonathan").

14. Psychohistorian King argues that autobiographical texts attempting to describe an American character or make sense of American experience do not simply reflect reality but have the power themselves to create character (*Iron* 7–8).

15. The first point comes from Couser, *American*, 25–26; Payne makes the second point in *Self*, 14. See also Payne's chapter 3, "The Paradox of Self."

16. Shea defines the spiritual autobiography genre as "creation myth written in the first person" and is among the first to argue that the genre is a key component informing American literary identity (*Spiritual* xvii). Additionally Edwards's "Narrative" in its unusual form and emphasis on "heart" contributes to American literature's romantic origins (182–83).

17. From the start Sarah Edwards's narrative makes plain the conflict between dedicating herself completely to God and attending to her family's involvement in community and ministerial rivalries. Between descriptions of night watches filled with spiritual experiences,

the narrative expresses repeatedly the all-too-real fears for the tenuousness of her husband's position "in advancing the work of grace in Northampton" (Dwight, *Life* 178).

18. For a fine discussion of Puritan doubt, see Morgan, *Visible*, esp. 70. For a more recent treatment, see Seed, "Exemplary," 40.

19. This sequence, in fact, distinguishes the narrative from other Puritan narratives as well, which typically *begin* with consciousness of sin. See, for instance, King, *Iron*, 14.

20. Shea remarks that this aspect of Edwards's narrative shows a kind of perfectionism, or that his sense of sin is greater than happiness over an increased awareness of grace (*Spiritual* 204–5). Granted Edwards allows that true saints "may be guilty of some kinds and degrees of backsliding, and may be soiled by particular temptations, and may fall into sin, yea great sins: but they can never fall away so, as to grow weary of religion, and the service of God, and habitually to dislike it and neglect it" nor "so as to continue no longer in a way of universal obedience" (*Works* 2:390).

Chapter 3: Pietism and the "Free Movement" of Self-Cultivation

1. For a more detailed account of Zinzendorf's Pietism in its historical context, see esp. chapter 4, "Zinzendorf," in Stoeffler's *German*, 131–67.

2. Hindmarsh's book provides a useful presentation of the many forms of evangelical conversion narratives in England from the mid-1730s through the mid-1780s, including Methodist, Moravian, and Calvinist narratives.

3. Some uncertainty seems to exist about precisely which *Ecce Homo* of Feti's Zinzendorf actually saw. Most believe that Zinzendorf was inspired by the one now hanging in Munich's Pinakothek. See Beyreuther, *Junge*, 169; Weinlick, *Count*, 42; Meyer et al., *Graf*, 168.

4. Kant's 1784 essay "Beantwortung der Frage: Was ist Aufklärung?" (Answer to the Question: What Is Enlightenment?) is a good place to begin on the subject of German Enlightenment. Nisbet's article on this essay, "Was," provides a useful starting point with the criticism in English.

5. As Kerry points out, the religious climate of Goethe's native Frankfurt was saturated with various Protestant denominations, orthodox and unorthodox, including a branch of Herrnhuters that Zinzendorf had established there in the 1730s (*Enlightenment* 27).

6. In an unusual combination of circumstances, von Klettenberg's manuscript was never published, nor has it been preserved, but it is known to have existed. See Becker-Cantarino, *Life*, 43. Even earlier in Goethe's career, Kerry argues that Goethe had already begun to experiment with blending aspects of Pietism into his fiction, particularly with the "secularized Pietist discourse" and "perspectival shift to interiority" of *Die Leiden des jungen Werthers* (The Sorrows of Young Werther) (*Enlightenment* 30). For a broad consideration of Goethe's involvement with Pietism, see Kemper and Schneider, *Goethe*, esp. chapters by Dohm and Soboth.

7. In the introduction to the English-language edition, Saine indicates that Pietist autobiography was a model for Goethe's own. And yet this demonstrated a remarkable departure from the religious form: "Although religion, religious sentiments, and the effort to come to terms with God and the world occupy a large part of the work, it is not Goethe's fear that impels the search, but rather his innate curiosity about the nature of things and his

. . . totally unshaken optimism about his own nature and about human nature in general" (11).

8. "Zwar verstärkte die pietistische Frömmigkeit des späteren 17. und 18. Jahrhunderts mit ihrer Forderung nach steter Introspektion und ihrer Betonung des Gefühls die Aufmerksamkeit des Einzelnen auf sich selbst" (Jacobs, *Wilhelm* 30–31).

9. "Aufgabe der Bildungsidee ist es, die Spannung zwischen dem Anspruch auf jeweils individuelle Selbstverwirklichung und der Geltung allgemeiner Gesetze zu lösen. Die Entwicklung des Einzelnen sollte ihr unverwechselbares Gepräge behalten und gleichwohl einer verbindlichen Norm folgen" (Jacobs, *Wilhelm* 35).

10. See Saine, "Time," 64. Seigel has, on a related note, discussed the connection between the religious "calling" and secular bildung throughout the novel in "Homology," esp. 354–55.

11. While composing my own translations of the correspondence, I have consulted Dieckmann's *Correspondence.*

12. In a letter dated June 28, 1796, Schiller later revised this position once he finished the novel and remarks on his admiration for the way book 8 resolves everything that seemed unresolved in book 6 (*Werke* 12:176). Other reactions, Boyle reports, include the cynical Frau von Stein's thought that book 6 simply contributed to the length (and earnings) of the manuscript; others such as Lavater thought that it indicated that "Goethe was after all about to become a Christian" (*Goethe* 2:269).

13. "Freilich weiß der arme Leser bei solchen Produktionen niemals wie er dran ist, denn er bedenkt nicht, daß er diese Bücher gar nicht in die Hand nehmen würde, wenn man nicht verstünde seine Denkkraft, seine Empfindung und seine Wißbegierde zum besten zu haben" (Goethe, *Sämtliche* 31:136).

14. For instance Saine believes that "the astute modern reader quickly discerns that the 'Beautiful Soul' is a sick woman indeed, and her autobiography . . . shows her as a model of how *not* to be and how *not* to live one's live, rather than as a model to be emulated" (introduction 10). See also Lukács's comments on Goethe's nuanced ironic critique of the Canoness throughout chapter 2 of *Goethe.*

15. Additionally Becker-Cantarino offers another feminist interpretation of the "Confessions": while this type of autobiography promoted "ethical and spiritual inwardness," in *Wilhelm Meister's Apprenticeship* "Goethe offered an ironic and slightly critical twist: his 'beautiful Soul' refuses to become a wife and mother for the sake of her piety, thus missing her 'natural' calling, and is in the end marginalized in the newly blossoming, totally patriarchal society created by and mostly for men—a reflection of the increasingly fixed gender roles and gender dichotomy in patriarchal Germany around 1800" (*Life* 43).

16. In book 5 the physician, who knew the Beautiful Soul during her lifetime, gives Wilhelm the manuscript of the "Confessions" to read to the rapidly declining Aurelie. As a true friend to the uncle, "he also admitted that he had found it most beneficial for sickly people, whose health could not be completely restored, to cultivate religious sentiments" (212). All translations of *Wilhelm Meister's Apprenticeship* come from the standard English edition of Goethe's collected works, translated by Eric A. Blackall.

17. As we have seen in Hindmarsh's comments on Zinzendorf's sense of conversion, the Canoness's own appears to be in line with the Count's with its rejection of "legal

preparation" in favor of "a childlike trust and radical identification with the love of the dying Jesus" (*Evangelical* 164). Indeed she explicitly rejects the rigid Franckean understanding of conversion held by the "pietist theologians at Halle" (Goethe, *Wilhelm* 236).

18. Most of the original community at Herrnhut comprised exiles from Moravia who were persecuted there for their religious practices.

19. In a rare moment of undisguised irritation, Goethe writes to Schiller, "to whom is it unknown that the Christians always appropriated everything that was rational and good in order to attribute it to the λόγος?" (Wie unwissend überhaupt diese Menschen sind, ist unglaublich; denn wem ist unbekannt, daß die Christen alles was von jeher vernünftig und gut war, sich dadurch zueigneten, daß sie es dem λόγος zuschrieben?)—an action to which he explicitly links the Canoness (Schiller, *Briefwechsel* 1:107).

20. For the polarized discussion the novel has inspired—its "poetisch" versus "prosaisch" values—from the time of its publication into the twentieth century, see Barner, "Geheime."

21. "Die zwey ersten sind heilige, die zwey andern sind wahre und menschliche Naturen; aber eben darum weil Natalie heilig und menschlich zugleich ist, so erscheint sie wie ein Engel, da die Stiftsdame nur eine Heilige, Therese nur eine vollkommene Irrdische ist" (Schiller, *Werke* 12:183).

22. "Nur die Philosophie kann das Philosophieren unschädlich machen; ohne sie führt es unausbleiblich zum Mysticism. (Die Stiftsdame selbst ist ein Beweis dafür. Ein gewißer aesthetischer Mangel machte ihr die Speculation zum Bedürfniß, und sie verirrte zur Herrenhuterey, weil ihr die Philosophie nicht zu Hülfe kam; als Mann hätte sie vielleicht alle Irrgänge der Metaphysic durchwandert)" (Schiller, *Werke* 12:199–200).

23. Of course to modern ears this conception of the ideal woman—and we must suppose her to be the novel's feminine ideal—has become quaint. This idealization of character additionally provides an instance of the potential misapplications of the *bildungsidee* into people's lives outside the world of the novel: one of the most powerful arguments to persuade someone to do or be something is to claim that it is in accordance with his or her nature. To resist this argument involves nothing less than redefining the sense of self on its deepest level.

24. "Sie wollten noch nicht mit einander zusammenfließen; jenes hatte er sich gleichsam geschaffen, und dieses schien fast *ihn* umschaffen zu wollen" (Goethe, *Sämtliche* 9:896).

25. For a psychoanalytic reading along these lines see, e.g., Edmunds, "Ich," 86–87.

26. See chapter 6 for a discussion on Melville's American version of a similar society. Symbolically the tower image represents ascent. In ancient Egyptian hieroglyphs, the tower denoted "height or the act of rising above the common level in life or society." Similarly the alchemist's furnace was shaped like a tower to suggest transformation and "to signify inversely that the metamorphosis of matter implied a process of ascension." See Cirlot, *Dictionary*, 344–45. It is not inconceivable that Goethe had something similar in mind when he gave the society its name, because these meanings directly reflect both the individual and political aspects of bildung that it advocates and enforces. For a focused discussion on the Turmgesellschaft, including the Freemasonry connection, see Barner, "Geheime."

27. A suitable visual corollary to this idea appears in Francisco de Goya's wonderfully ambiguous *El sueño de la razón produce monstruos*, or *The Sleep of Reason Produces Monsters* of *Los Caprichos*. By dramatizing the tensions between reason, romanticism, and religion, Goethe was clearly tapping into deep currents circulating throughout Europe at the time: *Wilhelm Meister's Apprenticeship* was completed in 1796, and Goya created *El sueño* one year later.

28. "Er tritt von einem leeren und unbestimmten Ideal in ein bestimmtes thätiges Leben, aber ohne die idealisierende Kraft dabey einzubüßen" (Schiller, *Werke* 12:194).

29. As Abel, Hirsch, and Langland have pointed out, Jane, "more than any other heroine, conforms to the male *bildungsheld*" (*Voyage* 15).

Chapter 4: "To enjoy my own faculties as well as to cultivate those of other people"

1. Most commentators on the novel take it more or less for granted that these male characters who play such powerful roles in the formation of Jane's character are drawn from either literary or biographical sources. In the case of Rochester, the usual precedents identified are Zamorna of Brontë's juvenilia (Gérin, introduction 21; Ratchford, *Legends* 213), Byron (Ratchford, *Legends* 221; Armstrong, *Desire* 203), and Brontë's tutor in Brussels, Constantin Heger (Harrison, *Clue* 161). St. John Rivers is most often linked to Henry Nussey (Winnifrith, *Brontës* 20–21; Barker, *Brontës* 451) or to famous missionary and Cambridge friend of Patrick Brontë, Henry Martyn (Thormählen, *Brontës* 215; Winnifrith, *Brontës* 31).

2. By recognizing Brontë's related affirmation of active Providence in *Jane Eyre*, I tend to agree more with critics such as Emily Griesinger, J. Jeffrey Franklin, Maria Lamonaca, Jerome Beaty, Robert F. George, and Marianne Thormählen over and against critics such as John Maynard and Sally Shuttleworth, who variously read religious allusions in the text as metaphors for the character's psychology or as deriving from strictly "natural" sources.

3. For all subsequent citations of the novel, I provide the chapter followed by page number.

4. To my mind the final two chapters of Beaty's *Misreading* provide the best and most unusually compelling account to date of St. John's power in its most heroic and most destructive moments. Other critics who have given due credit to St. John's role in Jane's self-formation include Moglen (*Charlotte* 139); Imlay (*Charlotte* 66); Rowe ("Fairy-Born" 89); and George ("Evangelical" 96).

5. Wolff clarifies the difference while at the same time indicating their close proximity in the Victorian religious "spectrum": Low Churchmen "generally referred to themselves as Evangelicals" and were "closest in outlook to dissenting churches" in comparison with High and Broad Churchmen (*Gains* 17). Wolff provides an excellent overview of the Church of England at the time in *Gains*, esp. 8–23. George's unpublished dissertation, "Evangelical," provides a historical contextualization of the novel within the eighteenth- and nineteenth-century Evangelical movements. Cf. J. Jeffrey Franklin's "Merging."

6. For more on the *Methodist Magazine*'s literary influence on Charlotte Brontë, see Talley's *Jane*. Cunningham credits Methodism as a "referent for passion" as well as providing a "rhetoric of passion" in the Brontës' work, or "extremes of feeling, behavior, and religious enthusiasm" (*Everywhere* 124–25).

7. For similar views see, e.g., Griesinger, "Charlotte," 46; and Myer, *Charlotte*, 60, 65. In an interesting if minor connection with the Revival nexus under discussion, Thormählen links Patrick Brontë's views with the Moravians. It was therefore no coincidence that when Anne Brontë fell ill at Miss Wooler's school she called for a local Moravian minister for comfort over the reportedly Calvinist Anglican clergymen connected with the school (*Brontës* 22). See also Anne Brontë's letter to Rev. D. Thom, December 30, 1848, in Charlotte Brontë's *Letters* (2:160n2).

8. See also Cunningham, *Everywhere*, 113, 116; and Harrison, *Clue*, 3. According to Griesinger, at Cambridge the curate of Patrick's tutor and mentor was the "Wesleyan missionary" Henry Martyn—who supported Patrick in seeking scholarships and whom many argue to be the model for St. John Rivers ("Charlotte" 44). On Patrick's many Methodist friends, including the widow of John Fletcher, a personal friend of John and Charles Wesley, see Barker, *Brontës*, 27.

9. As I have shown in chapter 1, the ongoing conflict between faith and doubt is evident even in the most dedicated—for instance on the very evening after Wesley's conversion experience, he reported that he was "much buffeted with temptations; but they fled away. They returned again and again" (*Journal* 1:467).

10. In the case of *Jane Eyre*, this debate began virtually upon its publication. Writing for the conservative *Quarterly Review*, Elizabeth Rigby condemned the novel as "pre-eminently an anti-Christian composition" ("Article V" 173).

11. Certainly the early letters to Ellen Nussey reflect Brontë's intense spiritual struggles, particularly with Calvinist dogma. In a letter from 1836, she writes, "if the Doctrine of Calvin be true I am already an outcast—You cannot imagine how hard rebellious and intractable all my feelings are—When I begin to study on the subject I almost grow blasphemous" (*Letters* 1:154).

12. The most famous form of this discussion appears, of course, in Gilbert and Gubar, *Madwoman*, 336–71. Cf. Rowe, "Fairy-Born," 83–85, and, more recently, Shuttleworth's *Charlotte*.

13. The article reviews both *Vanity Fair* and *Jane Eyre*. Of the latter Lady Eastlake wrote, "It is a very remarkable book: we have no remembrance of another combining such genuine power with such horrid taste" ("Article V" 163).

14. See Green, *Works*, 209. Green further notes that Wesley's abridged edition did not acknowledge Brooke's authorship.

15. Eagleton makes a sound argument for how St. John Rivers is an "extreme version of Jane herself" (*Myths* 19–20). Alternately in a suggestive psychoanalytic reading, Irene Taylor reads St. John as an embodying Brontë's own ambition "to be an apostle of art, her restless yearnings for spiritual liberty and intellectual excitement, for the 'wild, free' energy of the artist on her way to her promised land" (*Holy* 178). See also Knies, *Art*, 133.

16. Their shared feeling of exile and privation registers even on a physical level: after Jane is well enough to join the company at Moor House, as she dresses she observes that "my clothes hung loose on me; for I was much wasted" (Brontë, *Jane* 29, 349). Similarly Jane perceives that even St. John's attractive figure is "wasting away" in self-denial (32, 384): his cheek becomes "hollow," and "his hand looked wasted like his face" (33, 388).

17. For many more eighteenth-century ethical-philosophical perspectives on the affections, a good starting point is Raphael's *British Moralists* (an updated version of the classic Selby-Bigge edition).

18. See Filonowicz, *Fellow*, 52. Filonowicz considers "the notion of natural affection" to be the key to Shaftesbury's ethical system (50). For Shaftesbury "to be motivated by natural affection is to act neither irrationally nor blindly, but rather from robust recognition of the reality of others and of their weal or woe, flourishing or travail." Cf. Lockbridge, *Ethics*, esp. "Egoism and the Natural Affections" (45–53).

19. Irish moral philosopher Francis Hutcheson would continue with Shaftesbury's ideas by emphasizing "disinterested affection" as the primary motivating force for virtuous actions. See Hutcheson, "Inquiry," 278.

20. This image from Plato's *Phaedrus*, of the soul as a chariot guided by a dark horse and a light horse, is a convenient image encompassing the power, and the attempted control, of the passions. A reference appears in *Jane Eyre* as Jane reflects on St. John's suppression of his desire for Rosamond: "He curbed it, I think, as a resolute rider would curb a rearing steed" (31, 374).

21. The precise meaning of the word *powers* is ambiguous here and elsewhere in the text. Later Brontë uses it to imply some kind of sensible, "life quickening" force (Brontë, *Jane* 34, 414). Thormählen also remarks that the language of this passage indicates incomplete conversion (*Brontës* 208).

22. Many have harsh words for St. John's suppression of his sexual nature. Maynard calls St. John's "abundant sexual energy almost pathologically misdirected" into a "monomaniacal missionary zeal" (*Charlotte* 109); Moglen describes him as "sadistic" (*Charlotte* 136). Others go so far as to describe his presence in the novel as anti–life force, e.g., Auerbach (*Romantic* 200, 203).

23. In spite of its poetry, the scene is comic partly due to its sheer awkwardness: to be sure more than other genres, the radically limited point of view in the autobiographical mode is vulnerable to such devices when the narrator needs to reveal other characters' secret feelings and motives.

24. Based on these lines, Rich remarks that "what St. John offers Jane is perhaps the deepest lure for a spiritual woman, that of adopting a man's cause or career and making it her own" ("Jane" 103).

25. Many have commented on the contradiction in St. John's insistence on a loveless marriage: for instance both Moglen and Knies have likened his proposal to spiritual prostitution (according to Knies in contrast to the physical prostitution Rochester proposed [*Art* 134]). In Moglen's words "Jane recognizes that St. John would buy her body with the coin of spirituality" (*Charlotte* 138).

26. Those who seek similar or otherwise psychologically based explanations are modern heirs to Elizabeth Gaskell's skepticism. Gaskell attributes (at least the mysterious summons) to superstition and to Brontë's fragile nerves (*Life* 337). Moglen's reading is characteristic of reading Jane's response as explicitly sexual and "summoned by the sexual component of St. John's power, but it yields awareness and self-discovery instead of dread annihilation" (*Charlotte* 138). As such this experience amounts to Brontë's final affirmation

of the "dignity of human passion." Gilbert's similar reading concludes that Jane "was quite frankly replacing a Christian theology of renunciation with a more hedonistic theology of love" ("Jane" 367). Cf. Maynard, *Charlotte,* 136; Shuttleworth, *Charlotte,* 179; Myer, *Charlotte,* 71.

27. For readings closer in spirit to the present one, cf. Beaty, *Misreading,* 199–211; J. Jeffrey Franklin, "Merging," 481; Lamonaca, "Jane's," 251; and Thormählen, *Brontës,* 219. Griesinger offers a direct alternative to Gilbert's (see n. 26) by viewing the prayer scene as a "remarkable assertion of women's spiritual authority and an equally memorable rejection of the idea predominant among Victorians . . . that women must always be 'under' the spiritual authority of men" ("Charlotte" 52–55).

Chapter 5: "Faith in the immanence of spirit"

1. Cordery provides the language for this description of *David Copperfield,* though it should be remarked that his article explores some of the ways in which the novel critiques many of the values it overtly champions ("*David*" 372). Others who have notably discussed *Copperfield*'s place as the premier instance of the English bildungsroman include Barr ("Mourning"); McCarthy ("Making"); Maynard (*Beautiful*); and Jeffers (*Apprenticeships*). Hollington's "*David*" is, however, the only article to my knowledge devoted to an exclusive comparison between the novels as each applies to the bildungsroman genre.

2. Q. D. Leavis goes so far as to suggest that *Jane Eyre* was a probable inspiration for *David Copperfield* ("Dickens" 109); see also Tambling's introduction to the Penguin edition of *Copperfield* (xxiv).

3. I mean here bildungsroman loosely conceived—as a general novel of education or development—not in the sense of spiritual self-formation, by which I seek to characterize the genre.

4. On Fanny's conversion see Pope, *Dickens,* 32; Cunningham, *Everywhere,* 191–92.

5. Bradley, *Call,* 14; see more on Bradley in the introduction; Pope, *Dickens,* x.

6. Though on Dickens's part most agree this optimism noticeably declines as his career continues. As Walder remarks *David Copperfield* was "perhaps the last convincingly optimistic novel of Dickens's career" (*Dickens* 145). Further Dickens's optimism—at least in *David Copperfield*—is of a distinctly different texture from Wesley's: whereas Wesley is optimistic about God's grace as it may apply to anybody, Dickens strives to uphold the concordance of individual behavior with meet rewards or punishment here on earth.

7. I am here referring to the language of "the gloomy taint that was in the Murdstone blood" (Dickens, *David* chap. 4, 62), the implications of which I develop below. On Dickens's rejection of original sin, see, e.g., Cunningham, "Dickens," 267; and Oulton, *Literature,* 97. On Dickens's general avoidance of philosophical and theological doctrine, see, e.g., Newsom, "Dickens," 37; Cunningham, *Everywhere,* 190; and Walder, *Dickens,* 4.

8. See chapter 12, section 6, "The Religious Reaction," 348, 360. Stephen's criticism reveals perhaps more about his own skepticism and critical attitude toward Dissenters of the Second Evangelical Revival than it does about Wesley's original theology. His arguments at times amount to personal attack; he likens Wesley's appearance, for instance, to "a human gamecock" (*History* 348).

9. Ward compares Dickens's with Arnold's tactics against Dissenters: whereas Dickens employed a "rhetoric of repression" with the aim to exile Dissent from English culture, Arnold preferred (in *Culture and Anarchy*) the more practical "rhetoric of assimilation." Each individual Dissenter, for Arnold, should be treated as a "wayward citizen who must be re-educated and re-fitted for a role in national life" ("Transformed" 109).

10. Kent had already pointed out this contradiction in addition to the fact that Dissent was for the working classes the "religious counterpart of the democracy for which they yearned" (*Dickens* 94). Cf. Stephen's similar class-based criticism of Dissent (*History* 361).

11. Levine's "Dickens" provides a representative instance of the first critical perspective: before Levine, see Qualls, *Secular*, 86. Included among those who view Dickens's creative engagements with religion as dialogically engaged with rather than dialectically opposed to secularity are Larson, *Dickens*; and Karl Ashley Smith, *Dickens*. See also Cole, "Amen"; Newsom, "Dickens." Finally in *Literature* Oulton is one of the few critics to call into question the extent of Dickens's Broad Church liberalism.

12. Pope provides a comprehensive discussion of Dickens's involvement with social reform and the Evangelical community. The "practical environmentalism" of Evangelicals concerned itself with reforming everything from inner-city missions to sanitation practices (*Dickens* 8).

13. See also Forster (2:116). Lord Ashley, the Seventh Earl of Shaftesbury, served as chair of the Ragged School Union for forty years, from 1845 until 1885. Forster records that Dickens "spoke warmly of the services of Lord Ashley in connection with ragged schools" and that Shaftesbury dined with Dickens at Tavistock-house. It is interesting to observe the radical change in character of civic devotion from his eighteenth-century ancestor, the Fourth Earl.

14. See Pope, *Dickens*, 22–23; Buckley, *Season*, 40. Hardy, whom I shall discuss in greater detail below, characterizes Victorian conversion as not religious but "a turning from self-regard to love and social responsibility" (*Moral* 27). Others who advance similar arguments include Newey (*Scriptures* 3) and Walder (*Dickens* 113).

15. For Dawson the answer is affirmative, if not resoundingly, in the sense that David has achieved the status of Carlylian hero as man of letters.

16. The language here recalls Bakhtin's characterization of the bildungsroman as "the novel of human *emergence*," though, of course, the direction in which Bakhtin develops this idea diverges significantly from the approach presented here ("Bildungsroman" 21).

17. Needham's "Undisciplined" has been largely influential in informing the widely accepted reading of the novel as concerned with David's struggles toward heart-discipline.

18. Others, however, such as Polhemus view Dickens's privileging the child's point of view as a positive replacement for scripture. In *David Copperfield* "Dickens's values and faith . . . are child-centered, domestic, and expressly scriptural. . . . Equating novels—his own scripture—with children, he continues in *Copperfield* to develop the theme of faith in the child and to adapt and transmute . . . material from the actual Scripture to it" ("Favorite" 4).

19. This attribute of Dickens's also marks a basic difference between the English and the German bildungsroman. Jeffers writes that to move from *Wilhelm Meister* to *David Copperfield* "is to reverse the ratio between philosophy and character" and that "in England

there were more characters, if not more things, for a novelist to discover ideas *in*" (*Apprenticeships* 55).

20. For readers consulting other editions, I provide the chapter followed by page number for all subsequent citations from the novel.

21. The churchgoing scene in which Jane sits between David and his beloved Dora further recalls the Murdstones' decisive role in separating him from his mother. Many have discussed the psychological continuities between David's mother and Dora. See, e.g., Ayres, *Dissenting*, esp. chapter 2.

22. This differentiation marks an additional key difference from Goethe's plan for Wilhelm Meister: the middle-class Wilhelm is made to assimilate upward into the aristocratic class via the Tower Society, whereas Dickens causes David to shun aristocratic values and, by remaining middle-class, to further define its character and values. Of course the authors themselves were of the classes they extolled in turn.

23. Chap. 24, 368, and chap. 32, 462, respectively. Some critics have read David's and Steerforth's relationship in the direct terms of homosexual love; in my view Oulton's "Undisciplined" makes a more convincing case that, without denying its homoerotic elements, their relationship is better described contextually through mid-nineteenth century ideas of romantic friendship.

24. Cf. Buckley, who describes Steerforth as "the irresistible Byronic *homme fatale*" (*Season* 38).

25. Steerforth's death by water (the storm scene of chapter 55 is a masterpiece in sustained escalation) at the very scene of his original crime indicates that Providence is active in the world of the novel.

26. Cf. Jeffers, who attributes Steerforth's and David's "crisis of vocation" to a mutual lack of guiding fathers, which, in turn, indicates a larger crisis of the nation's middle class (*Apprenticeships* 70).

27. Regarding these virtues, Oulton remarks that "the importance accorded to earnestness and discipline, though redolent of evangelical thought, does not imply a need for expiation" (*Literature* 106).

28. Garnett points to George Orwell's famous objection, voiced in his "Charles Dickens" essay, to Agnes as "the real legless angel of Victorian romance" ("Why" 213). Forster is not much more sanguine in his appraisal; he finds the "spoilt foolishness and tenderness of the loving little child-wife, Dora" preferable to the "too unfailing wisdom and self-sacrificing goodness of the angel-wife, Agnes" (*Life* 2:133). Cf. Nelson on Dickens's preoccupation with "nubile girls," such as Agnes, who exemplify and inspire "moral change" in others ("Dickens" 33).

29. Newey advances a similar view: "This is the Dickensian epiphany: not a leaping of the spirit in the presence of the Divine or . . . of Nature, but a becoming of healthy emotional and moral instincts in anthropocentric contexts" (*Scriptures* 3).

30. Needham compares this chapter to the "Everlasting Nay" and "Everlasting Yea" of Carlyle's *Sartor Resartus* ("Undisciplined" 103); Buckley also makes the general comparison of the novels (*Season* 40).

31. In his comparative study of *David Copperfield* and Wordsworth's *Prelude*, Dawson notes that while Wordsworth "emphasizes the power inherent in the Alpine scene" (the

same could certainly be said about Shelley's Alpine rhapsodies), David recognizes it as "a sign of conversion" and begins to turn his mind back to work and civilization (*Victorian* 135). Dawson does not explore the spiritual dimensions of this conversion per se, but in drawing a contrast to his Romantic predecessors, he instead likens David's emotional crisis to John Stuart Mill's: "With his hard work and his need for success, David is no young Werther or Childe Harold" (132).

Chapter 6: *Pierre,* or Melville's Anarchic Calvinist Bildungsroman

1. Robertson-Lorant, *Melville,* 356; Parker, *Herman,* 1:625; Lieber, *Endless,* 114; Arvin, *Melville,* 30.

2. Review from *Washington National Era,* August 19, 1852 (Higgins and Parker, *Critical* 36–37).

3. On the country-to-city movement in the nineteenth-century American bildungsroman, cf. Seelye, "Pierre," 390; and Holman, *Windows,* 169.

4. De Tocqueville composed and published his four volumes throughout the 1830s, coincident in time with the second wave of the "neo-Edwardsianism" of Second Great Awakening ministers such as Charles Grandison Finney (1792–1875) and the "'new measures' revivalism" (Conforti, "Invention" 105).

5. Historian Sellers makes the most dramatic transposition from theological into economic contexts. Economically the Arminian/antinomian controversy appears as "the magical spirituality of a parochial and fatalist countryside against the self-reliant effort of a cosmopolitan and activist market. While arminian [*sic*] moralism sanctioned competitive individualism and the market's rewards of wealth and status, antinomian new birth recharged rural America's communal egalitarianism in resistance" (*Market* 30–31). This "*Kulturkampf* . . . would decide American destiny on the private battlegrounds of every human relationship"(31).

6. In 1776 American Methodists made up only 3 percent of churchgoers, but by 1850 their numbers claimed 34 percent (Reynolds, *Waking* 127). For a more detailed presentation and comparison of statistics for these as well as other Protestant sects up through the Civil War, see Timothy L. Smith, *Revivalism,* 20–21.

7. Wilson generally attributes nineteenth-century premillennialism to elite circles and postmillennialism to popular circles ("History" 134, 138).

8. To give one notable instance of the direct social activist overlap with the New Divinity, moral reformer Lyman Beecher was a student of Timothy Dwight, Jonathan Edwards's grandson. Beecher spearheaded the American Bible Society and was the father of Harriet Beecher Stowe and suffragist Isabella Beecher Hooker. Although twentieth-century writers such as James Baldwin have long since sensitized readers to *Uncle Tom's Cabin*'s limitations, it is undeniable that Stowe's work did significantly contribute to the growing national disgust with and active resistance to the institution of slavery. See Reynolds, *Waking,* 131–32.

9. For a good account of Melville's relationship with Hawthorne at the time of *Pierre*'s composition, see Milder, *Exiled,* 126, 137. Melville's biographers typically count Melville's domestic situation in 1851 as a significant contribution to the tensions in *Pierre,* particularly those involving the similarities between Mrs. Glendinning and Maria Gansevoort.

Robertson-Lorant further notes that like Melville's father, "Pierre's father lived in France, amassed a collection of prints and engravings and a library of domestic and foreign books, and died when his son was twelve" (*Melville* 309). Milder (*Exiled* 131) as well as Higgins and Parker (*Critical* 6) report that Melville's father may also have had an illegitimate daughter. Finally on Melville's growing antagonism with "Young America" and his publishers, see Reynolds, *Waking*, 272–73; and Higgins and Parker, *Critical*, 12.

10. Parker notes that Melville possessed a history of the Berkshires and marked the section of his copy discussing Edwards's presence there (*Herman* 1:795–96). With respect to Melville's overall preoccupation with the legacy of American Calvinism, Herbert has argued similarly to Arvin that the Calvinist "theocentric system gave [Melville] a fundamental idiom in which to comprehend himself and his world; problems of doctrine were for him continuous with problems of experience" (*Moby-Dick* 15).

11. Subsequent numeric citations of *Pierre* shall follow this order: book, chapter, and page number.

12. Cf. Wright: "The fate of Pierre, like that of Ahab, is all out of proportion to its original cause" (*Melville's* 124). On the novel's "ponderous" symbolism, see also H. Bruce Franklin, *Wake*, 100.

13. See Davis, *After*, 25–27. Cf. Douglas's contention that Pierre's rebellion (ironically destined to fail) begins once he "conceive[s] of virility" (*Feminization* 310).

14. *Wilhelm Meister's Apprenticeship* made more than a passing impression on Melville; he was quoting from the novel as late as 1857 on his trip to Italy. See *Journals*, 111, 485; and Braswell, *Melville's*, 16. See also Sealts, *Melville's*, 61, 179; and Bercaw, *Melville's*, 85, no. 304. Sealts notes that around the same time, while visiting the Berkshires in the summer of 1850, Melville also acquired *A History of the County of Berkshire* (see n. 10) (*Melville's* 62).

15. With respect to German authors, it comes as no surprise that, especially as he grew older, Melville aligned temperamentally more closely with Schopenhauer than with Goethe. Sealts observes that Melville was, in fact, reading Schopenhauer during his last illness (*Melville's* 130). See also Braswell, *Melville's*, 15.

16. Elsewhere, however, around this time Melville is more balanced and indeed shows great humor and understanding in his treatment of Goethe. Melville's scenario of Goethe urging a man incapacitated with a toothache to "live in the all" is one such instance. See his letter to Hawthorne, June 1, 1851 (*Correspondence* 188–94).

17. Pierre's absolutism is frequently likened to that of Ahab. On this and related interpretations, see Douglas, *Feminization*, 305; Wright, *Melville's*, 120; and Watkins, *Puritan*, 39. For another version of the ways in which Pierre's absolutism relates to New England Calvinism generally, Elliott reads Pierre's central conflict as his inability to reconcile himself either to the Calvinist doctrine of God's sovereignty or to Emerson's call to self-reliance ("Art" 344).

18. Braswell also reads Isabel symbolically as representing the "spiritual soul" (*Melville's* 95).

19. Pierre makes this association during their second meeting: "To Pierre's dilated senses Isabel seemed to swim in an electric fluid; the vivid buckler of her brow seemed as a magnetic plate" (7, 3, 151). Pierre later reflects that at that moment Isabel "had bound

him to her by an extraordinary spell—both physical and spiritual—which henceforth it had become impossible for him to break" (151).

20. This insight Melville later develops into the character of Bartleby. More generally through the Miss Pennies, Melville implicates the reform-based activities associated with the evangelicals of the Second Great Awakening.

21. While Isabel's Christlike qualities seem fairly overt here, I do not lean too heavily on the connection; rather it is one of the many ways in which she manifests qualities of the many-faceted Absolute.

22. In addition to meaning "if" in Greek, *ei* could also indicate the second person singular of the verb "to be." The significance of this depends on how well, if at all, Melville knew his Greek.

23. More recently critics such as Spanos, in *Herman*, and Grenberg, in *Some*, emphasize the pamphlet's ironical or satirical dimensions, whereas Schneider is among earlier readers who attribute to it a greater degree of seriousness on Melville's part. The notable early exception that serves as a basis for the former interpretations appears in Lawrance Thompson's *Melville's*. Thompson calls Plinlimmon's pamphlet a "hoax"; "a caustic and satirical representation of those ethical rules of conduct by which . . . the majority of professed . . . Christians in his day governed their conduct: rules of practicality, profitableness, expediency" (272, 276). See also Obuchowski, "Melville's."

24. Colacurcio in turn emphasizes the philosophical over the emotionalist perspective: he reads the "plausible cynic" Plinlimmon as suggesting that people like Pierre "ought indeed to adjust their expectations, learning to thank the system of natural being for the gift of natural life itself—and to regard universal protest both as naïve and as a form of ingratitude rather than of piety" ("Charity" 59–60).

25. On Pierre's absolutist rejection of Saddle Meadows and his general absolutist character, cf. Reynolds, *Beneath*, 160–61; Davis, *After*, 31; Arvin, *Melville*, 203; and Wright, *Melville's*, 120.

26. I have found no more than passing mention of Melville's choice in naming Plinlimmon after the third-century philosopher. Braswell writes that while Melville doesn't directly reference Plotinus's work, he would have had access to portions of it from various sources (*Melville's* 14); Bercaw does identify the *Selected Works of Plotinus* as one of Melville's sources (*Melville's* 109). The ironies of Melville's choice could bear expanding, considering the primary emphasis Plotinus puts upon the concept of spiritual correspondences. Consider just one example from the *Enneads* that bears significant similarities to Plinlimmon's idea of correspondence between the world of the senses and God's world (here the "Intellectual sphere"): "The loveliness that is in the sense-realm is an index of the nobleness of the Intellectual sphere, displaying its power and its goodness alike: and all things are forever linked; the one order Intellectual in its being, the other of sense; one self-existent, the other eternally taking its being by participation in that first, and to the full of its power reproducing the Intellectual nature" (48 "The Soul's Descent into the Body" §6; 204).

27. For one the conditions of the Apostles in many ways mirror Melville's own during the period of the novel's composition. The introductory essay in Higgins and Parker

provides the most complete reconstruction of his increasingly dire personal circumstances and its influence on the composition of *Pierre;* cf. the historical note appended to the Northwestern edition of *Pierre.*

28. See Melville, *Correspondence,* 190. The debate between Jefferson and his old rival John Adams on the nature of aristocracy in America would seem relevant here. Melville appears to be suggesting in *Pierre*—and perhaps among Melville's contemporaries—that the world of Adams has prevailed: whereas Pierre's natural virtues are condemned to poverty and obscurity, the pseudo-aristocracy of his cousin Glen's entrenched wealth and talent for "graceful attitudes" positions him to all expectations of worldly success and fulfillment. See Braden, "Ye," esp. Jefferson's letter to Adams, October 28, 1813 (101–8), and Adams's reply of November 15, 1813 (111–18).

29. Cf. Grenberg's assertion that Plinlimmon assumes the qualities of "the only God Melville can conceive of in 1852" (*Some* 141); in Pierre's reaction to Plinlimmon, "nowhere . . . do we find a more telling statement of the mid-nineteenth-century individual's sense of having been betrayed by God" (143).

30. "Bartleby, the Scrivener" was first published soon after *Pierre* in 1853; given the emphasis on the marked presence of the "gregarious lawyers" in the church, it seems that Melville had planted in *Pierre* many germinal elements of the short story, both in the character of Plotinus Plinlimmon as well as in the setting. As Davis has suggested, in "Bartleby" Melville continued the antinomian theme as well as took "self-reliance to its logical conclusion [and] stripped away the transcendental faith that a single source feeds and unites all radically separate selves" ("Not" 50). I am suggesting here that this process—one that reaches its lowest point in Bartleby's "catatonic stillness"—is well under way in *Pierre* and serves as precedent for the radical separation Davis identifies in the short story.

31. For a similar leap in what may be called an idée fixe for Melville, see also his letter to Hawthorne, April 16, 1851 (*Correspondence* 184–87).

Chapter 7: "An impulse more tender and more purely expectant"

1. See King, *Iron,* 85; Duban, "Reverent," 247; Edel, *Henry,* 29–30. It should be observed that the Edwards to which James was exposed was mediated through, as Duban notes, ministers associated with the New Divinity and Second Great Awakening such as Samuel Hopkins and Edward Beecher (*Nature* 17). As I have indicated in the introduction and chapter 6, these and other nineteenth-century ministers refashioned Edwards's Calvinism to various degrees to be more compatible with the "Methodized" nineteenth-century American evangelicals.

2. Recently in "Reverent" Duban has argued that the elder Henry James's most original contribution to the history of philosophy derives from his ability to combine the evolutionary rhetoric of New Science with Edwardsian theology. See also Duban's *Nature.*

3. Subsequent references refer to this work as "AS." Nadelman, however, cautions readers from reading the narrative as a merely objective history: she calls the elder James's autobiography a blend of literature and philosophy, a symbolic dramatization of his movement from Calvinism toward Swedenborgianism, "a story of spiritual awareness rather than a recitation of historical events" ("Creating" 258–59).

4. Duban concisely summarizes the thought of James the elder as a reconfiguration of Swedenborgian spiritualism, socialist politics, and Edwardsian understanding of virtue as "love of Being in general" (*Nature* 14).

5. It is interesting to note the central role the artist plays in James's millennial scheme: in the conclusion to his early lecture "The Principle of Universality in Art," he describes artists as "harbingers of the perfect man" who will lead humanity on to realize "true moral poise" (135–36). Nadleman describes how the elder James's millenarianism remains specifically Christian-based ("Creating" 251); Duban alternately describes how, for James, socialism serves as the replacement for Christ's Second Coming. See also King, *Iron,* 89.

6. As for conversion itself, in "A Very Long Letter"—another version of spiritual autobiography in epistolary form—James writes that as he was reading Paul's Epistle to the Romans, he was arrested by the words "*Faith cometh by hearing.* I said to myself, Faith then means belief of the truth, and not any magical operation in the bosom" (379). King interprets this passage to indicate that James thereby reconfigures but essentially preserves "the central tenet of his father's faith: *sola fides*" (*Iron* 113).

7. In "Autobiographical Sketch" James replaces this experience with Dewhurst's having suffered "a severe illness which befell me from a gun-shot wound in my arm" (35).

8. Habegger argues that the experience at Frogmore Cottage was due in part to its resembling the house in which James Sr. convalesced after the amputation that in turn caused him to reexperience his psychological reaction to that early trauma. "Once again," he writes, "James's abiding temptation, a constant and suicidally exacting abeyance toward the Almighty, was upon him" (*Father* 223).

9. For a detailed study of William's own crisis, including its many remarkable parallels to his father's, see King's chapter in *Iron,* "Conscience to Neurosis: William James."

10. The following accounts stand out among two central commonplaces in James criticism: first that James is not dogmatically religious but retains a distinctly moral/ethical religious sense (including a compelling awareness of the existence of evil); second that James more or less replaced religion with art itself. For the first point, see Lewis, "James's," 248; Meissner, *Henry,* 104; Daugherty, "James," 318; Brooks, *Melodramatic,* 5; and Paterson, *Novel,* 8. For the second point, see Jöttkandt, *Acting,* 13; Frederick, *Darkened,* 230; and Gale, "Religion," 71.

11. I am indebted to Hovanec's *Henry* for the direct reference James makes to *Wilhelm Meister* in "Professor Fargo." The story is an oddly shabby-sinister combination of Goethe and Hawthorne that follows the machinations of characters in a small American traveling show.

12. The choice of edition, 1881 or 1908, always influences critical readings of the novel. Bloom objects to the later edition for the reason that Isabel seems too intelligent to allow Osmond to deceive her (*How* 179). Baym's comparative analysis of the two versions suggests that the "matrix of values" shifts from the more socially based phenomenon of "independence" to the comparatively detached concept of "awareness" ("Revision" 183, 199). Apart from respecting the fact that James in his mature artistic judgment arranged the novel in 1908 as he wished to present it to posterity, I have chosen the New York Edition precisely because it demonstrates deeper interest in developing the ontological questions

of character over comparatively ephemeral concerns. For an excellent discussion of revision in *The Portrait of a Lady* and the thorny issues surrounding James's habits of revision generally and with respect to the New York Edition, see Horne, *Henry*.

13. For instance Jöttkandt reads the novel's "philosophical problem" as how to bridge the gap between intelligible truth and the "laws of the sensible world" (*Acting* 13). Jöttkandt's conclusion is, perhaps, less convincing when she argues that this bridge consists in Isabel's enacting the Kantian categorical imperative in her return to Rome (28).

14. Meissner and Pippin make some of the most compelling arguments in this vein: Pippin denounces Isabel's formless and unguided education that gave rise to ideas "half-baked, none of them really attached, connected, thought through, or deep" (*Henry* 130). Meissner more moderately reads the novel as a "cautionary tale about how the mind, however gifted perceptually, is prey to the hazards of a spectatorial understanding when it remains untempered by lived experience" (*Henry* 82).

15. Subsequent citations of *The Portrait of a Lady* include chapter and page.

16. Several feminist critics have provided important discussions surrounding Isabel's early education and environment, including comparisons with *Jane Eyre*. In "Seated" Hadley considers the kind of books Isabel reads and their particular effects on her character; Golden's *Images* argues that James offers a moral argument against women's unguided reading because it sets them up for disappointment with the realities of domestic life. Berkson remarks on the fact that Isabel's study room is emblematic of her enduring faults in perspective ("Why" 59).

17. This language appears to prefigure James's definition of a novel as he articulates it in "The Art of Fiction" (1884): "A novel is in its broadest definition a personal impression of life: that, to begin with, constitutes its value, which is greater or less according to the intensity of the impression" (29). Isabel's error seems to be that her impressions remain general when they should be intensely personal. In a related vein, many have described Isabel as an artist manqué: for two different interpretations of this idea, see Sabiston, *Prison*, 126, 137; and Tanner, "Fearful," 81.

18. For a full discussion on this topic, see the section "Perfecting Perfection" in chapter 2.

19. Many have developed the correlation James draws between the ghost at Gardencourt and suffering, and most agree that over the course of the novel, James moves Isabel from an Emersonian into a Hawthornian frame of mind. Matthiessen makes this connection in his contention that Isabel eventually must assume a necessary "discipline of suffering" (*Henry* 183); more recently Meissner argues that "James suggests it is only through suffering that we arrive at a position from which the truth begins to come into focus" (*Henry* 82), See also Jeffers, *Apprenticeships*, 208; and Weisbuch, "James," 226.

20. James is at his most economical in contrasting the two women's points of view in the scene in chapter 19 where Merle argues that "every human being has his shell and that you must take the shell into account"; Isabel retorts that "nothing that belongs to me is a measure of me" (*PL* 19, 253). For a good discussion of this scene, see Jöttkandt, *Acting*, 13.

21. Pippin notes another similarity between the two characters, that Isabel's definition of independence is remarkably and tragically close to Osmond's "irony and willful negation" (*Henry* 139).

22. Berkson has argued convincingly that Isabel's decision to marry Osmond is well in keeping with her character and ideals. She points out that Isabel's newfound financial independence adds concrete meaning to her defining impulse to give: because neither Warburton nor Goodwood have any real need of her fortune, the significance of her gift diminishes in proportion. By giving the gift of her fortune to Osmond, Isabel determines "tragically and ironically" that such an action will allow her to preserve the greatest independence and autonomy compared with a marriage to Goodwood or Warburton ("Why" 57, 62). For further discussion on Isabel's reverence for the institution of marriage, see Krook's "Problems."

23. Many commentators have discussed the ways in which James fulfills, or does not fulfill, the expectations he sets up in the preface. For a consideration that concentrates on the related themes of free will and self-determination that reads against the ideas and expectations of the preface, see Rawlings, "Vital"; and Westbrook, *Free,* 236–38.

24. The elder Henry James, too, makes a similar observation in his autobiography: "the dark silent night usually let in the spectral eye of God, and set me to wondering and pondering evermore how I should effectively baffle its gaze" ("AS" 40). See Edel's commentary on this in *Untried Years* (21–30).

25. Ralph makes this ironically irrelevant declaration during the scene in which they argue over Isabel's engagement (*PL* 34, 396).

26. Of these few Maynard most explicitly compares the novels' endings: "Like Jane and Rochester, Isabel and Osmond will always be together in the closest of society/association, but rather than the hopeful and progressive flesh-of-my-flesh, soul-of-my-soul intimacy of the Rochesters, the Osmonds attain only a superficially attractive stasis, indicative of hopelessness, fruitlessness, and weariness of their relation" (*Beautiful* 141). For other comparisons between the novels, see also n. 16.

27. The *Oxford English Dictionary* traces the first use of *rapture* in this sense to Jacques Cousteau's 1953 description: "l'ivresse des grandes profondeurs" (rapture, or "intoxication of the great depths").

28. Many earlier critics have discussed Isabel's reaction in terms of what Stein has called her "sexual inertia." In his article Stein rather quaintly contends that Isabel's obsession with "the abstractions of independence and freedom" makes her "oblivious to her role in nature," which in turn compels her to become a "sexless woman ("Portrait" 178).

29. The passage most frequently associated with the Rapture appears in 1 Thessalonians 4:15–17. The last verse reads, "Then we which are alive *and* remain shall be caught up [L. *rapiemur,* fr. *rapio,* to seize and carry off, etc.] together with them in the clouds, to meet the Lord in the air: and so shall we ever be with the Lord." Interestingly the *Oxford English Dictionary* records rapture both in the sense of rising to heaven but also in the sense of sinking "downe to the lowest hell." Jonathan Edwards, of course, often uses language in the former sense to describe his uplifting visions of Christ.

30. Most critics provide various explanations regarding *The Portrait of a Lady*'s enigmatic and innovative conclusion. Roughly, and with overlap, Isabel's motives are usually traced to three sources: moral, psychological, and philosophical. The majority adhere to the first; see, e.g., Oehlschlaeger, *Love,* 196; Pippin, *Henry,* 142–43; Sabiston, *Prison,* 135–36;

and Jeffers, *Apprenticeships,* 116. For discussion of psychological motive, see, e.g., Duban, *Nature,* 164; Horne, *Henry,* 220; and Maynard, *Beautiful,* 140. See Jöttkandt, *Acting,* 28, for a philosophical reading.

Coda

1. T. S. Eliot to his mother, March 29, 1919 (*Letters* 331); from Charles W. Eliot to T. S. Eliot, July 25, 1919 (384).

2. James, *American Scene,* 48, hereafter designated as *AS.*

3. For an excellent history of Park Street Church in the larger context of Boston's contentious interdenominational scene, see Bendroth, *Fundamentalists,* esp. chap. 9, "Brimstone Corner."

4. Dwight's ordination was presided over by Lyman Beecher; Beecher's son Edward succeeded Dwight in his duties in 1826. See Dwight, *Select Discourses,* xxxvii; Bendroth, *Fundamentalists,* 158.

5. The story of the saving process is in itself dramatic. A series of three short articles on Park Street Church that appeared between 1902 and 1904 in the *Congregationalist and Christian World* provides details from a contemporary perspective. By 1903 the *Herald* had apparently failed to pay a portion of the promised sum, and by the time James came to Boston in the following year, matters had changed once more. The final article, which was published July 2, 1904—the same year and month James was in Boston—notes that between the infighting of church members and the intervention of other community activists, the sale was prevented, and the church was able to retain its location. The overall tone of the 1904 article seems just as attentive to the church's "patriotic and educational" landmark status as to its role "as a strong center of evangelical faith and a valiant supporter of missionary and evangelistic enterprises" (8). Cf. Bendroth, *Fundamentalists,* 163.

WORKS CITED

Abel, Elizabeth, Marianne Hirsch, and Elizabeth Langland, eds. *The Voyage In: Fictions of Female Development.* Hanover, N.H.: University Press of New England, 1983.

Ahlstrom, Sydney E. *A Religious History of the American People.* 1972. 2nd ed. New Haven: Yale University Press, 2004.

Aldrich, Elizabeth Kaspar. "'The Children of These Fathers': The Origins of an Autobiographical Tradition in America." In *First Person Singular: Studies in American Autobiography,* ed. A. Robert Lee, 15–36. New York: St. Martin's, 1988.

Anderson, Quentin. "Practical and Visionary Americans." *American Scholar* 45, no. 3 (1976): 405–18.

Argyle, Gisela. *Germany as Model and Monster: Allusions in English Fiction, 1830s–1930s.* Montreal: McGill-Queen's University Press, 2002.

Armstrong, Nancy. *Desire and Domestic Fiction: A Political History of the Novel.* New York: Oxford University Press, 1987.

Arvin, Newton. *Melville.* New York: Sloane, 1950.

Auerbach, Nina. *Romantic Imprisonment: Women and Other Glorified Outcasts.* New York: Columbia University Press, 1985.

Ayers, Brenda. *Dissenting Women in Dickens' Novels: The Subversion of Domestic Ideology.* Westport, Conn.: Greenwood, 1998.

Bakhtin, Mikhail Mikhaĭlovich. "The Bildungsroman and Its Significance in the History of Realism." In *Speech Genres and Other Late Essays,* 10–59. Austin: University of Texas Press, 1986.

——. "Epic and the Novel." In *The Dialogic Imagination,* edited by Michael Holquist, translated by Caryl Emerson and Michael Holquist, 3–40. Austin: University of Texas Press, 1981.

Barker, Juliet. *The Brontës.* New York: St. Martin's, 1994.

Barner, Wilfried. "Geheime Lenkung. Zur Turmgesellschaft in Goethes Wilhelm Meister." In *Goethe's Narrative Fiction,* edited by William J. Lillyman, 85–109. Berlin: de Gruyter, 1983.

Barr, Alan P. "Mourning Becomes David: Loss and the Victorian Restoration of Young Copperfield." *Dickens Quarterly* 24, no. 2 (2007): 63–77.

Baym, Nina. "Revision and Thematic Change in *The Portrait of a Lady.*" *Modern Fiction Studies* 22, no. 2 (1976): 183–200.

Beaty, Jerome. *Misreading Jane Eyre: A Postformalist Paradigm.* Columbus: Ohio State University Press, 1996.

Becker-Cantarino, Barbara, ed. and trans. *The Life of Lady Johanna Eleonora Petersen, Written by Herself: Pietism and Women's Autobiography in Seventeenth-Century Germany.* Chicago: University of Chicago Press, 2005.

Bell, Matthew. *The German Tradition of Psychology in Literature and Thought, 1700–1840.* Cambridge: Cambridge University Press, 2005.

Bendroth, Margaret Lamberts. *Fundamentalists in the City: Conflict and Division in Boston's Churches, 1885–1950.* New York: Oxford University Press, 2005.

Bercaw, Mary K. *Melville's Sources.* Evanston, Ill.: Northwestern University Press, 1987.

Bercovitch, Sacvan. *The Puritan Origins of the American Self.* New Haven: Yale University Press, 1975.

——. "The Ritual of American Autobiography: Edwards, Franklin, Thoreau." *Revue Française d'Etudes Americaines* 7, no. 14 (1982): 139–50.

Berkson, Dorothy. "Why Does She Marry Osmond? The Education of Isabel Archer." *American Transcendental Quarterly* 60 (1986): 53–71.

Beyreuther, Erich. *Der Junge Zinzendorf.* Marburg: Francke-Buchhandlung, 1957.

Die Bibel oder Die Heilige Schrift des Alten und Neuen Testaments nach der deutschen Uebersetzung von Dr. Martin Luther. Leipzig: Brockhaus. 1805.

Block, James E. *A Nation of Agents: The American Path to a Modern Self and Society.* Cambridge, Mass.: Belknap Press of Harvard University Press, 2002.

Bloom, Harold. *How to Read and Why.* New York: Scribner, 2000.

Blumhofer, Edith L., and Randall Balmer, eds. *Modern Christian Revivals.* Urbana: University of Illinois Press, 1993.

Boyle, Nicholas. *Goethe: The Poet and the Age.* 2 vols. Oxford: Clarendon, 1991–2000.

Braden, Bruce, ed. *"Ye Will Say I Am No Christian": The Thomas Jefferson/John Adams Correspondence on Religion, Morals, and Values.* Amherst, N.Y.: Prometheus, 2006.

Bradley, Ian. *The Call to Seriousness: The Evangelical Impact on the Victorians.* New York: Macmillan, 1976.

Brantley, Richard E. *Coordinates of Anglo-American Romanticism: Wesley, Edwards, Carlyle and Emerson.* Gainesville: University Press of Florida, 1993.

——. *Locke, Wesley, and the Method of English Romanticism.* Gainesville: University Press of Florida, 1984.

Braswell, William. *Melville's Religious Thought: An Essay in Interpretation.* 1943. New York: Pageant Books, 1959.

Bredahl, A. Carl, Jr. *Melville's Angles of Vision.* Gainesville: University Press of Florida, 1972.

Breitenbach, William. "Piety *and* Moralism: Edwards and the New Divinity." In *Jonathan Edwards and the American Experience,* edited by Nathan O. Hatch and Harry S. Stout, 177–204. New York: Oxford University Press, 1988.

Brontë, Charlotte. *Jane Eyre.* New York: Barnes & Noble, 1993.

——. *Letters.* 2 vols. Edited by Margaret Smith. Oxford: Oxford University Press, 1995–2000.

Brooks, Peter. *The Melodramatic Imagination: Balzac, Henry James, Melodrama, and the Mode of Excess.* New Haven: Yale University Press, 1976.

Buckley, Jerome Hamilton. *Season of Youth: The Bildungsroman from Dickens to Golding.* Cambridge, Mass.: Harvard University Press, 1974.

——. *The Victorian Temper.* Cambridge, Mass.: Harvard University Press, 1951.

Caldwell, Patricia. *The Puritan Conversion Narrative: The Beginnings of American Expression.* Cambridge: Cambridge University Press, 1983.

Carton, Evan. "What Feels an American? Evident Selves and Alienable Emotions in the New Man's World." In *Boys Don't Cry? Rethinking Narratives of Masculinity and Emotion in the U.S.,* edited by Milette Shamir and Jennifer Travis, 23–43. New York: Columbia University Press, 2002.

Carwardine, Richard. "The Second Great Awakening in Comparative Perspective: Revivals and Culture in the United States and Britain." In *Modern Christian Revivals,* edited by Edith L. Blumhofer and Randall Balmer, 84–100. Urbana: University of Illinois Press, 1993.

——. *Transatlantic Revivalism: Popular Evangelicalism in Britain and America, 1790–1865.* Westport, Conn.: Greenwood, 1978.

Chadwick, Owen. *The Victorian Church.* 2 vols. New York: Oxford University Press, 1966.

"Charles Dickens and Fictitious Literature." *Wesleyan-Methodist Magazine,* October 1853, 948–53.

Chase, Richard. *The American Novel and Its Tradition.* London: Bell, 1958.

Chesterton, G. K. *Charles Dickens.* London: Methuen, 1907.

Cirlot, J. E. *A Dictionary of Symbols.* Translated by Jack Sage. New York: Dorset, 1971.

Clapper, Gregory. "'True Religion' and the Affections: A Study of John Wesley's Abridgement of Jonathan Edwards's *Treatise on the Religious Affections.*" In *Wesleyan Theology Today,* edited by Theodore Runyon, 416–23. Nashville: Kingswood Books, 1985.

Cocalis, Susan L. "The Transformation of Bildung from an Image to an Ideal." *Monatshefte* 70, no. 4 (1978): 399–414.

Colacurcio, Michael. "Charity and Its Discontents: Pity and Politics in Melville's Fiction." In *There before Us: Religion, Literature, and Culture from Emerson to Wendell Berry,* edited by Roger Lundin, 49–79. Grand Rapids, Mich.: Eerdmans, 2007.

Cole, Natalie Bell. "'Amen in a Wrong Place': Charles Dickens Imagines the Victorian Church." In *Victorian Religious Discourse: New Directions in Criticism,* edited by Jude V. Nixon, 205–34. New York: Palgrave Macmillan, 2004.

Conforti, Joseph. "The Invention of the Great Awakening, 1795–1842." *Early American Literature* 26, no. 2 (1991): 99–118.

Conner, Frederick William. *Cosmic Optimism: A Study of the Interpretation of Evolution by American Poets from Emerson to Robinson.* Gainesville: University Press of Florida, 1949.

Cordery, Gareth. "*David Copperfield.*" *Companion to Charles Dickens,* edited by David Paroissien, 369–79. Oxford: Blackwell, 2008.

Cotton, John. "A Treatise of the Covenant of Grace." In *The Puritans in America: A Narrative Anthology,* edited by Alan Heimert and Andrew Delbanco. Cambridge, Mass.: Harvard University Press, 1985.

Couser, G. Thomas. *American Autobiography: The Prophetic Mode.* Amherst: University of Massachusetts Press, 1979.

Culler, A. Dwight. *The Poetry of Tennyson.* New Haven: Yale University Press, 1977.

Cunningham, Valentine. "Dickens and Christianity." In *Companion to Charles Dickens,* edited by David Paroissien, 255–76. Oxford: Blackwell, 2008.

——. *Everywhere Spoken Against: Dissent in the Victorian Novel.* Oxford: Clarendon, 1975.

Daugherty, Sarah B. "James, Renan, and the Religion of Consciousness." *Comparative Literature Studies* 16, no. 4 (1979): 318–31.

Davis, Clark. *After the Whale: Melville in the Wake of "Moby-Dick."* Tuscaloosa: University of Alabama Press, 1995.

——. "'Not like Any Form of Activity': Waiting in Emerson, Melville, and Weil." *Common Knowledge* 15, no. 1 (2009): 39–58.

Dawson, Carl. *Victorian Noon: English Literature in 1850.* Baltimore: Johns Hopkins University Press, 1979.

Delaney, Paul. *British Autobiography in the Seventeenth Century.* London: Routledge, 1969.

Dickens, Charles. *David Copperfield.* Edited by Jeremy Tambling. New York: Penguin, 2004.

——. *Sketches by Boz.* Edited by Michael Slater. Columbus: Ohio State University Press, 1994.

Dieckmann, Liselotte, trans. Introduction to *Correspondence between Goethe and Schiller: 1794–1805,* ix–xvi. New York: Lang, 1994.

Dilthey, Wilhelm. *Das Erlebnis und die Dichtung: Lessing, Goethe, Novalis, Hölderlin.* Göttingen: Vandenhoeck & Ruprecht, 1970.

——. *Gesammelte Schriften.* Bd. 6. Stuttgart: Teubner, 1958.

——. "The Imagination of the Poet: Elements for a Poetics." Translated by Louis Agosta and Rudolf A. Makkreel. In *Selected Works,* vol. 5, edited by Rudolf A. Makkreel and Frithjof Rodi, 29–174. Princeton: Princeton University Press, 1985.

——. *Das Leben Schleiermachers.* Vol. 1. Berlin: Reimer, 1870.

Douglas, Ann. *The Feminization of American Culture.* 1977. New York: Anchor, 1988.

Dreyer, Frederick. "Evangelical Thought: John Wesley and Jonathan Edwards." *Albion* 19, no. 2 (1987): 177–92.

——. "Faith and Experience in the Thought of John Wesley." *American Historical Review* 88 (1983): 12–30.

Duban, James. *The Nature of True Virtue: Theology, Psychology, and Politics in the Writings of Henry James, Sr.* Madison, N.J.: Fairleigh Dickinson University Press, 2001.

——. "'A Reverent and Obedient Evolution': Jonathan Edwards, the New Science, and the Socialism of Henry James Sr." *Journal of Speculative Philosophy* 23, no. 3 (2009): 244–61.

Dupee, F. W., ed. *The Question of Henry James.* New York: Holt, 1945.

Dwight, Sereno Edwards. *The Life of President Edwards.* New York: Carvill, 1830.

——. *Select Discourses of Sereno Edwards Dwight, D.D.: Pastor of Park Street Church, Boston, and President of Hamilton College in New York.* Boston: Crocker & Brewster, 1851.

Eagleton, Terry. *Myths of Power: A Marxist Study of the Brontës.* New York: Palgrave, 1975.

Ebner, Dean. *Autobiography in Seventeenth-Century England: Theology and the Self.* The Hague: Mouton, 1971.

Edel, Leon. *Henry James: The Untried Years.* London: Hart-Davis, 1953.

Edmunds, Kathryn R. "'Ich bin gebildet genug . . . um zu lieben und zu trauern': Wilhelm Meister's Apprenticeship in Mourning." *Germanic Review* 71, no. 2 (1996): 83–100.

Edwards, Jonathan. "A Divine and Supernatural Light." In *Works,* vol. 17, edited by Mark Valeri, 405–26. New Haven: Yale University Press, 1999.

——. "The Mind." In *Works,* vol. 6, edited by Wallace E. Anderson, 332–93. New Haven: Yale University Press, 1980.

——. "Personal Narrative." In *Works,* vol. 16, edited by Harry S. Stout, 790–804. New Haven: Yale University Press, 1998.

——. "The 'Spider' Letter." In *Works,* vol. 6, edited by Wallace E. Anderson, 163–69. New Haven: Yale University Press, 1980.

——. "A Treatise Concerning Religious Affections." In *Works,* vol. 2, edited by John E. Smith, 365–76. New Haven: Yale University Press, 1959.

Eliot, T. S. *Letters.* Vol. 1. Edited by Valerie Holt. New York: Harcourt, 1988.

Elliott, Emory. "Art, Religion, and the Problem of Authority in *Pierre.*" In *Ideology and Classic American Literature,* edited by Sacvan Bercovitch and Myra Jehlen, 337–51. Cambridge: Cambridge University Press, 1986.

Ellis, Lorna. *Appearing to Diminish: Female Development and the British Bildungsroman, 1750–1850.* Lewisburg, Penn.: Bucknell University Press, 1999.

English, John C. "John Wesley and the English Enlightenment: An 'Appeal to Men of Reason and Religion.'" *Studies on Voltaire and the Eighteenth Century* 263 (1989): 400–403.

Fessenden, Tracy. *Culture and Redemption: Religion, the Secular, and American Literature.* Princeton: Princeton University Press, 2007.

Filonowicz, Joseph Duke. *Fellow-Feeling and the Moral Life.* Cambridge: Cambridge University Press, 2008.

Finney, Charles G. "What a Revival of Religion Is." 1835. In *Religion in America,* edited by James T. Baker, 135–40. Belmont, Cal.: Thompson, 2006.

Flory, Wendy Stallard. "Melville and Isabel: The Author and the Woman within the 'Inside Narrative' of *Pierre.*" In *Melville and Women,* edited by Elizabeth Schultz and Haskell Springer, 121–40. Kent, Ohio: Kent State University Press, 2006.

Forster, John. *The Life of Charles Dickens.* 1870. 2 vols. New York: Scribner, 1902.

Fraiman, Susan. *Unbecoming Women: British Women Writers and the Novel of Development.* New York: Columbia University Press, 1993.

Franklin, H. Bruce. *The Wake of the Gods: Melville's Mythology.* Stanford: Stanford University Press, 1963.

Franklin, J. Jeffrey. "The Merging of Spiritualities: Jane Eyre as Missionary of Love." *Nineteenth-Century Literature* 49, no. 4 (1995): 456–82.

Frederick, John T. *The Darkened Sky: Nineteenth-Century American Novelists and Religion.* Notre Dame: University of Notre Dame Press, 1969.

Gale, Robert L. "Religion Imagery in Henry James's Fiction." *Modern Fiction Studies* 3, no. 1 (1957): 64–72.

Gallagher, Susan VanZanten. "*Jane Eyre* and Christianity." In *Approaches to Teaching Brontë's "Jane Eyre,"* edited by Diane Long Hoeveler and Beth Lau, 62–68. New York: MLA, 1993.

Garnett, Robert R. "Why Not Sophy? Desire and Agnes in *David Copperfield.*" *Dickens Quarterly* 14, no. 4 (1997): 213–31.

Gaskell, Elizabeth. *The Life of Charlotte Brontë.* 1857. Oxford: Oxford University Press, 1996.

George, Robert F. "The Evangelical Revival and Charlotte Brontë's *Jane Eyre.*" Ph.D. diss. University of Florida, 1981.

Gérin, Winifred. Introduction to *Five Novelettes,* by Charlotte Brontë. London: Folio, 1971.

Gilbert, Sandra M. "*Jane Eyre* and the Secrets of Furious Lovemaking." *Novel* 31, no. 3 (1998): 351–72.

Gilbert, Sandra M., and Susan Gubar. *The Madwoman in the Attic: The Woman Writer and the Nineteenth-Century Literary Imagination.* New Haven: Yale University Press, 1979.

Goethe, Johann Wolfgang von. *Sämtliche Werke.* Vol. 9. Edited by Wilhelm Voßkamp and Herbert Jaumann. Frankfurt: Deutscher Klassiker, 1992.

——. Sämtliche Werke. Vol. 14. Edited by Klaus-Detlef Müller. Frankfurt: Deutscher Klassiker, 1996.

——. *Sämtliche Werke.* Vol. 31. Edited by Volker C. Dörr and Norbert Oellers. Frankfurt: Deutscher Klassiker, 1998.

——. *Wilhelm Meister's Apprenticeship.* Vol. 9 of *The Collected Works.* Edited and translated by Eric A. Blackall. Princeton: Princeton University Press, 1989.

Golden, Catherine J. *Images of the Woman Reader in Victorian British and American Fiction.* Gainesville: University Press of Florida, 2003.

Goozé, Marjanne E., ed. *Challenging Separate Spheres: Female Bildung in Eighteenth- and Nineteenth-Century Germany.* Oxford: Lang, 2007.

Gordis, Lisa M. "The Conversion Narrative in Early America." In *Companion to the Literatures of Colonial America,* edited by Susan Castillo and Ivy Schweitzer, 369–86. Oxford: Blackwell, 2005.

Green, Richard. *The Works of John and Charles Wesley: A Bibliography.* 2nd ed. London: Methodist Publishing House, 1906.

Grenberg, Bruce L. *Some Other World to Find: Quest and Negation in the Works of Herman Melville.* Urbana: University of Illinois Press, 1989.

Griesinger, Emily. "Charlotte Brontë's Religion: Faith, Feminism, and *Jane Eyre.*" *Christianity and Literature* 58, no. 1 (2008): 29–59.

Griffith, John. "Jonathan Edwards as a Literary Artist." *Criticism* 15, no. 2 (1973): 156–73.

Gunn, Giles, ed. *Henry James, Sr.: A Selection of His Writings.* Chicago: ALA, 1974.

Habegger, Alfred. *The Father: A Life of Henry James, Sr.* New York: Farrar, Straus & Giroux, 1994.

Hadley, Tessa. "Seated Alone with a Book . . ." *Henry James Review* 26, no. 3 (Fall): 229–36.

Haigwood, Laura. "*Jane Eyre,* Eros, and Evangelicalism." *Victorian Newsletter* 104 (2003): 4–12.

Hardin, James, ed. *Reflection and Action: Essays on the Bildungsroman.* Columbia: University of South Carolina Press, 1991.

Hardy, Barbara. *The Moral Art of Dickens.* London: Athlone, 1970.

Haroutunian, Joseph. *Piety versus Moralism: The Passing of the New England Theology.* 1932. Hamden, Conn.: Archon, 1964.

Harrison, G. Elsie. *The Clue to the Brontës.* London: Methuen, 1948.

Hatch, Nathan O. *The Democratization of American Christianity.* New Haven: Yale University Press, 1989.

Herbert, T. Walker, Jr. *Moby-Dick and Calvinism: A World Dismantled.* New Brunswick, N.J.: Rutgers University Press, 1977.

Higgins, Brian, and Hershel Parker. *Critical Essays on Herman Melville's "Pierre; or, the Ambiguities."* Boston: Hall, 1983.

Higginson, Francis Wentworth. "Henry James, Jr." 1879. In *The Magnificent Activist: The Writings of Thomas Wentworth Higginson*, edited by Howard N. Meyer, 581–86. Cambridge, Mass.: Da Capo Press, 2000.

Hindley, J. Clifford. "The Philosophy of Enthusiasm: A Study in the Origins of 'Experimental Theology.'" *London Quarterly and Holborn Review* 182 (1957): 99–109, 199–210.

Hindmarsh, D. Bruce. *The Evangelical Conversion Narrative: Spiritual Autobiography in Early Modern England.* Oxford: Oxford University Press, 2005.

Hirsch, Marianne. "Spiritual bildung: The Beautiful Soul as Paradigm." In *The Voyage In: Fictions of Female Development*, 23–48. Hanover, N.H.: University Press of New England, 1983.

Hollington, Michael. "*David Copperfield* and *Wilhelm Meister*: A Preliminary *Rapprochement*." *Q/W/E/R/T/Y* 6 (1996): 129–38.

Holman, C. Hugh. *Windows on the World: Essays on American Social Fiction.* Knoxville: University of Tennessee Press, 1979.

Horne, Philip. *Henry James and Revision.* Oxford: Clarendon, 1990.

House, Humphry. *The Dickens World.* 2nd ed. London: Oxford University Press, 1941.

Hovanec, Evelyn A. *Henry James and Germany.* Amsterdam: Rodopi, 1978.

Howe, Susanne. *Wilhelm Meister and His English Kinsmen: Apprentices to Life.* New York: Columbia University Press, 1930.

Hutcheson, Francis. "An Inquiry Concerning the Original of Our Ideas of Virtue or Moral Good." 1725. In *British Moralists: 1650–1800*, edited by D. D. Raphael, 261–99. Oxford: Oxford University Press, 1969.

Imbarrato, Susan Clair. "Early American Autobiography." In *Oxford Handbook of Early American Literature*, edited by Kevin J. Hayes, 395–414. Oxford: Oxford University Press, 2008.

Imlay, Elizabeth. *Charlotte Brontë and the Mysteries of Love: Myth and Allegory in Jane Eyre.* New York: St. Martin's, 1989.

"In Brief." *Congregationalist and Christian World*, April 11, 1903, 513.

Jacobs, Jürgen. *Wilhelm Meister und seine Brüder: Untersuchungen zum deutschen Bildungsroman.* Munich: Fink, 1972.

James, Henry. *The American Scene.* 1907. Edited by Leon Edel. Bloomington: Indiana University Press, 1968.

——. "The Art of Fiction." In *The House of Fiction*, edited by Leon Edel, 23–46. London: Hart-Davis, 1957.

——. *Complete Notebooks.* Edited by Leon Edel and Lyall H. Powers. New York: Oxford University Press, 1987.

——. *Henry James: A Life in Letters.* Edited by Philip Horne. New York: Viking, 1999.

——. "Johann Wolfgang von Goethe." 1865. In *Literary Criticism*, edited by Leon Edel and Mark Wilson, 944–49. New York: Library of America, 1984.

——. *Notebooks of Henry James.* Edited by F. O. Matthiessen. New York: Oxford University Press, 1947.

——. "Notes of a Son and Brother." 1914. In *Autobiography*, edited by Frederick W. Dupee, 239–546. New York: Criterion, 1956.

——. *The Portrait of a Lady.* Edited by Geoffrey Moore. New York: Penguin, 1984.

———. "A Small Boy and Others." 1913. In *Autobiography,* edited by Frederick W. Dupee, 3–238. New York: Criterion, 1956.

James, Henry, Sr. "Autobiographical Sketch." 1884. In *Henry James, Sr.: A Selection of His Writings,* edited by Giles Gunn, 34–53. Chicago: ALA, 1974.

———. "Society the Redeemed Form of Man." 1879. In *Henry James, Sr.: A Selection of His Writings,* edited by Giles Gunn, 54–68. Chicago: ALA, 1974.

———. "The Principle of Universality in Art." 1850–51. In *Lectures and Miscellanies,* 101–36. New York: Redfield, 1852.

———. "A Very Long Letter." In *Lectures and Miscellanies,* 375–406. New York: Redfield, 1852.

James, William. *The Varieties of Religious Experience: A Study in Human Nature.* Centenary Edition. Edited by Eugene Taylor and Jeremy Carrette. London: Routledge, 2002.

Jay, Elizabeth. *The Religion of the Heart: Anglican Evangelicalism and the Nineteenth-Century Novel.* Oxford: Clarendon, 1979.

Jeffers, Thomas. *Apprenticeships: The Bildungsroman from Goethe to Santayana.* New York: Palgrave Macmillan, 2005.

———. "Forms of Misprision: The Early and Mid-Victorian Reception of Goethe's *Bildungsidee.*" *University of Toronto Quarterly* 57, no. 4 (1988): 501–15.

Jöttkandt, Sigi. *Acting Beautifully: Henry James and the Ethical Aesthetic.* Albany: SUNY Press, 2005.

Kant, Immanuel. "Beantwortung der Frage: Was ist Aufklärung?" 1784. In *Werke,* vol. 8,S33–42. Edited by Heinrich Maier. Berlin: de Gruyter, 1968.

Kemper, Hans-Georg, and Hans Schneider, eds. *Goethe und der Pietsmus.* Halle: Verlag der Franckeschen Stiftungen, 2001.

Kent, William. *Dickens and Religion.* London: Watts, 1930.

Kerry, Paul E. *Enlightenment Thought in the Writings of Goethe: A Contribution to the History of Ideas.* Rochester, N.Y.: Camden House, 2001.

King, John Owen, III. *The Iron of Melancholy: Structures of Spiritual Conversion in America from the Puritan Conscience to Victorian Neurosis.* Middleton, Conn.: Wesleyan University Press, 1983.

Knies, Earl A. *The Art of Charlotte Brontë.* Athens: Ohio University Press, 1969.

Kontje, Todd. *The German Bildungsroman: History of a National Genre.* Columbia, S.C.: Camden House, 1993.

Krook, Dorothea. "Two Problems in *The Portrait of a Lady.*" In *Twentieth-Century Interpretations of "The Portrait of a Lady,"* edited by Peter Buitenhuis, 97–106. Englewood Cliffs, N.J.: Prentice-Hall, 1968.

Lamonaca, Maria. "Jane's Crown of Thorns: Feminism and Christianity in *Jane Eyre.*" *Studies in the Novel* 34, no. 3 (2002): 245–63.

Larson, Janet L. *Dickens and the Broken Scripture.* Athens: University of Georgia Press, 1985.

Leavis, Q. D. "Dickens and Tolstoy: The Case for a Serious View of *David Copperfield.*" In *Dickens the Novelist,* by F. R. Leavis and Q. D. Leavis, 34–117. London: Chatto & Windus, 1970.

Levine, George. *Darwin and the Novelists: Patterns of Science in Victorian Fiction.* Cambridge, Mass.: Harvard University Press, 1988.

———. "Dickens, Secularism, and Agency." In *Contemporary Dickens*, edited by Eileen Gillooly and Deirdre David, 13–34. Columbus: Ohio State University Press, 2009.

———. "Jane, David, and the Bildungsroman." In *How to Read the Victorian Novel*, 81–99. Malden, Mass.: Blackwell, 2008.

———. *Realism, Ethics and Secularism: Essays on Victorian Literature and Science.* Cambridge: Cambridge University Press, 2008.

Lewis, Pericles. "James's Sick Souls." *Henry James Review* 22, no. 3 (2001): 248–58.

Lieber, Todd M. *Endless Experiments: Essays on the Heroic Experience in American Romanticism.* Columbus: Ohio State University Press, 1973.

Lockbridge, Lawrence S. *The Ethics of Romanticism.* Cambridge: Cambridge University Press, 1989.

Lukács, Georg. *Goethe und Seine Zeit.* Berlin: Aufbau, 1949.

Maclear, James Fulton. "'The Heart of New England Rent': The Mystical Element in Early Puritan History." *Mississippi Valley Historical Review* 42, no. 4 (1956): 621–52.

Mahoney, Dennis F. "The Apprenticeship of the Reader: the Bildungsroman of the 'Age of Goethe.'" 1986. In *Reflection and Action: Essays on the Bildungsroman*, edited by James Hardin, 91–117. Columbia: University of South Carolina Press, 1991.

Maier, Sarah E. "Portraits of the Girl-Child: Female Bildungsroman in Victorian Fiction." *Literature Compass* 4, no. 1 (2007): 317–35.

Martini, Fritz. "Bildungsroman: Term and Theory." In *Reflection and Action: Essays on the Bildungsroman*, edited by James Hardin, 1–25. Columbia: University of South Carolina Press, 1991.

———. "Der Bildungsroman: Zur Geschichte des Wortes und der Theorie." *Deutsche Vierteljahrsschrift für Literaturwissenschaft und Geistegeschichte* 35 (1961): 44–63.

Marsden, George M. *Jonathan Edwards: A Life.* New Haven: Yale University Press, 2003.

Matthews, Rex D. "'With Eyes of Faith': Spiritual Experience and the Knowledge of God in the Theology of John Wesley." In *Wesleyan Theology Today*, edited by Theodore Runyon, 406–15. Nashville: Kingswood Books, 1985.

Matthiessen, F.O. *American Renaissance.* London: Oxford University Press, 1941.

———. *Henry James: The Major Phase.* London: Oxford University Press, 1944.

Maynard, John. "The Bildungsroman." In *A Companion to the Victorian Novel*, edited by Patrick Brantlinger and William B. Thesing, 279–301. Malden, Mass.: Blackwell, 2002.

———. *Charlotte Brontë and Sexuality.* Cambridge: Cambridge University Press, 1984.

———. "The Brontës and Religion." In *Cambridge Companion to the Brontës*, 192–213. Cambridge: Cambridge University Press, 2002.

Maynard, Lee Anna. *Beautiful Boredom: Idleness and Feminine Self-Realization in the Victorian Novel.* Jefferson, N.C.: McFarland, 2009.

McCarthy, Patrick. "Making for Home: David Copperfield and His Fellow Travelers." In *Homes and Homelessness in the Victorian Imagination*, edited by Murray Baumgarten and H. M. Daleski, 21–32. New York: AMS, 1998.

M'Clintock, Rev. John. *Cyclopaedia of Biblical, Theological, and Ecclesiastical Literature.* Vol. 5. New York: Harper, 1878.

McNees, Eleanor, ed. *The Development of the Novel: Literary Sources and Documents.* 3 vols. Mountfield, East Sussex: Helm Information, 2006.

Mealey, Mark T. "Tilting at Windmills: John Wesley's Reading of John Locke's Epistemology." *Bulletin of the John Rylands University Library of Manchester* 85, no. 2–3 (2003): 331–46.

Meckier, Jerome. *Hidden Rivalries in Victorian Fiction: Dickens, Realism, and Revaluation.* Lexington: University Press of Kentucky, 1987.

Meissner, Collin. *Henry James and the Language of Experience.* Cambridge: Cambridge University Press, 1999.

Melville, Herman. *Correspondence.* Edited by Lynn Horth. Evanston, Ill.: Northwestern University Press, 1993.

——. *Journals.* Edited by Howard C. Horsford and Lynn Horth. Evanston, Ill.: Northwestern University Press, 1989.

——. *Moby-Dick.* 1851. New York: Modern Library, 2000.

——. *Pierre.* 1852. Edited by Harrison Hayford, Hershel Parker, and G. Thomas Tanselle. Evanston, Ill.: Northwestern University Press, 1971.

Meyer, Dietrich, et al. *Graf ohne Grenzen: Leben und Werk von Nikolaus Ludwig Graf von Zinzendorf.* Herrnhut: Comeniusbuchhandlung Herrnhut, 2000.

Meyer, Howard N., ed. *The Magnificent Activist: The Writings of Thomas Wentworth Higginson.* Cambridge, Mass.: Da Capo, 2000.

Milder, Robert. *Exiled Royalties: Melville and the Life We Imagine.* Oxford: Oxford University Press, 2006.

Miller, Perry. "Jonathan Edwards and the Sense of the Heart." *Harvard Theological Review* 41, no. 2 (1948): 123–45.

Moglen, Helene. *Charlotte Brontë: The Self Conceived.* New York: Norton, 1976.

Moretti, Franco. *The Way of the World: The Bildungsroman in European Culture.* 2nd ed. Translated by Albert Sbragia. London: Verso, 2000.

Morgan, Edmund S. *Visible Saints: The History of a Puritan Idea.* New York: New York University Press, 1963.

Moseley, James G., Jr. *A Complex Inheritance: The Idea of Self-Transcendence in the Theology of Henry James Sr., and the Novels of Henry James.* Missoula, Mon.: Scholars, 1975.

Myer, Valerie Grosvenor. *Charlotte Brontë: Truculent Spirit.* London: Vision, 1987.

Nadelman, Heather L. "Creating an Immortal Life: A Consideration of the Autobiography of Henry James, Sr." *New England Quarterly* 66, no. 2 (1993): 247–68.

Needham, Gwendolyn B. "The Undisciplined Heart of David Copperfield." *Nineteenth-Century Fiction* 9., no 2 (1954): 81–107.

Nelson, Harland N. "Dickens, Religion, and Nubile Girls." *Dickens Quarterly* 14, no. 1 (1997): 33–38.

Newey, Vincent. *The Scriptures of Charles Dickens: Novels of Ideology, Novels of the Self.* Aldershot: Ashgate, 2004.

Newsom, Robert. "Dickens and the Goods." *Contemporary Dickens,* edited by Eileen Gillooly and Deirdre David, 35–52. Columbus: Ohio State University Press, 2009.

Nisbet, H. B. "'Was ist *Aufklärung*?': The Concept of Enlightenment in Eighteenth-Century Germany." *Journal of European Studies* 12, no. 2 (1982): 77–95.

Noll, Mark A. "Jonathan Edwards as a Figure in Literary History." In *Jonathan Edwards and the American Experience,* edited by Nathan O. Hatch and Harry S. Stout, 260–87. New York: Oxford University Press, 1988.

Norton, Robert E. *Herder's Aesthetics and the European Enlightenment.* Ithaca, N.Y.: Cornell University Press, 1991.

Obuchowski, Peter A. "Melville's *Pierre:* Plinlimmon as a Satirist Satirized." *CLA Journal* 39, no. 4 (1996): 489–97.

Oehlschlaeger, Fritz. *Love and Good Reasons: Postliberal Approaches to Christian Ethics and Literature.* Durham, N.C.: Duke University Press, 2003.

Orcibal, J. "The Theological Originality of John Wesley and Continental Spirituality." Translated by R. J. A. Sharp. In *A History of the Methodist Church in Great Britain,* vol. 1, edited by Rupert E. Davies and E. Gordon Rupp,83–111. London: Epworth, 1965.

Oulton, Carolyn W. de la L. *Literature and Religion in Mid-Victorian England: From Dickens to Eliot.* New York: Palgrave Macmillan, 2003.

———. "'My Undisciplined Heart': Romantic Friendship in *David Copperfield.*" *Dickens Quarterly* 21, no. 3 (2004): 157–69.

Outler, Albert C., ed. *John Wesley.* New York: Oxford University Press, 1964.

"Park Street Church and Its Problem." *Congregationalist and Christian World,* July 2, 1904, 8–9.

"Park Street Church, Boston, and Its Problem." *Congregationalist and Christian World,* December 13, 1902, 1.

Parker, Hershel. *Herman Melville: A Biography.* 2 vols. Baltimore: Johns Hopkins University Press, 1996.

Paterson, John. *The Novel as Faith: The Gospel According to James, Hardy, Conrad, Joyce, Lawrence, and Virginia Woolf.* Boston: Gambit, 1973.

Payne, Rodger M. *The Self and the Sacred: Conversion and Autobiography in Early American Protestantism.* Knoxville: University of Tennessee Press, 1998.

Petrie, Paul R. "Hawthorne in Time of Schism: 'The Gentle Boy' and the Second Great Awakening." In *Early Protestantism and American Culture,* edited by Michael Schuldiner, 150–78. Lewiston, N.Y.: Mellen, 1996.

Phillips, Marion J. "Charlotte Brontë and the Priesthood of All Believers." *Brontë Studies* 20, no. 3 (1991): 145–55.

———. "Charlotte Brontë's Favourite Preacher: Frederick Denison John Maurice (1805–1872)." *Brontë Studies* 20, no. 2 (1990): 77–88.

Pickering, Samuel, Jr. *The Moral Tradition in English Fiction: 1785–1850.* Hanover, N.H.: University Press of New England, 1976.

Pippin, Robert. *Henry James and Modern Moral Life.* Cambridge: Cambridge University Press, 2000.

Pitts, Carolyn. "Church of the Ascension (Protestant Episcopal)." In *National Register of Historic Places Inventory—Nomination Form.* Washington, D.C.: National Park Service, History Division, 1986.

Plotinus. *The Six Enneads.* Translated by Stephen MacKenna and B. S. Page. Chicago: Benton, 1952.

Polhemus, Robert M. "The Favorite Child: David Copperfield and the Scriptural Issue of Child-Wives." In *Homes and Homelessness in the Victorian Imagination,* edited by Murray Baumgarten and H. M. Daleski, 3–20. New York: AMS, 1998.

Pope, Norris. *Dickens and Charity.* New York: Columbia University Press, 1978.

Porteous, N.W. "Image of God." *Interpreter's Dictionary of the Bible.* Ed. George Arthur Buttrick et al. New York: Abingdon Press, 1962.

Qualls, Barry V. *The Secular Pilgrims of Victorian Fiction: The Novel as Book of Life.* Cambridge: Cambridge University Press, 1982.

Rack, Henry. *Reasonable Enthusiast: John Wesley and the Rise of Methodism.* 2nd ed. Nashville: Abingdon, 1992.

Raphael, D. D. *British Moralists, 1650–1800.* Oxford: Clarendon, 1969.

Ratchford, Fannie E., ed. *Legends of Angria.* By Charlotte Brontë. New Haven: Yale University Press, 1933.

Rawlings, Peter. "Vital Illusions in *The Portrait of a Lady.*" In *Companion to Henry James,* edited by Greg W. Zacharias, 70–87. Oxford: Wiley-Blackwell, 2008.

Reilly, Robert J. "Henry James and the Morality of Fiction." *American Literature* 39, no. 1 (1967): 1–30.

Reynolds, David S. *Beneath the American Renaissance: The Subversive Imagination in the Age of Emerson and Melville.* New York: Knopf, 1988.

——. *Waking Giant: America in the Age of Jackson.* New York: HarperCollins, 2008.

Rich, Adrienne. "Jane Eyre: The Temptations of a Motherless Woman." In *On Lies, Secrets, and Silence,* 89–107. New York: Norton, 1979.

[Rigby, Elizabeth]. "Article V." *Quarterly Review* 84, no. 167 (1848):153–85.

Rivers, Isabel. *Reason, Grace and Sentiment: A Study of the Language of Religion and Ethics in England, 1660–1780.* Vol. 1, *Whichcote to Wesley.* Cambridge: Cambridge University Press, 1991.

Robertson-Lorant, Laurie. *Melville: A Biography.* New York: Clarkson Potter, 1996.

Rogers, Charles. "John Wesley and Jonathan Edwards." *Duke Divinity School Review* 31, no. 1 (1966): 20–38.

Rowe, Karen E. "'Fairy-Born and Human-Bred': Jane Eyre's Education in Romance." In *The Voyage In: Fictions of Female Development,* edited by Elizabeth Abel, Marianne Hirsch, and Elizabeth Langland, 69–89. Hanover, N.H.: University Press of New England, 1983.

Runyon, Theodore. "The Role of Experience in Religion." *International Journal for the Philosophy of Religion.* 31, no. 2–3 (1992): 187–94.

Sabiston, Elizabeth Jean. *The Prison of Womanhood: Four Provincial Heroines in Nineteenth-Century Fiction.* New York: St. Martin's, 1987.

Saine, Thomas P. Introduction to *From My Life: Poetry and Truth.* By Johann Wolfgang von Goethe. New York: Suhrkamp, 1987.

——. "Was *Wilhelm Meisters Lehrjahre* Really Supposed to Be a Bildungsroman?" In *Reflection and Action: Essays on the Bildungsroman,* edited by James Hardin, 118–41. Columbia: University of South Carolina Press, 1991.

——. "What Time Is It in *Wilhelm Meisters Lehrjahre*?" In *Horizonte: Festschrift für Herbert Lehnert zum 65. Geburtstag,* edited by Hannelore Mundt, Egon Schwarz, and William J. Lillyman, 52–69. Tübingen: Niemeyer, 1990.

Sammons, Jeffrey L. "The Mystery of the Missing Bildungsroman; or, What Happened to Wilhelm Meister's Legacy?" *Genre* 14, no. 2 (1981): 229–46.

Schiller, Friedrich. *Briefe.* Vol. 1. Edited by Georg Kurscheidt. Frankfurt: Deutscher Klassiker Verlag, 2002.

——. *Briefwechsel zwischen Schiller und Goethe, 1794–1805.* Vol. 1. Stuttgart: Union Deutsche Verlagsgesellschaft, 1890.

——. *Werke und Briefe.* Vols. 11–12. Edited by Norbert Oellers. Frankfurt: Deutscher Klassiker, 2002.

Schneider, Herbert W. *A History of American Philosophy.* 1946. New York: Columbia University Press, 1963.

Sealts, Merton M., Jr. *Melville's Reading.* 1948. Columbia: University of South Carolina Press, 1988.

Seed, David. "Exemplary Selves: Jonathan Edwards and Benjamin Franklin." In *First Person Singular: Studies in American Autobiography,* edited by A. Robert Lee, 37–56. New York: St. Martin's, 1988.

Seelye, John. "*Pierre, Kavanagh,* and the Unitarian Perplex." In *Melville's Evermoving Dawn,* edited by John Bryant and Robert Milder, 375–91. Kent, Ohio: Kent State University Press, 1997.

Seigel, Jerrold. "Homology and Bildung: Herder, Humboldt, and Goethe." In *The Idea of the Self: Thought and Experience in Western Europe since the Seventeenth Century,* 332–60. Cambridge: Cambridge University Press, 2005.

Sellers, Charles. *The Market Revolution: Jacksonian America, 1815–1846.* New York: Oxford University Press, 1991.

Shaffner, Randolph P. *The Apprenticeship Novel: Studies in the Bildungsroman as a Regulative Type in Western Literature with a Focus on Three Classic Representatives by Goethe, Maugham, and Mann.* New York: Lang, 1984.

Shaftesbury, Anthony Ashley Cooper. "An Inquiry Concerning Virtue, or Merit." In *British Moralists: 1650–1800,* edited by D. D. Raphael, 169–88. Oxford: Oxford University Press, 1969.

Sharf, Robert H. "Experience." In *Critical Terms for Religious Studies,* edited by Mark C. Taylor, 94–116. Chicago: University of Chicago Press, 1998.

Shea, Daniel. *Spiritual Autobiography in Early America.* Madison: University of Wisconsin Press, 1968.

Shuttleworth, Sally. *Charlotte Brontë and Victorian Psychology.* Cambridge: Cambridge University Press, 1996.

Smith, John E., Harry S. Stout, and Kenneth P. Minkema, eds. *A Jonathan Edwards Reader.* New Haven: Yale University Press, 1995.

Smith, Karl Ashley. *Dickens and the Unreal City: Searching for Spiritual Significance in Nineteenth-Century London.* New York: Palgrave Macmillan, 2008.

Smith, Timothy L. *Revivalism and Social Reform: American Protestantism on the Eve of the Civil War.* 1957. 2nd ed. Baltimore: Johns Hopkins University Press, 1980.

Smith, Zadie. "North West London Blues." *New York Review of Books,* July 12, 2012: 10–12.

Spanos, William V. *Herman Melville and the American Calling: The Fiction after "Moby-Dick," 1851–1857.* Albany: SUNY Press, 2008.

Stein, William Bysshe. "*The Portrait of a Lady:* Vis Inertae." *Western Humanities Review* 13 (1959): 177–90.

Steinecke, Hartmut. "The Novel and the Individual." Translated by James Hardin. In *Reflection and Action: Essays on the Bildungsroman,* edited by James Hardin, 69–96. Columbia: University of South Carolina Press, 1991.

Stephen, Leslie. *History of English Thought in the Eighteenth Century.* 1876. Vol. 2. New York: Harcourt Brace, 1962.

Stewart, Randall. *American Literature and Christian Doctrine.* Baton Rouge: Louisiana State University Press, 1958.

Stoeffler, F. Ernest, ed. *Continental Pietism and Early American Christianity.* Grand Rapids, Mich.: Eerdmans, 1976.

——. *German Pietism during the Eighteenth Century.* Studies in the History of Religions 24. Leiden: Brill, 1973.

Swales, Martin. *The German Bildungsroman from Wieland to Hesse.* Princeton: Princeton University Press, 1978.

——. "Irony and the Novel: Reflections on the German Bildungsroman." In *Reflection and Action: Essays on the Bildungsroman,* edited by James Hardin, 46–68. Columbia: University of South Carolina Press, 1991.

Sweeney, Douglas. "Edwards and His Mantle: The Historiography of the New England Theology." *New England Quarterly* 71, no. 1 (1998): 97–119.

Swift, Donald C. *Religion and the American Experience.* New York: Sharpe, 1998.

Talley, Lee A. *Jane Eyre*'s Little-Known Debt to the *Methodist Magazine.*" *Brontë Studies* 33, no. 2 (2008): 109–19.

Tanner, Tony. "The Fearful Self." In *Twentieth-Century Interpretations of "The Portrait of a Lady,"* edited by Peter Buitenhuis, 67–83. Englewood Cliffs, N.J.: Prentice-Hall, 1968.

Tate, Andrew. "Tell the Story: Re-imagining Victorian Conversion Narratives." In *Shaping Belief: Culture, Politics and Religion in Nineteenth-Century Writing,* edited by Victoria Morgan and Clare Williams, 3–19. Liverpool: Liverpool University Press, 2008.

Taylor, Eugene. *Shadow Culture: Psychology and Spirituality in America.* Washington, D.C.: Counterpoint, 1999.

Taylor, Irene. *Holy Ghosts: The Male Muses of Emily and Charlotte Brontë.* New York: Columbia University Press, 1990.

Tennyson, G. B. "The Bildungsroman in Nineteenth-Century English Literature." In *Medieval Epic to the "Epic Theater" of Brecht,* edited by Rosario P. Armato and John M. Spalek, 135–46. Los Angeles: University of Southern California Press, 1968.

Thackeray, William Makepeace. "To William Smith Williams, 23 October 1847." In *Letters and Private Papers,* vol. 2, edited by Gordon N. Ray, 318–19. London: Oxford University Press, 1946.

Thompson, G. R., and Eric Carl Link. *Neutral Ground: New Traditionalism and the American Romance Controversy.* Baton Rouge: Louisiana State University Press, 1999.

Thompson, Lawrance. *Melville's Quarrel with God.* Princeton: Princeton University Press, 1952.

Thormählen, Marianne. *The Brontës and Religion.* Cambridge: Cambridge University Press, 1999.

Tocqueville, Alexis de. *Democracy in America.* 2 vols. Translated by Henry Reeve. New York: Collier, 1900.

Todorov, Tzvetan. *The Fantastic: A Structural Approach to a Literary Genre.* Translated by Richard Howard. Cleveland: Press of Case Western Reserve University, 1973.

Tolstoy, Leo. "Letter to James Ley, 21 January 1904." In *Letters,* vol. 2, edited by R. F. Christian, 637. New York: Scribner, 1978.

Underhill, Evelyn. *Mysticism.* 1911. New York: Dutton, 1961.

Underwood, Grant. "'Awash in a Sea of Faith': America and the Second Great Awakening." In *Lectures on Religion and the Founding of the American Republic,* 97–107. Provo, Utah: Brigham Young University Press, 2003.

Walder, Dennis. *Dickens and Religion.* London: Allen & Unwin, 1981.

Walker, Williston. *A History of the Christian Church.* 3rd ed. New York: Scribner, 1970.

Ward, David A. "Transformed Religion: Matthew Arnold and the Refining of Dissent." *Renascence* 53, no. 2 (2001): 97–117.

Watkins, Floyd C. "Melville's Plotinus Plinlimmon and Pierre." In *Reality and Myth: Essays in American Literature,* 39–51. Nashville: Vanderbilt University Press, 1964.

Watkins, Owen C. *The Puritan Experience: Studies in Spiritual Autobiography.* New York: Schocken Books, 1972.

Watts, Isaac. *The Doctrine of the Passions Explain'd and Improv'd: or, A Brief and Comprehensive Scheme of the Natural Affections.* London: Hett & Brackstone, 1739.

Weddle, David L. "The Image of the Self in Jonathan Edwards: A Study of Autobiography and Theology." *Journal of the American Academy of Religion* 43, no. 1 (1975): 70–83.

Weinlick, John R. *Count Zinzendorf.* New York: Abingdon, 1956.

——. "Moravianism in the American Colonies." In *Continental Pietism and Early American Christianity,* edited by F. Ernest Stoeffler, 123–63. Grand Rapids, Mich: Eerdmans, 1976.

Weisbuch, Robert. "Henry James and the Idea of Evil." In *The Cambridge Companion to Henry James,* edited by Jonathan Freedman, 102–19. Cambridge: Cambridge University Press, 1998.

——. "James and the American Sacred." *Henry James Review* 22, no. 3 (2001): 217–28.

Wesley, John. *Journal.* 8 vols. Edited by Nehemiah Curnock. London: Epworth, 1960.

——. *Letters.* 8 vols. Edited by John Teleford. London: Epworth, 1960.

——. "A Plain Account of Christian Perfection." In *Works,* vol. 11, 366–446. Grand Rapids, Mich.: Zondervan, 1958.

——. *A Plain Account of Genuine Christianity.* Bristol: Farley, 1755.

Westbrook, Perry D. *Free Will and Determinism in American Literature.* Rutherford, N.J.: Fairleigh Dickinson University Press, 1979.

Whaling, Frank, ed. and intro. *John and Charles Wesley: Selected Prayers, Hymns, Journal Notes, Sermons, Letters and Treatises.* New York: Paulist, 1981.

Williams, Peter W. *America's Religions: From Their Origins to the Twenty-First Century.* Urbana: University of Illinois Press, 1990.

Wilson, John F. "History, Redemption, and the Millennium." In *Jonathan Edwards and the American Experience,* edited by Nathan O. Hatch and Harry S. Stout, 131–41. New York: Oxford University Press, 1988.

Winnifrith, Tom. *The Brontës and Their Background: Romance and Reality*. London: Macmillan, 1973.

Wolff, Robert Lee. *Gains and Losses: Novels of Faith and Doubt in Victorian England*. New York: Garland, 1977.

Wright, Natalia. *Melville's Use of the Bible*. New York: Octagon, 1969.

Yousef, Nancy. "The Poverty of Charity: Dickensian Sympathy." In *Contemporary Dickens*, edited by Eileen Gillooly and Deirdre David, 53–74. Columbus: Ohio State University Press, 2009.

INDEX

ABOUT THE AUTHOR

KELSEY L. BENNETT'S articles and essays have appeared in *Brontë Studies, New Criterion, Colorado Review, Notes on Contemporary Literature,* and elsewhere. Bennett lives in Gunnison, Colorado, and serves on the English faculty at Western State Colorado University.

CPSIA information can be obtained at www.ICGtesting.com
Printed in the USA
LVOW12*1109190814

399790LV00003B/7/P